GW00469745

Dilemmas of
Liberal Democracies

Tavistock Studies in Sociology

General Editor: FRANK PARKIN

Dilemmas of Liberal Democracies

STUDIES IN FRED HIRSCH'S
'SOCIAL LIMITS TO GROWTH'

EDITED BY
ADRIAN ELLIS AND KRISHAN KUMAR

TAVISTOCK PUBLICATIONS
LONDON AND NEW YORK

First published in 1983 by
Tavistock Publications Ltd
11 New Fetter Lane, London EC4P 4EE

Published in the USA by
Tavistock Publications
in association with Methuen, Inc.
733 Third Avenue, New York, NY 10017

Photoset by Rowland Phototypesetting Ltd
Bury St Edmunds, Suffolk, and printed in
Great Britain at the University Press,
Cambridge

British Library Cataloguing in
  Publication Data

Dilemmas of liberal democracies: studies in
Fred Hirsch's Social limits to growth. –
(Tavistock studies in sociology)
1. Economic development – Social aspects
– Addresses, essays, lectures, etc.
I. Ellis, Adrian   II. Kumar, Krishan
III. Hirsch, Fred
339.5'09172'   HD82
ISBN 0-422-78460-5
ISBN 0-422-78470-2 Pbk

Library of Congress Cataloging in
  Publication Data

Dilemmas of liberal democracies.
(Tavistock studies in sociology)
Bibliography: p.
Includes index.
1. Economic development – Social aspects
– Addresses, essays, lectures. 2. Hirsch,
Fred. Social limits to growth – Addresses,
essays, lectures. I. Ellis,
Adrian, 1956–. II. Kumar, Krishan.
III. Hirsch, Fred. Social limits to growth.
IV. Series.
HD88.D54
1983   306'.3   83-13207
ISBN 0-422-78460-5
ISBN 0-422-78470-2 (pbk.)

Contents

Notes on contributors

COLIN CROUCH was born in 1944 and educated at the London School of Economics and Political Science and at Nuffield College, Oxford. He is now a reader in sociology at the LSE. He is the author of *The Student Revolt* (1970), *Class Conflict and the Industrial Relations Crisis* (1977), *Trade Unions: The Logic of Collective Action* (1982), *The Politics of Industrial Relations* (1979 and 1982), and of articles and Fabian Society pamphlets in the fields of social stratification, industrial relations, and social policy, and editor (with L. N. Lindberg and others) of *Stress and Contradiction in Modern Capitalism* (1975), of *British Political Sociology Yearbook, Volume III: Participation in Politics* (1977), (with A. Pizzorno) of *The Resurgence of Class Conflict in Western Europe since 1968*, two volumes (1978), and of *State and Economy in Contemporary Capitalism* (1979). He is a former chairman of the Fabian Society.

ADRIAN ELLIS was born in 1956 and graduated from University College, Oxford in 1979. He undertook postgraduate work at the London School of Economics and was a College Lecturer in Politics at University College Oxford in 1980–81. He is a former Research Adviser to the Acton Society. He joined the Civil Service in 1981 and is currently working in the Management and Personnel Office. His contribution to and editorial work on this book were undertaken in a personal capacity and any views expressed in it should not be taken as representing those of his employer.

ANDREW GAMBLE was born in 1947 and educated at Cambridge and Durham universities. He has lectured in politics at Sheffield University since 1973, where he is currently Reader in Politics. His books include *The Conservative Nation* (1974) and *Britain in Decline* (1981).

JONATHAN GERSHUNY was born in 1949 and educated at Loughborough, Strathclyde, and Sussex universities. He is the author of *After Industrial Society* (1978), *Social Innovation and the Division of Labour* (1983), and (with Ian Miles) *The New Service Economy* (1983), as well as numerous articles. He is currently Senior Fellow at the Science Policy Research Unit, Sussex University.

JOHN GRAY was born in 1948, and educated at Exeter College, Oxford. He is a Fellow of Jesus College, Oxford and University Lecturer in Politics. His book, *Mill on Liberty: A Defence*, was published by Routledge and Kegan Paul and the International Library of Philosophy in February 1983. His current research projects include book-length studies of F. A. Hayek's conception of spontaneous social order and of the philosophical background of Marx's social theory.

JOHN HALL was born in 1949. He was educated at Oxford, Pennsylvania State University, and the London School of Economics. He has been Lecturer in Sociology at the University of Southampton since 1975. He is the author of *The Sociology of Literature* (1979), *Diagnoses of Our Time* (1981), and a forthcoming Penguin book on world history, as well as of numerous articles in scholarly and popular journals.

ANTHONY HEATH was born in 1942, and educated at Cambridge University. He taught at Cambridge before becoming a Fellow of Jesus College, Oxford, and University Lecturer in Sociology in 1970. His books include *Rational Choice and Social Exchange* (1976), *Origins and Destinations* (with A. H. Halsey and J. M. Ridge) (1980), and *Social Mobility* (1981). He is currently working on class and gender in education and employment.

KRISHAN KUMAR was born in 1942, and educated at St John's College, Cambridge, and the London School of Economics. Since 1967 he has lectured in Sociology at the University of Kent at Canterbury, where he is currently Reader in Sociology. During 1972–73 he was a Producer in the Talks and Documentaries Department of the BBC, and in 1979–80 he was a Visiting Fellow in the Sociology Department at Harvard

Preface

Neither of us knew Fred Hirsch; nor is this book conceived in the spirit of a tribute or homage to him, in the usual sense of a collection *in memoriam*. But a tribute of some kind it is, of course. It is a tribute to a thinker who, in a regrettably brief working life, produced an impressive series of contributions to economic and political analysis; and it is a tribute in particular to the power and fertility of one of these contributions, his book *Social Limits to Growth*.

When *Social Limits* appeared in 1977, it was immediately hailed for raising in a compelling form some of the most important and urgent questions facing present-day Western societies. Hirsch's actual originality, in detail at any rate, is questionable. What is not questionable is the power of his synthesis, and the range and complexity of the material that he presents so brilliantly. Others had been dissatisfied with the narrowness of the discussion surrounding the 'physical limits to growth', and the dominance of the public debate by the issues this posed. It was Hirsch who gave that debate a new and wider dimension. He crystallized fears and anxieties of a different kind that had been present throughout the post-war boom, but that had been largely suppressed by the sheer dazzle and success of economic growth. When that growth faltered, as it did in the 1970s, it was possible to see that the conflicts and frustrations of the slow growth era stemmed not so much from the cessation of growth as from the surfacing of tendencies long at work in the liberal democracies of the West. Or at least Hirsch made us see it that way. *Social Limits to Growth* presented an analysis of our current predicament in terms which suggested more deeply rooted causes of the crisis.

Undeniably much of Hirsch's appeal was that he unified within a single analytic framework problems which had preoccupied different disciplines in their characteristically separate ways, and in their segmented social areas. Economists were exercised by what seemed the failure of Keynesian economics to continue to ensure orderly growth. Political scientists had discovered the 'economic contradictions of democracy', the tendency for social democracies to be driven into crisis by an electoral mechanism which tempted political parties to offer more than they could ever hope to deliver. Sociologists had concerned themselves with the 'crisis of legitimation' in modern capitalism, the extent to which capitalist societies erode the moral basis of their own social order and so unleash fierce social conflicts. Hirsch encompassed all these areas of concern, drawing freely on their respective disciplines without letting himself be limited by the perspective of any one of them.

It is not necessary here to offer a formal summary of Hirsch's argument. This is done sufficiently in the various contributions to this volume, and what these suggest, indeed, is that a short summary would be very difficult, and less profitable than might be expected. This is at first surprising, in view of the explicitly schematic character of much of Hirsch's book, and the many summaries which he himself gives at various points. But second and subsequent readings distinctly confirm what on the first reading occasions only a slight perplexity, that Hirsch does not in fact follow a single consistent line of argument. This conduces to a degree of ambivalence and ambiguity in both concepts and argument which is noted by several contributors (e.g. Ellis and Heath, Gershuny), and which is richly exploited by Hirsch himself. It gives him the freedom to range over a remarkably wide range of topics, of interest to students of many disciplines as well as to politically interested readers of all kinds. It also permits 'hidden' and alternative readings of key concepts and themes, which suggest different lines of analysis and prescription from Hirsch's own. All this is generally to the good, of course, and is no doubt one reason why the book has continued to fascinate so many readers. But it also means that any attempt at a short summary is more than usually doomed to do an injustice to the richness and subtlety of its many but sometimes inconsistent themes.

So, for instance, in the first part of the book the formal analysis of the 'positional economy' – Hirsch's main conceptual innovation – occupies pride of place. Hirsch identifies a hitherto neglected realm of scarcity, concerned largely with non-material satisfaction, which becomes the central arena of conflict once societies have passed beyond a certain stage of material growth. Since however the satisfactions of this realm are of a 'zero-sum' kind – that is, they depend essentially on restricted access or possession – the hopes of progress through economic growth are blasted. What the few have today the many *cannot* have tomorrow. Nevertheless it is rational for each individual to strive to improve his position, for to stand still is to slip back. This explains 'the paradox of affluence', the fact that we all continue to strive for economic advance even though it persistently disappoints when we achieve it. This in turn leads to the 'distributional compulsion', the intensified concern to get a better slice of the pie since the pie cannot grow any bigger in the desired form. Hence, too, our 'reluctant collectivism', the increasing resort to collective action and state intervention not to achieve social goals but to pursue private ends in the face of the frustrations engendered by individually orientated behaviour.

This line of argument is developed with a wealth of illustrative detail for most of the first half of the book. In the second half a new theme increasingly takes over. This is the 'depletion of the moral legacy' of capitalism. The phrase is itself ambiguous, in that it refers not to a morality that capitalism itself creates but rather one that is a fortunate inheritance from its pre-capitalist past. Hirsch's argument is that capitalism rests on this pre-capitalist social morality, that it is highly vulnerable without it, but that nevertheless the very principle of the capitalist ethic of self-interest and individual maximization undermines this morality. There is an obvious link with the earlier part of the analysis, in so far as the erosion of the pre-capitalist morality, by removing self-imposed restraints, heightens the conflicts over distribution. But it is equally clear that what Hirsch offers is two quite separate explanations of what drives the system into crisis. Economic growth by itself drags the positional realm into the centre of the social struggle. If the pre-capitalist morality has been adequate to the phase of material growth, there is no reason to think that it will be adequate to cope with the conflicts of the positional economy, which by Hirsch's own account are of an inherently frustrating nature. It is a quite different matter – but equally plausible – to explain the intensity of distributional struggles by the decline of a pre-capitalist, religiously based, ethic of restraint. Certainly Hirsch warms very much to this latter theme – one, incidentally, that he shares with many other current social commentators – and from the shape of the book one suspects that it may well have grown on him, to the point almost of superseding the earlier analysis in explanatory importance.

The various contributors take their lead, in a sense, from this very generosity of Hirsch's themes. Some engage directly with Hirsch's concepts and argument. Heath and Ellis and Gershuny are critical both of the concept of the 'positional economy' and of Hirsch's account of the consequences of economic growth. Others treat Hirsch more as a point of departure, as supplying an agenda of questions and issues to be discussed in the light of their own particular interests. Plant and Gray both discuss the implications of the declining moral legitimacy of capitalism, but while Plant (like Hirsch) sees some hope in a regenerated social democratic consensus, Gray regards such a cure as worse than the disease. Hall and Crouch oppose the 'no growth' advocacy of some of Hirsch's interpreters, and, partly taking their lead from Hirsch, stress by contrast both the desirability and the possibility of renewed economic growth. Using the example of post-war economic policy in Britain, Gamble largely accepts Hirsch's characterization of our dilemmas, but considers his prescriptions for a new social morality do not go far enough. Taylor-Gooby, however, questions the accuracy of Hirsch's portrayal of recent history, and on the basis of an examination of the impact of post-war social policy suggests that Hirsch has accepted too readily the ideology of the welfare state. Kumar and Lane are yet more oblique to Hirsch. Kumar endorses Hirsch's view of the significance of a pre-capitalist morality for the functioning of capitalism, but considers that Schumpeter provides a more satisfying and fruitful account both of the source of that morality and of its eventual displacement. Lane, finally, in a comparison of the rationality of markets and politics, accepts (with Hirsch) the limitations and failures of market rationality, but bleakly concludes, contrary to Hirsch's hopes, that it is greatly superior to the rationality of the political sphere in liberal democratic societies, and suggests that the latter might do better to adopt a market model in its operations.

Many of the contributors to this volume are critical of Hirsch, some seriously so. All share the conviction that he has raised the issues that matter, and has presented them in a form that cannot be ignored. It is a measure of his achievement, and the best kind of tribute to Fred Hirsch, that his book should excite so many minds, even in disagreement. We are certain that it will continue to do so for a long time to come.

The Acton Society provided the stimulus for this volume. Early drafts of some of these papers were presented at a series of seminars in its basement meeting room at 9 Poland Street, London. We are grateful to its Trustees for their support for this project, and especially grateful to its secretary, Jackie Lebe, for her invaluable help in putting together the essays. Thanks are also due to Frank Parkin, of Magdalen College, Oxford, for his ready response to the idea of this volume, and for his sympathetic support throughout.

ADRIAN ELLIS
KRISHAN KUMAR

1 Positional competition, or an offer you can't refuse?[1]

ADRIAN ELLIS and ANTHONY HEATH

One

The academic division of labour in the social sciences is increasingly coming to be seen as inappropriate to the sorts of problems that many of those working within its disciplines are attempting to understand. Areas of one discipline are being integrated into – some would say poached by – adjacent ones through the application of a single methodological framework to both. This is particularly the case with economic science, which is adding ever greater areas of political and social life to its traditional domain of monetary exchange.

Many of the insights gathered from the application of the methods of economics to the domain usually occupied by political scientists and sociologists have been elegantly simple. The dividends have usually come from *ad hoc* applications ('soft social choice') rather than from the development of more theoretically sophisticated models, despite the facility economists appear to have in elaborating such models. Those who are not economists are inclined to explain this by suggesting that the conceptual inadequacy of the assumptions behind these models are such that they are only appropriate to 'one-off' situations, where the idea that political or social agents are rational, self-interested 'utility maximizers' is tenable. Economists, on the other hand, tend to favour an explanation based on the relative youth of the approach or empirical difficulties in testing it rather than on any more theoretically intractable problems in the approach.

Whatever the reasons for greater success of soft social choice compared with econometrically more sophisticated approaches, Olson's notion of the Logic of Collective Action (Olson 1965), Downs's hypotheses concerning the behaviour of electorally competitive parties (Downs 1957), and Hirschman's analysis of the choices between Exit, Voice, and Loyalty (Hirschman 1970) all appear to be cases in point. Hirsch's notion of the competition for positional goods appears to fit into this tradition. It is elegantly simple and has apparently strong explanatory power in dealing with unforeseen political and social side effects of economic growth. 'Positional competition' has therefore slipped rapidly into the vocabulary of social science alongside such notions as 'the voters' paradox', 'the prisoner's dilemma', 'minimum winning coalitions', and 'selective incentives'.

This chapter attempts, first, to demonstrate that the notion of positional competition cannot solve the problems Hirsch sets it and, second, to provide an alternative solution. We shall begin by describing the essential features of Hirsch's argument and the problems inherent in his approach. We shall then develop the notion of 'coerced exchange' as an alternative explanation, and conclude with a discussion of the wider political and social implications of our analysis.

Two

Social Limits is concerned with the political and social effects of two largely unnoticed and, incidentally, utterly distinct sources of market failure. 'Market failure' here means the failure of the invisible hand of individualistic competitive behaviour to ensure an identity between the sum of the individual costs and benefits confronting individual decision-makers and the total confronting society as a whole. The first source of failure Hirsch concentrates on, and the focus of this chapter, is the inability of the market to deal with competition for goods whose supply is innately limited. Hirsch calls these 'positional goods' because one's *relative* economic position rather than absolute level of income will determine one's command over them. According to Hirsch, the existence of such goods and their method of distribution solve two apparent paradoxes: the 'paradox of affluence', and the 'distributional compulsion'. In full, these are:

'Why has economic advance become and remained so compelling a goal to us all as individuals, even when it yields disappointing fruits when most, if not all, of us achieve it?' (Hirsch 1977: 1)

and

'Why has modern society become so concerned with distribution – with division of the pie – when it is clear that the great majority can raise their living standards only through production of a larger pie?' (Hirsch 1977: 1)

Hirsch's second source of market failure, and one that we will not be discussing in this chapter, is an increase in 'the area of commercialization' and an associated depletion of the 'moral legacy' of pre-capitalism. Hirsch's argument is that the market system can only function if there is a framework of social obligations on which it can rest, but that growth in commercialization tends to undermine these foundations. In this way the market system 'may sabotage its own foundations' (Hirsch 1977: 143).

In order to understand how Hirsch uses the concept of positional goods to explain his paradoxes it is necessary to look at these goods in rather more detail. There is, he says, an analytical distinction that can be made concerning the goods and services that are distributed in the market: namely between those necessarily limited in supply and for which competition is therefore zero-sum, and those that can be increased through the process of economic growth and for which competition is therefore, over time, positive sum. A positional good is thus one for which competition is necessarily and forever zero-sum as, irrespective of the method of distribution, supply cannot be increased. In contrast a material good is one which the process of economic growth can provide more of (as with, say, cookers or typewriters).

Hirsch distinguishes various types of positional good. There are the ones that are unavoidably scarce, as for example an Old Master or a secluded country cottage in a scenic yet accessible area, and there are ones whose value varies in inverse proportion to the volume of such goods produced, as for example a car on a potentially over-crowded road, or a 'snob good', valued not for its intrinsic qualities but for the prestige accruing to its ownership. One additional point should be made about positional goods here. If Hirsch's argument is to run, the positional goods in question must all be luxury goods, that is to say their income elasticity of demand over time should be greater than unity. If this is not the case, then demand for these goods will not increase with economic growth – individuals will not spend a larger proportion of their income on them as they become richer. For this reason in the rest of this chapter 'positional goods' should be taken to mean 'positional goods which are also luxury goods'.

Having defined positional goods and assumed them to play a significant part in economic life, we can now see how Hirsch uses them to explain the paradox of affluence and the distributional compulsion. In order to do this he introduces a further important notion, that of 'intermediate' or 'defensive' consumption. Defensive consumption is the consumption of goods that are a means to a final good rather than goods of intrinsic value to a consumer:

> 'Because [positional goods] are allocated by an auction process or its equivalent, relative rather than absolute command over resources deployed in the auction process will determine one's take. This struggle for relative shares will absorb real resources that add to the consumption expenditure necessary to achieve given ends and in this sense add to "needs". So if one's own income remains unchanged while the income of other people rises, one's command over the positional sector will fall.'   (Hirsch 1977: 102)

In other words there is an economic inefficiency stemming from positional goods which leads to increased defensive consumption being necessary for the same level of want satisfaction. People have to run faster and faster to stay both relatively and absolutely where they are.

Hence, Hirsch argues, the existence of positional goods leads to a flaw in the ideological attraction of growth. Liberal and social democratic philosophies usually regard growth as an alternative to the redistribution of wealth. However, if growth cannot provide positional goods, and people increasingly desire these goods as their demands for material goods are met, distributional conflict may be expected to reappear. The existence of these goods constitutes a 'social limit to growth'. Their existence is, however, obscured by conventional economic indicators such as GDP because these indicators are usually read with an assumption that all consumption contributes directly towards 'want satisfaction', that is all consumption is 'final'. The economic inefficiency stemming from positional competition means that increased 'intermediate' or 'defensive' consumption is necessary for the same level of want satisfaction. Take leadership positions, one of Hirsch's examples of a positional good: as competition for them becomes more acute, there is greater and greater channelling through suitable educational qualifications. This results in socially wasteful 'credentialism', a futile paper chase in which ever higher qualifications of marginal relevance to the content of the job are required in order for one to maintain access to it; but this fact escapes the statistics upon which economic analysis is based, and this omission is an important factor in explaining why both the existence of, and the inefficiency of, positional competition have gone largely unnoticed.

Thus, through the notion of positional competition and its tendency to encourage defensive consumption, Hirsch accounts for the paradox of affluence: growth definitionally cannot fulfil the promise of putting the worse-off in society tomorrow where the better-off are today, and attempts to fulfil that promise lead to frustrations on the part of the aspirants to, and possessors of, positional goods. The distributional compulsion is also explained: given this failure, redistribution is naturally embraced as the only method of ensuring a 'slice of the pie'. (It is perhaps worth mentioning that another facet of the distributional compulsion is explained by Hirsch through reference to his second source of market failure – that of the erosion of normative constraints on selfish behaviour – and is not dealt with in this chapter.)

The following two sections are concerned with two sets of criticisms that can be levelled at Hirsch's argument. The first is that the types of positional good that fulfil his criteria of being in inelastic supply (i.e., positional goods) and having income elasticity of demand (i.e., luxury goods) are smaller than Hirsch assumes and the explanatory weight the remaining types must bear is implausibly increased (Section Three). The second criticism is that there is a hiatus in Hirsch's causal reasoning: he fails to make a causal link between defensive consumption and competition for positional goods, and as defensive consumption is both necessary and sufficient to explain his two paradoxes, the notion of positional competition is redundant in his explanation (Section Four).

Three

THE LINK BETWEEN POSITIONAL COMPETITION AND GROWTH

As we have seen, Hirsch is concerned with luxury goods in inelastic supply. Their inelastic supply and the greater demand for them as societies grow rich are the reasons why any effects stemming from their existence are cumulative over time. Jonathan Gershuny has dealt with some of the empirical questions surrounding positional goods in the next chapter. The point here is that not all the goods which Hirsch calls positional fulfil his criteria. In order to understand why not, it is helpful to look at each of Hirsch's categories of positional good in turn.

The first category of good Hirsch mentions but, like other economists, dismisses, are those which are factors of production and are nearing physical exhaustion. He concurs with the majority of economists – and disagrees with environmentalists and ecologists – that there is considerable scope for substitution of factors of production. If resources are limited – they are, of course, finite – then these limitations have not yet been reached. He therefore turns his attention to 'scarcities of consumption' and isolates three types, marked I, II (1), and II (2) in *Figure 1*.

I Physical scarcity

Physical scarcities of consumption clearly may be, as Hirsch argues, luxury goods, but as physical scarcities rather than social scarcities, they do not play a very important part in Hirsch's analysis which, after all, is called *'Social' Limits to Growth*. However, in so far as they do, there are two weaknesses in his argument. First, land, even as a consumption good rather than as a factor of production, is not in as inelastic a supply as he suggests. Experiments in multiple ownership, time-sharing of holiday homes, and the opening of private parks to the public have expanded rather than contracted access to rural areas. To use as a counter-argument that less satisfaction will be derived if the home is not empty when the owner is absent is to turn a physical scarcity into a 'pure social scarcity' or snob good. Second, competition for Old Masters will not lead to Armageddon. (Incidentally, they would appear to be in very elastic supply, whether through forgery, discovery, or the march of time.) Even assuming a value-consensus throughout all levels of society about the

Figure 1   A categorization of consumption scarcity

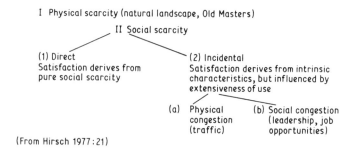

(From Hirsch 1977: 21)

desirability of such goods as Old Masters or holiday cottages, which is far from obvious, Hirsch does not demonstrate that pure physical scarcities play a significant part in people's lives, and, from the examples he gives, it is difficult to imagine that he could do so.

II (1) Direct social scarcity

In Hirsch's next category of positional good, it is the scarcities themselves that give satisfaction. This Hirsch calls 'pure social scarcity' but it is more easily intelligible simply as 'snob value'. Certain goods are not enjoyed for any intrinsic qualities they may have but because they are rare or expensive and possession of them is therefore indicative of relative position or social status. Their value is in direct proportion to their scarcity. Unlike medals for bravery, however, or respect for having run the four-minute mile or invented the internal combustion engine, these goods, and therefore the respect accruing to their possession, are distributed through the market.

Hirsch argues that snob goods are luxury goods and states that 'luxury goods are used here in the sense of a commodity or service for which, as income rises, effective demand rises more than proportionately – that is one with a high income elasticity of demand' (Hirsch 1977: 32). Hobbes presented an identical thesis about the income elasticity of snob goods: 'All men naturally strive for honour and preferment but chiefly those who are least troubled with caring for necessary things' (Thomas 1965: 191). There is, however, an ambiguity in the concept of a luxury good which could lead to the exclusion of snob goods from any category of positional goods. While snob goods are luxury goods *within a given income structure* (i.e. as one's income rises relative to other people's, one's demand for snob goods increases), it is not at all obvious that they are luxury goods *over time* (i.e. as the society as a whole gets richer, demand throughout the population increases). In other words the demand for snob goods may be analogous to the propensity to save in Keynes's schema, which increases with income cross-sectionally but not over time. In proving the former one does not prove the latter, but Hirsch assumes that in proving a good to be a luxury in the cross-sectional sense he has therefore demonstrated that 'as general standards of living rise, demand for luxuries becomes more generally diffused throughout the population' (Hirsch 1977: 66).

There are three ways in which the observed cross-sectional tendency for demand for snob goods to increase proportionately faster than income and Hirsch's (and Hobbes's) posited long-run tendency might be linked, two of which are implicit in his argument. The first way in which the two might be connected, and superficially the most plausible, is to argue that people will be frustrated if they believe that economic growth will bring snob goods or rather the attributes (status and prestige) which attach themselves to the consumers of these goods. As the volume of these goods increases or as the costs of production decline, their prestige is eroded. The aspiring owners will be frustrated because once having gained these goods, they discover – along with many others – that they have the good but not the status. The original owners of the previously scarce good are frustrated because their status-attributes are being eroded.

There are however a number of problems with this line of argument. First, there is an assumption that people are aware of the status of prestige accruing to the ownership of the goods *before* they have obtained them. Assume, for example, that the top 2 per cent of the population have strings of pearls. As cultured pearls become more widely available another, say, 8 per cent of the population purchase them, on the assumption that they will gain the same deference that the original 2 per cent enjoyed as a result of their possession of the good and the relative position which ownership signified. As the 8 per cent join the 2 per cent they discover that they do not enjoy the deference they expected. But whilst the prestige accruing to the 10 per cent is less than that accruing to the 2 per cent, how do the lower 8 per cent know? They have no standards of comparison precisely because they were not in the original 2 per cent. As regards the frustration of the old-guard rather than the *nouveaux riches*, it is surely the case that snob value is transferred to other, relatively more scarce goods. Yesterday's common-or-garden pearl becomes today's pearl with a specific *provenance*.

What constitutes a snob good changes apace with economic growth and whilst this does not necessarily lead to net increase in well-being it is not an element of material growth which causes increased frustrations. A further problem with this argument is that it assumes snob goods are *entirely* wanted for their snob value rather than being intrinsically desirable but carrying with them 'windfall' gains in prestige. If it is the latter which is the case rather than the former then the area of economic growth with no welfare pay-off is still further reduced, as it will merely be the windfall gains which economic growth devalues.

A second way in which the two conceptions of luxury good might be connected is by introducing the idea that as basic needs are satisfied, the demand for unneeded luxury goods increases (Hirsch 1977: 32, 66). These goods include snob goods which definitionally give satisfaction because they are not needed. However, needs are protean things, which is why the concept is assiduously avoided in most economic literature.

Beyond the subsistence economy, which Britain may reasonably be assumed to have left behind before Hirsch's paradox became apparent, most needs are socially determined. For the link between cross-sectional and long-run tendencies to be made it would have to be demonstrated first that the individual's assessment of his needs is growing more slowly than the command over resources that economic growth provides him with, and that, within the freedom which this shortfall of needs over resources provides, there is an increasing tendency for individuals to opt for the pursuit of snob goods rather than other luxury goods. Hirsch makes no attempt to demonstrate either and it is far from obvious that the first hurdle could be passed, never mind the second.

A third relation between snob goods and growth, albeit one which Hirsch does not consider, is that economic growth might lead to an equalization of incomes; that is, change the *relative* income structure and thus make the fact that snob goods are luxury goods within that income structure relevant again. However, whilst the interpretation of figures on income and wealth are disputed at length there is little doubt that within the period with which Hirsch is concerned, the Keynesian heyday, there has been insufficient redistribution for this argument to be brought to bear. (See Peter Taylor-Gooby's chapter in this volume for a vigorous support of this view.)

As none of these posited links between the long-run and cross-sectional tendencies for demand for snob goods to grow proportionately faster than income has been made firm, the conclusion must be that although 'pure social scarcity' constitutes a social limit to growth in the sense that growth cannot bring prestige to all, it is not one which can be used to explain either of Hirsch's first two paradoxes, as it is a social limit which exists potentially in any society at any period. It was a limit which even Adam Smith claimed to be acute:

> '[It] is chiefly from regard to the sentiments of mankind that we pursue riches and avoid poverty. For to what purpose is all the toil and bustle of this world? What is the end of avarice and ambition, of the pursuit of wealth, of power, of pre-eminence? To be observed, to be attended to, to be taken notice of with sympathy, complacency and appreciation, are all the advantages which we can propose to derive from it. *It is the vanity, not the ease or the pleasure which interests us.*'
>
> (quoted in Hirschman 1977: 108; italics added)

II (2) Incidental social scarcity

Much of Hirsch's analysis, however, is not concerned with physical scarcity or direct social scarcity but with incidental social scarcity, that is, with goods whose satisfaction is influenced by the extensiveness of use. Hirsch's examples include automobiles, educational qualifications (as a means to leadership positions), and suburban housing. These are the 'core' positional goods. As with the other two forms of scarcity, however, the distinction between the cross-section and the time-series would appear to be crucial. We must distinguish between the overcrowding of a *specific* plant, road, occupation, or suburb within an existing economic and social structure and the increase in *general* of overcrowding, externalities, and so on over time. There is a difference between being unable to increase congestion-free transport given a stock of roads, and being unable to increase the stock of roads itself. This is a difference which is vital for Hirsch and, again, in demonstrating the former he assumes the latter.

A further serious error is that in the case of incidental social scarcity Hirsch seems to equate positional good with public good. Consider his example of suburbanization. He writes:

'If the process of suburbanization is unimpeded by planning or other restrictions, excess demand for this positional good involves, in the first instance, a process of *crowding* that changes – and beyond some point, worsens – the quality of suburban characteristics. This development in turn induces creation of new suburbs with undefiled characteristics, but since these also in time tend to attract demand that is excessive for the maintenance of maximum quality, the leapfrogging process will tend to continue.

This leapfrogging process involves potential social waste, in so far as the combined result of the series of individual moves leaves all concerned worse off than they would be if they concerted their actions in the knowledge of the likely responses by others. Those involved in the process are victims of "the tyranny of small decisions".'

(Hirsch 1977: 39–40)

The tyranny of small decisions is the usual tyranny of the market, and the fact that the combined result of a series of individual moves leaves all concerned worse off than they would be if they concerted their actions is a defining feature of a collective good. Incidental social scarcity in this case seems to be synonymous with collective goods. The peace and quiet of a suburb is a collective good that can be destroyed by the individual pursuit of self-interest just as, in the absence of collective controls, clean air tends to be polluted by self-interested profit-maximizers. Most of the other examples of incidental social scarcity which Hirsch gives would appear to have the same features.

Now it is not immediately obvious that there is anything to be gained by amalgamating the concepts of positional good and collective good. It may well be true that there is a high income elasticity of demand for collective goods over time: it does indeed tend to be rich societies which worry about air pollution and the conservation of the countryside. But there is nothing in the concept of collective good to explain the paradox of affluence or the distributional compulsion. True, individual action leads to the under-provision of collective goods, and in that sense to market failure, but there is also a standard solution to the problem, namely social regulation. Unless we postulate a tendency for social regulation to become more difficult as societies become richer, there is no reason to suppose that collective goods will become a source of increasing frustration. And one could just as plausibly argue that an increased demand for collective goods will lead to a reduced concern about distributional issues as people come to focus more on collective benefits than on individual position within the hierarchy.

The one exception is that of leadership. Hirsch recognizes that, 'since jobs or other positions at the top of a hierarchy almost always have high status, which is generally valued in itself, they also have some attributes of pure social scarcity' (Hirsch 1977: 22); but rather curiously he prefers to regard them as valued primarily for their intrinsic attractions and therefore assigns them to the category of incidental social scarcity. This is puzzling because the concept of leadership, unlike those of roads, cars, or even suburbs, is inherently *relational.* There cannot be leaders without followers. We can in principle all have cars or live in low-density housing or go to university but we cannot all be leaders. We must therefore accept that leadership is a positional good not a collective one.

Four

In Section Three it was argued that only one of the three categories of scarcity Hirsch describes – that of incidental social scarcity – fulfils his criteria for being positional, and that within even this category there may be fewer examples of positional goods than Hirsch believes. The implication is that the causal significance of these remaining goods would have to be far greater than Hirsch originally assumed if their existence is to explain his two paradoxes. The purpose of the next section is to argue that even were this not the case, and there was an abundance of goods which fulfilled Hirsch's criteria, their existence would be neither necessary nor sufficient to explain his paradoxes.

Analytical categories are interesting largely in so far as they provide the bases upon which to build causal models. The interest of Hirsch's distinction between positional goods and material goods is that he builds upon it the idea that the existence of the former sort of good causes a market failure. However, he is unable to do this. Let us re-examine in more detail his argument concerning leadership positions and credentialism outlined in the second section of this chapter.

Three assumptions, which will be accepted at their face value here, are prerequisites in Hirsch's argument: first, leadership positions are in inelastic supply; and second, demand for these goods has income elasticity greater than unity. In other words we are not producing any more of them, but as people get richer in absolute terms *and* relative terms they are prepared to devote a greater proportion of their incomes to the attainment of these goods. There is a *latent* demand for them diffused throughout the population which manifests itself when individuals have reached a given level of command over resources. They are not, as Peter Wilby once described education, 'a middle-class taste, like wholemeal bread'. These assumptions link the demand for these goods cumulatively to economic growth. Third, leadership positions and other goods with similar inelasticities of supply and high income elasticities of demand constitute a 'significant' proportion of total goods. This third assumption ensures that any effects attributable to their existence will be, for all the ambiguity of the phrase, 'socially important'. For the sake of simplicity it will be assumed here that if they can explain any parts of the paradox they can explain all of it.

The obvious hiatus in Hirsch's argument is that there is no *a priori* reason why positional goods should not be distributed in the same way as material goods; namely by some form of auction. The fact that some positional goods, like some material goods, are not so distributed is not contingent upon their being positional but depends upon different factors according to each positional good under consideration. In the case of leadership positions and credentialism, it is not the inelasticities of supply which cause the wasteful absorption of finite resources, the paradox of affluence, and the distributional compulsion; rather, we shall argue, it is due to purely contingent features of the educational system which do not have their source in positional competition. Hirsch himself concedes the contingent nature of screening but does not fully face the implications. He agrees that 'There is no reason, in principle, why these scarcities too [leadership] should not be allocated by auction' (1977: 29) a mechanism which 'absorbs no economic resources and represents merely a transfer of claims to resources' (1977: 31). But he suggests that there are powerful reasons why the auction will not typically be used and why screening is likely to be the more usual method for allocating coveted jobs. He writes:

'Flexibility in relative pay in different occupations is inhibited by a number of factors. These include (1) conventional pay differentials or norms; (2) high "transactions" costs in filling senior posts from outside the firm or organization or department, resulting both from necessary on-the-job training and from the cost of acquiring information about the capability of potential candidates; and (3) the ability of existing incumbents in superior jobs to influence their own pay scales either through the exercise of economic power over their contribution to "team" productivity, or more simply through their access to relevant scarce information.'   (Hirsch 1977: 43)

Now Hirsch is probably correct in arguing that there is little flexibility in pay differentials. This is no new phenomenon and applies to inferior jobs as much as it does to superior ones. And it does not on its own entail the conclusion that jobs will instead be allocated by a wasteful process of educational screening. Indeed, there is little evidence that *top* jobs actually are allocated in this way. Educational screening is used largely as an entry mechanism, rather than as a promotion mechanism. Educational qualifications are used, for example, to select students for medical school, to select management trainees or recruits to the trainee grades in the civil service. But the further you progress in your professional, managerial, or administrative career the less relevant your initial educational qualifications become. To be sure, promotion up the career ladder is not organized through an auction; candidates are 'screened' and interviewed in the ways with which we are all familiar, but it is not obvious that this absorbs unnecessary resources or leads to market failure. Nor does Hirsch make any effort to show that it does. The resources deployed in selecting candidates for promotion to top jobs can probably be justified by the information they contribute towards the decision and it is not immediately obvious that there will be any divergence between the private and social returns.

The defensive consumption and market failure with which Hirsch is concerned, therefore, come in the competition for the educational entry qualifications and not with the selection of candidates for promotion to top jobs. So how well does his argument fare here? Our answer is that it is no more successful because the defensive consumption has a different explanation that has nothing to do with positional competition. Rather, the defensive consumption and absorption of real resources arise from the fact that (1) educational information is 'free' to the potential employer, (2) educational qualifications are only imperfectly correlated with job potential, and (3) access to educational institutions is not strictly rationed. Let us consider these points in turn.

The employer recruiting new entrants from school or university has little relevant information about their job potential apart from their academic qualifications. This information, however, is free to him (although not to the society at large) and allows him to make a rough ordering of candidates' suitability. Since it is free, it is not worth his while obtaining more accurate but more expensive information for himself – and anyway he can weed out bad choices before they do too much damage.

So far there is no inefficiency. Indeed, a national system of educational testing can be seen as a public good which avoids the need for wasteful duplication of selection tests by individual employers. The waste only arises because candidates compete to obtain the educational qualifications stipulated by the examining boards, leapfrogging each other but making no (or little) contribution to overall productivity. It is here that the divergence between the private and social rates of return occurs. There is nothing inevitable about this situation, however. It so happens that the content of school and university qualifications is on the whole (or at least is believed to be) rather irrelevant to eventual job performance, but in principle schools could teach and/or examine skills which were more relevant. The fact, if it is a fact, that extra years of schooling improve one's position in the queue for jobs but do not improve one's job skills may be simply a reflection of the current content of the syllabus. There is no incentive for employers to test for job skills, since the existing tests are 'good enough' value, but it does not follow that better tests and/or training could not be devised.

Even if we accept defeat on this front and make do with the existing system of testing, the waste is still not inevitable. The reason is again the public goods one. The market failure arises because of the 'tyranny of small decisions', but the tyranny can be overthrown in the usual way by instituting an appropriate social rule. If it is true that appropriate tests cannot be devised to encourage candidates to improve their skills rather than just their ranking, what we need to do is ration the different levels of education. This is to a large extent already done with university education, but the earlier decisions about when to leave school are left much more to the individual pupil and his family, and this is why the tyranny of small decisions can operate. In principle, however, there is no reason why access to the sixth form should not be rationed in just the same way as access to university. The crucial point is that the number of students attending different educational institutions can be set at the levels dictated by the social rates of return. Once this is done, testing and screening can be carried out in the usual way without waste of social resources. In summary, therefore, selection for leadership positions does not have to be through educational screening (and often is not), and educational screening does not necessarily have to involve a waste of resources.

The division between positional and material goods is now less interesting than at first appeared. Hirsch spends much of *Social Limits* elaborating and referring to the concept of positional competition, but it ends up as a synonym for, rather than an explanation of, the market's failure to reflect social costs at individual level. Inelasticity of supply and elasticity of demand, the original criteria for a positional good, prove to be neither necessary nor sufficient conditions for defensive consumption such as credentialism.

To recap, Hirsch attempts to explain the paradox of affluence through the idea that competition for positional goods leads in turn to defensive consumption, a distinct form of market failure. On investigation, however, 'positional competition' proves to be unable to explain this failure. He attempts to explain the 'distributional compulsion' through the idea that positional goods cannot be increased through the process of economic growth and therefore people will demand access to them through a redistribution of the present stock. The main criticism here is that Hirsch states rather than demonstrates the importance of these goods and mistakenly assumes that in showing how untraded interdependencies lead to a *misrepresentation* of satisfaction levels in conventional growth figures he has also explained why frustration at the distribution should be increasing. In order to do this he would need to explore the structure of normative expectations in liberal democracies, an undertaking Hirsch believes unnecessary for his argument.

The importance and failure of the liberal democratic 'ideology of growth' is a major theme in *Social Limits* but the connection between its failure and the response of society is undeveloped. That there are certain promises that growth cannot fulfil is clear but it is not clear why people should have ever believed that growth could fulfil these promises. The link is undeveloped because Hirsch eschews arguments based on the 'psychological re-evaluation' of the benefits of growth (Hirsch 1977: 7) such as those of Sam Brittan (1975).

A final misgiving about this part of *Social Limits* is that it never adequately confronts the fact that the distributional dissent he describes appears to have increased as economic growth has slowed. This must, within his argument, either be coincidence or the direction of causation must run from frustration to stagnation rather than the other way round. However, if this is the case Hirsch needs to suggest why frustrations have arisen at different absolute levels of economic welfare in different countries, where positional goods will be of differing importance. As

Schumpeter pointed out, the failure of economic growth need not be perceived as permanent for frustrations to appear:

> 'Any pro-capitalist argument must rest on long-run considerations. In the short run it is profits and inefficiencies which dominate the picture. In order to accept his lot the leveller or chartist of old would have to confront comfort himself with hopes for his great grandchildren. . . . For the masses it is the short-run view which counts. Like Louis XV they feel "après nous la deluge" and from the standpoint of the individualistic utilitarian they are of course perfectly rational if they feel like that.'   (Schumpeter 1976: 144)

The slower the growth the more rational such an attitude, as there is a smaller difference between the short-run and long-run outcomes. (In addition, one of the themes of Parts Two and Three of *Social Limits* is that such individualistic utilitarians are on the increase.)

Five

The distinguishing trait of the goods which Hirsch considers in *Social Limits* is not that they are positional but that competition for them is *coerced* (Heath 1976: 19). Coerced competition is competition in which the *status quo* is not an option. Most market exchanges are assumed to be voluntary; that is to say that the motive for entering into them is that one is better off after an exchange than before, as is the case with barter exchanges. However, the exchanges for the goods with which Hirsch is concerned are not voluntary, in that although one is better off participating in them than not, one is not necessarily better off after having participated than before. They approximate closer to the pattern of the highwayman's 'your money or your life' than to Robinson Crusoe and Man Friday exchanging oranges for apples in the textbooks of neo-classical micro-economics.

To take an example of a coerced market transaction: Radio Luxembourg has recently advertised a £5.00 package which includes tape-recorded advice and examples of letters of application designed to improve purchasers' chances of success at job interviews. Assuming the product is an effective one and that there is not a significant multiplier effect which expands the job market through the financial success of the venture, one's job chances are adversely affected simply by doing nothing. Either one joins in and sends off £5.00 or one gets left behind. Either way there is no aggregate benefit in such an exchange and consumption of the product, although recorded in the National Accounts as final and therefore an increase in GDP, is what Hirsch rightly deems 'defensive'. Indeed, if one has to run to stay where one is in the job queue it adversely affects aggregate welfare.

It is this argument which Hirsch is implicitly applying to the race for educational qualifications. Hirsch's contention is that there are certain goods – positional goods – which, however distributed, will lead to a paradox of affluence and increased distributional conflict as demand for them increases through the process of economic growth. The contention here is that there are certain forms of exchange which, whatever the goods under consideration, will lead to the phenomena Hirsch associated with affluence. The difference between the notions of positional and coerced competition is that the former aspires to be explanatory whilst the latter is descriptive. So far, no reason has been offered as to why coerced exchanges should increase with economic growth. However, there are a number of possibilities here. First, in a very general way we can expect economic growth to involve changes in supply and demand and hence in relative prices that make some people worse off (although others better off) and in that respect require them to run faster in order to stay in the same place. As an example of this consider the case of suburbanization which Hirsch deals with at some length. His picture is one of leapfrogging: people move to the suburbs to escape from the congestion of the city and to be near the quiet of the countryside, but as economic growth continues people move even further out so that those in the original suburb now find themselves cut off from the country.

Now the crucial point here (as with all Hirsch's examples) is that the action of others makes one worse off than before – the *status quo ante* is not an option for the original suburbanites. They find that the new building in the green belt has reduced their amenities – new building that has been permitted by economic growth. But this is in fact only a special case of a very general aspect of economic growth. In the short run, increased incomes may increase demand for certain goods so that existing purchasers find they have to pay more for their goods than they have been used to. For example, economic growth may increase the demand for, say, smoked salmon, and reduce that for fish and chips; relative prices will change and the erstwhile consumers of smoked salmon will find that they have to pay more for their customary pleasures than before. Most people would hardly regard this loss of satisfaction on the part of traditional consumers of smoked salmon as a serious side-effect of economic growth, although we may note that Hirsch, in the context of tourism, observes that 'if the increased activity of tourists at large deprives only one of their number of a satisfaction previously available, orthodox economic analysis provides no basis for judging the increase in tourism to be of net benefit' (Hirsch 1977: 38). One is inclined to retort 'so much the worse for economics', because economic growth is almost always going to bring gains to some but losses to others. Indeed, it probably goes even further than this; an individual, even the consumer of smoked salmon, is likely to find that growth has made him better off in some respects although worse off in others.

Of course, in the long run the increased demand for salmon may encourage new methods of fish farming, and the economies of scale may bring the price down so that in the end even the traditional consumer has benefited from the increased demand. If this happens, he hardly has good grounds for complaint, but unfortunately consumers probably do not always wait for the long run to decide whether to complain or not. Indeed, it may be precisely the short-run fluctuations in relative wages and prices that cause the most dissent and protest. Here we must make a sharp distinction between the economic concept of utility and want satisfaction and the sociological concept of satisfaction and relative deprivation. Economic growth may increase want satisfaction as measured by consumption of goods and services, but the changing relativities may also generate a greater chorus of protests and relative deprivation. In short, change will rarely entail a smooth transition to a new Pareto optimum; there will almost always be some losers who find they are coerced into new exchanges on worse terms than before.

The problem of changing relativities is clearly endemic in a society where goods and services are exchanged through the market, but there are further reasons why the problem may become particularly acute with economic growth. Technical change and innovation are one of the mainsprings of economic growth, but are bound to bring about defensive expenditure and coerced exchanges for many people. Suppose, for example, that a company introduces a new and superior model, such as a corrosion-free car at the same price as previous, inferior models. Clearly, this disadvantages existing car owners in one respect – they now have a less marketable asset in their present models; equally clearly it disadvantages competing manufacturers who have to engage in 'defensive investment' if they are to retain their share of the market. Indeed, it could be argued that this kind of innovation is a 'collective bad' for the manufacturers and that they have an interest in clubbing together to outlaw such changes (hence of course the need for anti-cartel legislation). Technological change may also increase the scope for coerced exchanges through the greater uncertainty that it generates. To take two obvious examples, again from the labour market: the interdependence engendered by technological change makes the marginal productivity of labour extremely difficult to measure – what is the marginal productivity of a skilled power worker who can darken a conurbation at the turn of a switch? In addition, technological change alters the criteria by which performance might be judged, as demands for new skills develop and old ones die. The perfection of indicators is constantly subverted by the changing criteria they must simulate.

Finally, one of the slightly paradoxical results of the development of information technology has been the potential for coerced exchanges that it has produced. It is quite easy to see how information might increase uncertainty: the fewer facts one has to hand, the easier it is to develop a hypothesis to fit those facts. Certainty is not synonymous with truth. As more and more information becomes available which is pertinent to any given situation, then the need to develop one's hypotheses to integrate that information becomes more acute. In such cases there is often a divergence between the social gains from this process and the private costs. For example, it has been argued that the rapid dissemination of information on exchange rates through the adoption of information technology by exchange dealers has increased the instability (and uncertainty) of exchange rates. It is a moot point whether over time the increased information flow provided will lead to a net increase in efficiency or not. What is clear is that for *any individual dealer* the situation constitutes a coerced exchange. A dealer has a choice of not acquiring the technology and therefore being at a disadvantage *vis-à-vis* his competitors, or acquiring it along with his competitors and being in a similar or worse position than in the *status quo*.

This last example underlines an important difference between the idea of positional competition and that of coerced exchange. The argument of this section has been that one cause of coerced exchange has been the entreprenurial exploitation of uncertainty. Unlike positional competition it is entirely unclear whether over time such exploitation moves society towards or away from expectations which more closely approximate reality (a reality which the exploitation itself alters). What is clear is that for the individual involved rather than for society as a whole, the game he is involved in is negative or zero-sum. A competitive struggle to produce more accurate information is likely *ceteris paribus* to lead to aggregate increases in economic welfare even if it is heavily redistributional. A competitive struggle to produce more and more effective disinformation is less likely to do so. One cannot, therefore, dismiss the possible merits of coerced exchanges in the same way that Hirsch dismisses the benefits of competition for positional goods: although the effects at individual level may lead to Hirsch's paradox of affluence or his distributional struggle, it is the possible hiatus between the individual and collective benefits that makes policy implications very difficult to evaluate.

Six

This critique is as guilty as Hirsch's in 'lacking a quantitative dimension', but one can none the less analytically isolate the occurrence of coerced exchanges in the market with relative ease and certainly with no more difficulty than one can isolate, for example, the abuse of power by monopoly suppliers of goods or services. However, even though there may be a case for banning certain goods which create coerced exchanges, there are a number of reasons why such an act by, for example, a 'Commission for Coerced Exchanges' might be problematic.

The first follows directly from the point made at the end of the concluding section: the short-term effects of such exchanges may be unpleasant for the individuals involved but it is unclear whether the longer-term effects of any particular exchange will prove to be benign or malign. Schumpeter argued that the long-term effects of monopoly may be collectively beneficial rather than otherwise since monopoly creates an entrepreneurial incentive to innovate. The same case may be put for coerced exchanges.

Second, as indicated above, there is an entreprenurial incentive to create such exchanges, and to intervene to diminish their effects would lead to frustrations not only on the part of the individual entrepreneur but also on the part of the consumer who wishes to purchase such an individually benign product, despite its collective inefficiencies. Were one to ban, for example, either the Radio Luxembourg advertised tapes or information technology used for dissemination of information on exchange rates, one can easily see how, provided the goods were effective, the incentive to turn to the black market to procure them would be acute. (Especially so if Hirsch and other contributors to this volume are correct in suggesting that such intervention would be collective interference in *ever more acute* economic individualism.)

If the suggestion in the previous section that uncertainty is increasing with rapid technological change is a correct one, then the dilemmas of intervention are likely to become more rather than less acute. One is faced with, on the one hand, a choice between the economically suboptimal results of laissez faire and the individual frustrations that are engendered by coerced exchanges and, on the other hand, economic intervention which is likely to incur the wrath of the very groups it is designed to protect. Whether or not coerced exchanges prove to constitute a significant proportion of total economic exchange is an empirical question, but it is fascinating that they have been overlooked in conventional economic analysis, which is built up from a pattern of voluntary exchange based on barter. One of the political justifications of the market has traditionally been that it maximized choice by decentralizing decisions to those who had the best information about how to take them. However, the attractiveness of this maximization of choice is dependent upon the voluntary nature of choices: once the barter analogy is broken, one finds it difficult to see the intrinsic *political* attraction of market choice. Outside the market one is often presented with coerced exchanges which present one with choices which one would wish to avoid ('your money or your life' for example), and any link between the maximization of choice and the maximization of freedom is wholly dependent upon those choices being voluntary ones and the *status quo* being an option in the choice. Once it is realized that market exchanges do not necessarily approximate to voluntary exchanges, then the political rather than economic attraction of the market is called into question. Whereas the concept of positional good draws attention to the supposed social *limits* to growth, then, the concept of coerced exchange emphasizes the social *costs* of growth. The usual comfortable assumption about growth was always that it brought benefits to all without introducing unpleasant issues of redistribution. Hirsch rightly challenges the assumption, but for the wrong reason. Our counter-argument is that growth is inevitably painful if pursued through the free play of market forces. There may be *net* increases in welfare, but the net increase will always conceal movements in opposite directions, at least in the short run. Changing relativities will inevitably cause dissatisfaction and distributional questions about the fairness of the new differentials. The paradoxes of affluence are thus no longer paradoxes if we see them as the consequences of change. Change is painful, and many of the struggles Britain has seen in recent years can be regarded as being intended to secure growth without the painful consequences of change. Demands for security of employment and fair wage differentials may have nothing to do with the social limits to growth but much to do with the desire to minimize the social costs of growth. Indeed, it may be that many people in Britain prefer more stability to more growth, and it may not be entirely fanciful to suppose that this has something to do with Britain's low rate of economic growth.

Note

1. An earlier version of some of the points in Sections Two and Three of this chapter appeared in the Political Studies Association of the United Kingdom's short articles journal *Politics* (Ellis 1981: 9–12).

References

BRITTAN, S. (1975) The Economic Contradictions of Democracy. *British Journal of Political Science* 5: 129–59.

DOWNS, A. (1957) *An Economic Theory of Democracy*. New York: Harper and Row.

ELLIS, A. (1981) The Paradox of Affluence. *Politics* 1 (1): 9–12.

HEATH, A. F. (1976) *Rational Choice and Social Exchange*. Cambridge: Cambridge University Press.

HIRSCH, F. (1977) *Social Limits to Growth*. London: Routledge and Kegan Paul.

HIRSCHMAN, A. O. (1970) *Exit, Voice and Loyalty*. Cambridge, Mass.: Harvard University Press.

——— (1977) *The Passions and the Interests; Political Arguments for Capitalism before Its Triumph*. Princeton: Princeton University Press.

OLSON, M. (1965) *The Logic of Collective Action*. New York: Schocken.

SCHUMPETER, J. (1976) *Capitalism, Socialism and Democracy*. London: Allen and Unwin.

THOMAS, K. (1965) The Social Origins of Hobbes's Political Thought. In K. C. Brown (ed.) *Hobbes Studies*. Oxford: Blackwell.

2 Technical change and 'social limits'

JONATHAN GERSHUNY

Some personal notes

I first read Professor Hirsch's book while sitting on a veranda of an otherwise deserted small hotel on a mountainside several thousand feet above the town of Aosta, with a view of the valley at my feet. I was at the end of a holiday. I had driven several thousand miles across Europe, swum in the Mediterranean (not too crowded early in the summer), spent some days in Venice (whence I had gone on a whim from Ravenna); now I had some days of relaxation in which to read and to walk in the hills before returning to Sussex. I cannot now think of *Social Limits* without reflecting on the ironical contrast between the substance of the book and the circumstances in which I read it.

I found the book moving, vigorous, humane, and witty. Its author's warm personality and kind intelligence communicated themselves vividly to me through every paragraph. It discussed issues that had long troubled me. I wanted to agree with its conclusions, but I could not do so. The more I think about its central thesis the more convinced I become of its error. The arguments seem to me to amount to a selfish defence of middle-class privilege – or, to be more precise, to the belated defence of a particular set of middle-class privileges, recently won, in historical terms, and still more newly lost, as a result of the post-war betterment in working-class life-styles. The implications of the thesis now seem to me illiberal and anti-progressive.

How is it that such an evidently nice man, in such a well-argued and attractive book, should provoke me to such hostility? In this paper I shall try to demonstrate that Hirsch made a number of errors. He committed a classic historicist fallacy, a generalization from cross-sectional, single time-point evidence, to a prediction of change over time. His account entirely omits one major issue: the question of whether technological change may alleviate the natural and socially generated scarcities which might otherwise inhibit genuine economic growth. But these are matters of merely technical controversy; I shall also try to look beyond them, to explain the reason for my antipathy to his argument.

Ultimately his condemnation of the consequences of economic growth seems to me to reflect his own position in society. He was of a class, and of a generation, which, it is true, did not reap any startling benefits from the economic growth of the 1950s and 1960s. Professor Hirsch, I suspect, grew up during the 1930s in circumstances in which domestic comforts, ample leisure time, interesting recreation, personal mobility, could be taken for granted; others, however, brought up in less privileged surroundings, have only recently come to similar circum-stances – and have done so as a consequence of economic growth. What Professor Hirsch saw as the degradation of life-styles due to social congestion, others might see as . . . redistribution of the benefits of society. I shall present some empirical material in support of this alternative view; but let us start by considering the more technical issues.

The 'Social Limits' thesis

The argument rests on what is in effect a theory of consumption, which distinguishes between the different sorts of satisfaction that an individual derives from different sorts of commodities. Commodities which satisfy the more basic human needs – e.g. for nourishment – give satisfaction strictly in relation to their intrinsic characteristics. So food, to a man on the breadline, is valued for its inherent nutritive qualities. The only constraint on the possibilities for economic growth to increase the supply of this sort of commodity is physical scarcity – ultimately the Malthusian scarcity of land on which to produce food. The Club of Rome's original *Limits to Growth* argument related to physical scarcity in this sense. But when we turn to commodities which satisfy what might be considered luxury requirements, we observe that characteristics other than the intrinsic qualities become important determinants of the satisfaction they generate. Extrinsic characteristics are now important – specifically the social context of the use of the commodities.

Hirsch identifies two ways in which the social context impinges on the satisfaction derived from the use of commodities. There are constraints which result from congestion: thus the satisfaction derived from a motor car is limited by the state of crowding on the roads (which in turn reflects the number of other people who have cars); or, to choose another, more abstract, of Hirsch's examples, the sort of job which may be obtained with a particular level of educational qualification depends on the number of other people who have attained that level. Of course, the supply of a commodity to other people does not *necessarily* diminish the satisfaction that an individual derives from consumption. On the contrary, the car owner needs some other car owners in order to justify the construction of roads; the well-educated individual gets the best economic return from his education in a society that has a sufficient level of general education to maintain an efficient modern economy. In these cases, the social context of consumption only constrains satisfaction when the commodities are *over*-supplied.

But Hirsch points to a second category, of cases where *any* increase in the supply of the commodity to others decreases the satisfaction derived by the individual. There is some satisfaction in, say, the possession of an Old Master painting, entirely extrinsic to the painting itself, that may be actually diminished by the discovery of a lost hoard of that Master's works. There is a class of benefit derived by the owner of the only weekend cottage on the shores of an isolated lake that is lost by the construction, however discreetly, of even one more cottage on the lake. Social cachet that depends on the exclusivity of possession of commodities is necessarily diminished by any increase in the supply of such commodities.

These two categories add up, in Hirsch's account, to a new sort of constraint on the possibilities for economic growth to add to human well-being. In addition to the Malthusian physical constraints, there is a new range of Hirschian social constraints. We can all build ladders and stand on them. We cannot all stand on each other's shoulders.

So far, I can see no objection. There clearly are some classes of satisfaction which depend on exclusivity and cannot logically be extended through any process of economic growth (or indeed by any mechanism whatsoever). But how numerous are these cases? What part of economic growth can be attributed to the vain attempt to evade Hirschian scarcity? And how do we evaluate the cases where the extension of supply of a commodity both reduces the level of 'extrinsic characteristic-related' satisfaction (i.e. its exclusivity) – and yet at the same time increases the level of 'intrinsic characteristic-related' satisfaction (i.e. the real material benefits to its individual consumers)? It is in the answers to these questions that I am forced to part company with Professor Hirsch.

A Marxian paradox

The really challenging part of Hirsch's argument is his analysis of the relationship between what he terms the 'material economy' ('output amenable to continued increase in productivity per unit of labour input' (Hirsch 1977: 27), and the 'positional economy' which supplies all those commodities which are subject to Hirschian scarcity either because of the constraints of congestion or of exclusivity. Economic growth must by definition take place entirely in the material economy. And yet, as more and more of our 'basic' material needs are satisfied, so our aspirations turn to the satisfaction of the more immaterial needs, the provision for which lies in the positional economy.

As we get richer, we want more personal services, which are considered not to be amenable to labour productivity growth; the increasing productivity in the material economy enables a growth in demand for services which therefore bids up their prices. In addition (though this is an aspect of the argument that Hirsch does not stress) the rising wages in the material economy induce a similar rise in wages in the personal services sector, in the name of 'maintaining pay differentials'; the fact that these differential-maintaining pay rises in the service sector, unlike those in the material economy, do not relate to any labour productivity growth also leads to a rise in the relative prices of services.

We may all want services, but we cannot all have servants (since *inter alia* some of us would have to *be* servants). The growth of the material economy simultaneously increases the wages of service workers and the money available to be spent on them, yet productivity in the service sector remains constant. Result: inflation, and the crisis of the welfare state.

And, as we get richer, we also want to improve our social status. Naturally, an individual seeking to advance relative to others in the society would seek to acquire commodities associated with the positional economy. He or she might hope to acquire status at the expense of some other individual. But what if we *all* seek advancement?

The commodities of the positional economy are naturally limited in supply; an increase in demand for them tends to inflate their prices. So we look to the commodities of the material economy to fulfil the same function. Our real material needs are now satisfied, but we use material commodities as proxies for the immaterial ones; we buy goods, not for themselves, but for the status that we believe they will confer on us (Hirsch refers to this practice as 'the new commodity fetishism'). While real positional commodities are in scarce supply, these proxies are not – the economic growth that enables us to buy material status goods, enables our neighbour to buy them as well, and frustrate our purpose in doing so. We cannot all simultaneously advance our status – or at least, when we try to do so, we all end up exactly where we started in relation to each other.

Hirsch borrows a powerful image from Young and Wilmott's *The Symmetrical Family* (1973: 167). It presents the developing society in the guise of a long, slowly marching column. From time to time the vanguard wheels to right or left; one by one, the following ranks wheel on the same spot. The spacing between the ranks represents the income distribution, it remains essentially unchanged; yet, to Young and Willmott, this is social progress – each rank does advance in material terms. Hirsch's rebuttal is of course that if the purpose of each forward step is to advance *relative to the rank ahead*, then no progress is made.

If the pursuit of positional advantage is really the aim of consumption of the products of the material economy, why do we not recognize its fatuity, and abandon it in favour of, say, Zen Buddhism? Hirsch explains this succinctly:

> 'Taking part in the scramble [for advancement] is fully rational for any individual in his own actions, since in these actions he (or she) never confronts the distinction between what is available as a result of getting ahead of others and what is available from a general advance shared by all.'   (Hirsch 1977: 10, my parentheses)

What is available to each individual is not available to all individuals.

Once we have seen economic growth in these terms (the individually rational in hot pursuit of the collectively unachievable) our attention turns to its costs. We can find no statistical evidence that inhabitants of rich countries are happier than inhabitants of poor countries, or that people get happier as their countries get richer, but only that the relatively poor in a country are less happy than the relatively rich – a problem that general economic expansion cannot alleviate (Hirsch 1977: 111–14). And we see the congested roads, the populated countryside, the crowded seaside. We see the poor put-upon consumer frantically trying to use all his consumer durables – simultaneously, since time itself has become congested. (See the quotation in Staffan Linder (1971: 73).) The sorry trudge of the rearguard of the marching column is across ground broken and muddied by the forward ranks.

So this is the argument. Our material needs are satisfied, so we become increasingly concerned to advance our status. But the positional economy is not susceptible to economic growth, so we attempt to use the material economy, which is susceptible to growth, as a proxy – we transfer some of the function of the positional to the material. While this attempt may appear rational to any single individual, if the whole society attempts to advance in this way, nothing whatsoever can be achieved other than the generation of what conventional economists are pleased to term 'externalities' – pollution, congestion, and the wasteful depletion of resources. Hirsch has effectively restated Marx's well-known paradox. Economic growth offers us the membership of the sorts of clubs we would not wish to belong to if they would have us as members.

An alternative theory of consumption

This seems a strong case, but it rests heavily on Hirsch's analysis of the motives for consumption. If it is true that the main reason for the growth in demand for consumer goods is the pursuit of the status they are presumed to confer on the consumer, then his argument stands as a weighty criticism of the central aspiration of all developed economies. But if on the contrary we can show that the main motive for this consumption has something to do with some intrinsic characteristics of the goods – that the extrinsic, position-conferring function of goods is in general a subsidiary motive for their purchase – then the argument is revealed as rather less fundamentally important. In this section I shall discuss an alternative theory of consumption, one that I hope will plausibly suggest that post-war economic growth did – and future economic growth might still – produce real material benefits for the great majority. But the issue is largely an empirical one; in a following section I shall produce some unusual evidence of the actual effects of growth in the material economy.

The conventional economists' position was once that demand for a commodity reflected two things – a 'need' for that commodity combined with an ability to pay for particular quantities of it at particular rates. Innovators such as Galbraith and Lancaster have made it apparent that there is nothing immutable about these 'needs' – indeed, to the extent that there are any genuinely immutable requirements involved, Galbraith's arguments suggest that these are the institutional requirements of the producers rather than of the consumers. Lancaster argues that 'goods are not goods' but rather bundles of desirable characteristics perceived by the purchaser, this perception being in part at least determined by the producer's packaging and presentation. Hirsch's contribution to this line of argument is to stress that among this bundle of characteristics is the social status supposed to attach to possession of the product.

My work, over the last few years – and partly stimulated by my reading of Hirsch's book – has been devoted to the development of an alternative version of Lancaster's theory of consumption. This alternative theory also relies on a notion of need for particular characteristics of products; in my case these characteristics relate specifically to the way, the *purpose* for which the products are used. In my approach 'needs' refer to the requirements for the 'final service functions' that all commodities ultimately fulfil; we do not have needs for particular commodities, rather, we have certain requirements which might be satisfied in various different ways by different combinations of commodities.

This is not a mere conceptual device; we can describe these requirements empirically. With a comprehensive list of such service functions, we can classify each item of final expenditure, each final purchase of a commodity in an economy by its purpose. *Table 1* outlines such a classificatory exercise, using the expenditure categories of the European System of National Accounts. It identifies ten service functions – nutritional, shelter, domestic, entertainment, transport, educational, medical, governmental, and other – though of course this list could be either longer or shorter depending on the purpose.

Each item of final consumption, by households or collective agencies such as governments or charities, can be classified as relating to one of these functions (investment expenditure is treated as intermediate output for these purposes). Obviously relating to each of the final functions will be a number of very different commodities. There will be finished final services, privately purchased, or furnished collectively, which provide for the final function directly. And there will be various other commodities – materials, consumer durables, material infrastructure, intermediate services – which provide for similar functions indirectly; they are used in what I have elsewhere termed the 'informal' production of services: economic activity outside the measured money economy, producing the final services we actually consume. Thus, to satisfy the 'transport' function, for example, we employ a mixture of final services produced in the money economy – buses and trains and taxis – and final services produced informally – car or bicycle travel – which employ products (i.e. cars and bicycles) from the formal economy as intermediate inputs to the final transport service function. We either buy final services, or buy goods and make the services ourselves.

Over extended periods of time we can see, in the distribution of final expenditure classified in the manner outlined in *Table 1*, two quite different classes of systematic change. First we can see a change in the

Table 1 Purposes of household and government final expenditure, classified by function and by type of commodity*

'function' classification	'commodity' classification		
	primary and manufactured goods	marketed services	non-marketed services
a. food, drink, tobacco	food, drink, tobacco (D1)		
b. shelter, clothing	rent, fuel and power, clothing and footwear (D2, D3)	personal care and effects (D81)	housing and community amenities (sewers, etc.) (G6)
c. domestic functions	furniture, furnishings, appliances, utensils and repairs to these (D41 to D44)	household operation and domestic services (D45, D46)	social security and welfare services (G5)
d. entertainment	equipment, accessories, and repairs to these, books, etc. (D71, D73)	entertainment, recreation, cultural, hotels, cafes, etc., package tours (D72, D83, D84)	recreational, cultural and religious services (G7)
e. transport, communications	personal transport equipment and operation (D61, D62)	purchased transport and communications services (D63, D64)	roads, waterways, communications, and their administration subsidies (G8.5, G8.6, G8.7)

functions provided mainly by households

functions provided mainly by governments

	goods	services	public services
f. education		purchased education (D74)	public education (G3)
g. medical functions	medical and pharmaceutical products and appliances (D51, D52)	purchased medical services, medical insurance service charges (D53, D54, D55)	public health services (G4)
h. other government functions			general public services and economic services excluding transport and communications (G1, G8.1 to G8.4, G8.8)
i. defence			defence (G2)
j. functions n.e.s.	goods n.e.s. (D82)	Services n.e.s. (D85, D86)	other public services n.e.s. (G9)

ESA Classification and Coding of the Purposes of Final Consumption of Households. ESA 1979 Table 7. (The same as Table 6.1, SNA, UN, New York 1968).

ESA Classification and Coding of the Purposes of General Government. ESA 1979, Table 8. (The same as Table 5.3, SNA, New York, 1968.)

* References in parentheses to classifications of the European System of Integrated Economic Accounts (ESA).

distribution of expenditure by 'final services function'. We see, through-out the developed world, a shift in the balance of expenditure away from the more basic categories of nutrition and shelter towards the more luxury categories of domestic services, entertainment, transport, educa-tion, and medicine. (Evidence for this proposition is discussed at length in Gershuny and Miles (1983).)

This is of course quite in accord with Hirsch's argument. Basic needs being satisfied, we want sophisticated services. Hirsch argues however that these sophisticated services are in necessarily short supply. We cannot all have domestic servants, professional musicians entertaining us in our drawing rooms, personal chauffeurs. But could equivalent final service functions not be provided for by other means? At this point we have to consider a second class of systematic change in expenditure patterns over time.

In addition to the shift towards the satisfaction of the more sophisti-cated final service functions, we may also see a shift away from the purchase of some finished final services towards expenditure on mate-rials, consumer durables, intermediate services. This reflects a change in the mode of provision for particular final service functions. As the relative costs, and the technical performances, of alternative means for providing for particular functions change, so households change the technical means they employ to satisfy them. We now use cars instead of buses, washing machines instead of laundries, televisions instead of music halls.

The post-war decades saw substantial changes of this sort in three of the service function categories – domestic, entertainment, and transport. The growing demand for the satisfaction of these functions did indeed have a Hirschian effect on the availability and quality of the finished final services associated with these functions. The prices of these services rose; overall consumption of them declined. This is clearly what Hirsch describes as congestion: the increased effective demand eventually leads to a reduction in output as prices rise, quality falls, and customers go elsewhere. And some people – precisely those people who were pre-viously in a position to purchase the final services and now are not – will certainly feel themselves worse-off as a result.

But the question we must ask ourselves is: what is the overall balance of consequences between those who are worse-off and those who are better-off? Because others who previously were ill-provided with these service functions are now better provided. Admittedly the extrinsic characteristics that previously attached to the satisfaction of the particu-lar function have been degraded. But is the *only* reason that we want sophisticated services that the nobs on the hill have them? Presumably we would place *some* value on having the clean and convenient housing, the frequent changes of clothing, the occasional changes of scene, the regular access to entertainment that is enabled by the self-serviced, consumer durable owning mode of service provision – even though access to these does not imply the social status that once it did.

An extension of the same argument applies to those more luxurious final service functions which have not in the past been subject to innovations in their mode of provision. The post-war decades saw an expansion in the provision of educational and medical services. But we would certainly not consider that the current level of provision of these is satisfactory. And it is rather difficult, at least in countries like Britain, to see how the levels of provision could be substantially improved by simple extensions to the existing system. Clearly we have Hirschian congestion here: to provide all the educational and medical services we might conceivably want, we would all have to *be* doctors or teachers. An impasse?

Not necessarily: just as we had, in the 1950s and 1960s, innovations in the mode of provision for domestic and transport and entertainment services, based on a particular set of technologies developed in the 1930s and before (the fractional horsepower electric motor, the valve, the television tube, the internal combustion engine), so we might imagine future innovations in the mode of provision of educational and medical services involving technologies we have already developed (the micro-computer, the video-recorder, the satellite and fibre-optic telecommunications links). The Open University is a harbinger, though we have hardly started to consider the variety of possible social forms that such innovations might take. Of course, there will be negative effects, just as there were in the historical examples. The new modes of provision will tend to price some particular sorts of personal services in these categories beyond the pockets of all but a diminishing number of plutocrats. The hour-long supervision of one undergraduate by one university professor may disappear as we adopt some of the techniques of the Open University. But can we really justify the persistence of a society which provides this sort of education – to 5 per cent of its population?

Social innovation versus Hirschian scarcity

So the central point of my argument against Hirsch concerns the mutability of his social scarcities, and in the evaluation of the costs that arise because of them. Hirsch sees the proliferation of demand for consumer durables as the vain striving for positional advancement. My argument should not be interpreted as denying the existence of a positional component in this proliferation; the extrinsic, positional characteristics of the products certainly explains some part of this sort of growth. But nevertheless, it must surely be wrong to ignore completely the intrinsic characteristics – the uses to which consumer durables, and their associated consumable materials and infrastructures and intermediate services, are put.

Hirsch sees, in the spread of consumer durables, an attempt to achieve the aims of the positional economy through the material economy – an attempt that is, if not individually at least collectively, quite irrational. The approach that I have outlined, considering innovation in the mode of provision of service functions, suggests a subtly different process: particular sorts of final service provision, which were previously placed within the positional economy by reason of their resistance to improvement in the efficiency of their production, are, by the application of new techniques and forms of social organization, removed to the material economy. The consumption of the commodities which provide for these particular service functions necessarily lose their positional connotation – since they are now in plentiful, not scarce, supply. Some people accordingly lose the possession of positional goods. But others gain materially. Hirsch concentrates our attention on the loss, and distracts us from the gain.

The overall process of development implied by this approach to consumption theory is quite different from 'the slow march'. In important respects, the rear ranks tread different ground to the forward. The change in the mode of provision of the service functions means a very real change in life-style. The poor, when they attain equivalent levels of provision of a particular service function to those enjoyed by the rich at some previous point in time, do not have the same pattern of activities as the rich did; and probably the dynamics of Hirschian congestion mean that the rich no longer have this pattern of life either. The well-serviced households of the rich meant the employment of servants; the rich and the poor now may both have well-serviced houses, but many fewer of the rich have servants. The marching column moves sideways as well as forwards.

And it is by no means clear that the forward ranks always take the leading role in promoting the innovative modes of provision of services. To choose one example from the data we shall consider in the following section: in the 1930s listening to the radio seems to have been largely an activity of the poor, rather than of the rich; yet this was clearly the harbinger of the dominant leisure activity (watching TV) of both the rich and the poor in the post-war period.

The central error in Hirsch's approach is the identification of particular sorts of needs with particular sorts of consumption. There are in fact no necessary connections between classes of need and consumption categories. The connection is mediated by technology – the particular means, the techniques and forms of organization that households adopt to satisfy their needs. The social improvement that comes with economic growth is provided, not so much by the technical change that makes particular material commodities cheaper and hence more widely available, as by this other, *domestic* technical change – change in the way households combine purchased commodities to produce the services they actually consume. Change in the mode of provision of final service functions means that the poor do not consume the things the rich used to consume – rather that new, shared patterns emerge; an effective sort of equalization, as the examples in the following section will show, lowering some standards for the richer classes perhaps, but raising standards for the poorer.

Changing activities in a period of economic growth

So far the argument is no more than theory. Hirsch introduces a particular analytical perspective to describe the effects of economic growth; I counterpose an alternative perspective. Both ways of approaching the problem will certainly have some validity – but the question we must now consider is: which is the more suitable? There is no single correct answer to this question, since (I will return to this later) the choice between our two perspectives is ultimately a matter of politics. But nevertheless empirical evidence can make a substantial contribution to our understanding of the problem. The degradation of life-styles described by Hirsch does have one particular empirical manifestation – that daily life becomes progressively more congested, with time devoted increasingly to activities related to the consumption of material goods, and with a decreasing amount of uncommitted leisure time.

The alternative perspective does not produce a directly contrary prediction and there is nothing in the argument to suggest that this time congestion will necessarily increase. It does however suggest that, during periods of economic growth, we might expect to see two other sorts of change in people's time-use patterns not predicted within the Hirschian perspective. We would expect to find that as the poorer groups in society gain access to particular sorts of services not previously open to them, so the differences between the activity patterns of richer and poorer groups in the society get smaller. And in relation to particular classes of services, particular 'service functions', the proportion of time spent in the direct consumption of final services produced by groups in the formal economy should decline relative to the proportion of time spent in what might be considered 'self-service' activities.

My argument, in this empirical discussion, as in the foregoing more theoretical sections, is that the reduction in differences between the social classes' access to services which is enabled by self-servicing, and in particular the improvement in the position of the worse-off sectors of society, should be set against the Hirschian costs of economic growth to the better-off.

Hirsch himself discusses the effects of economic growth on time use patterns quite extensively (for example in Chapter 5). But he does so through the medium of anecdotes and theoretical models rather than substantial empirical material. The reason for this is that when he wrote, there was virtually no historical time-series data on time use patterns available to him. Since then, however, some longitudinal collections of time-series data have started to become available. My research group at Sussex has been responsible for one such exercise; we now have comparable data for the UK for 1974 and 1975, 1961, and, with some reservations, 1937. We can use this information to discover the relative weight of the Hirschian time congestion and the redistribution of activity patterns suggested by my approach. I shall exhibit just two pieces of evidence, concerning change in housewives' domestic work, and the distribution of leisure between different types of activity.

The first of these is the more dramatic. There has been extensive discussion of the consequences of the spread of domestic equipment for housework (see Robinson and Converse 1972; Robinson, Converse, and Szalai 1972; Vanek 1974), the conclusions of which seem to be that, surprisingly, the supposed labour-saving equipment seems to have increased the amount of domestic work. Vanek, for example, in a widely cited article, suggests that housework time for housewives actually increased, between about 1930 and the mid-1960s, from about 445 minutes per average day, to about 470 minutes. Robinson and Converse (1972) similarly report that: 'The time spent on chores associated with the upkeep and management of a home and family, including care of the children and shopping for food, . . . is remarkably higher in our 1965/6 data than in the studies from the 1930s.'

This striking evidence would seem to lend strong support to Hirsch's thesis. After all, the diffusion of these same 'labour-saving' domestic appliances constitutes a large part of the benefits that any apologist for economic growth must cite as the positive consequence of the social and economic changes of the 1950s and 1960s. (And a large portion of the overall growth in output of developed economies during these decades must relate to the expansion of the industries producing these appliances.) If the result of the spread of these devices has been in fact to increase the amount of housework, then whatever new services they generate must be set against the extra time spent using them. It looks as if, far from liberating her, the acquisition of new capital equipment for house cleaning, clothes washing, and cooking has involved the average American housewife in more of the traditional domestic activities. The new possessions, it seems, burden us with new but unrewarding ways of spending our time. The evidence might be construed as an example of Hirschian time congestion.

Some part of this evidence for the USA is paralleled by our data for the UK. It does appear from our material that the time spent in housework by the average UK housewife did rise quite significantly between 1937 and 1961. Our estimates are very similar to the American ones, both in their absolute level and in the change over the decades. Are we then forced to accept that a process of Hirschian time congestion has really taken place?

We can place a quite different interpretation on the evidence. The original time-use diaries, from which the American evidence derives, have disappeared; the surviving material consists of tables constructed by the original researchers themselves. This means that certain sorts of information, particular ways of tabulating the data, which would not have been of interest to American sociologists of the 1920s, or to the agricultural economists who collected the most extensive and best documented data of the period, cannot now be reconstructed. In particular, we do not have information about domestic work time broken down by social class. Our UK investigations, however, have unearthed the original 1937 diaries, together with a wealth of background information about the diarists, amply sufficient to enable us to ascribe their social class.

Figure 2 plots the change in housewives' work time between 1937 and 1975, for working- and middle-class groups separately (weighting the 1937 data to give the same proportion of women with children as in the 1961 sample), and for an (appropriately weighted) average of the two groups. For the average group we see a pattern very much as described by the American researchers, in which housework time increases from the 1930s to the 1960s. But the explanation for this is revealed when we disaggregate the sample by social class. It is not that housework time is increasing marginally for all, but rather that housework time is increasing markedly for some – middle-class – women, while substantially decreasing, from the mid-1950s onwards, for other – working-class – women.

There are quite clearly two different processes at work. The first is the increase in housework time consequent on the loss of domestic servants from middle-class households. This is substantiated by the fact that

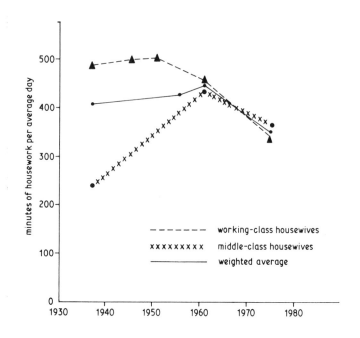

Figure 2 Housewives' domestic work (non-employed, or part-time-employed women)

Sources: 1937   Mass Observation manuscript diaries
                (Gershuny and Thomas 1983, forthcoming)

           1951   Mass Observation Ltd, *The Housewives' Day*
                (working class only)

           1956   Mass Observation Ltd, *The Housewives' Day*
                (middle and working classes averaged)

           1961   BBC Audience Research Department data
           1974/75 (Gershuny and Thomas 1983, forthcoming)

those few housewife diarists from 1937 whom we classified as middle class, even though their households had no servants, did as much or even more housework than their working-class equivalents. The second trend is the reduction in housework time in working-class households, which we may suspect relates to the diffusion of domestic equipment. We cannot prove this suspicion – but the fact that the same trend holds when we control for employment status, and for the presence of children in the household, at least rules out these alternative explanations.

So what emerges from the data is not Hirschian time congestion, but rather the redistribution of access to services suggested by my alternative model. The middle-class households lose their access to the fully 'serviced' mode of provision of domestic services. They have had to increase the amount of unpaid labour they contribute to their own domestic servicing, and (in so far at least as the loss of servants has meant the move to less spacious accommodation) the standard of domestic services they consume may actually have declined over the whole period covered by this figure.

By contrast, the working-class households' contribution of unpaid labour to their own domestic services has declined dramatically. And few people, comparing their memories of working-class domestic life in the 1930s to current conditions, would be tempted to argue that the physical conditions of life are in any way inferior. A balanced appraisal of the changes would be, it seems to me, that the middle classes – and particularly middle-class women – may have partly lost their previously privileged position in this sphere of life, but the working classes (for these purposes, say 70 per cent of the population – the proportion of people who could never have expected to employ domestic servants) have gained considerably. And this redistribution of the benefits of society has taken place through the agency of the change in the social and technical organization of the provision of domestic services resulting from economic growth.

The second piece of evidence can be dealt with more briefly. *Table 2* sets out the allocation of leisure time by various different demographic groups to various different categories of leisure activity. The leisure activities are classified here in a manner analogous to *Table 1*. It identifies three different categories of leisure ('spectator', 'sociable', and 'other at home') and two alternative modes of provision ('serviced' and 'self-serviced'). In the 'spectator' category, television and radio would count as 'self-serviced', while going to the theatre or cinema, or watching sporting events where they happen, would be 'serviced'; in the 'sociable' category, seeing friends or going to parties would be 'self-serviced', while going to restaurants, pubs, and so on, would be classed as 'serviced'.

Table 2a *Allocation of leisure time (mins per average day) (ages 25–45; excluding leisure travel)*

		middle class			working class		
		self-serviced	serviced	total	self-serviced	serviced	total
employed men, with children							
spectator	1937	19	31	50	76	17	93
	1961	118	23	141	144	10	155
	1975	120	18	138	151	18	169
sociable	1937	95	24	119	7	7	14
	1961	32	10	42	25	13	38
	1975	46	18	64	49	30	79
other	1937	–	–	94	–	–	126
	1961	–	–	67	–	–	52
	1975	–	–	79	–	–	53
employed men, no children							
spectator	1937	11	71	82	26	55	81
	1961	95	18	113	155	27	182
	1975	98	26	124	161	12	173
sociable	1937	56	38	94	12	43	55
	1961	49	24	73	43	17	60
	1975	65	47	112	56	23	79
other	1937	–	–	141	–	–	132
	1961	–	–	65	–	–	42
	1975	–	–	54	–	–	55
non-employed women, with children							
spectator	1937	1	64	65	24	27	51
	1961	103	12	115	156	8	164
	1975	120	14	134	167	10	177
sociable	1937	63	104	167	27	3	30
	1961	46	11	57	44	7	51
	1975	67	11	78	87	11	98
other	1937	–	–	114	–	–	94
	1961	–	–	100	–	–	77
	1975	–	–	104	–	–	79

Tables 2a and *b* demonstrate two things quite clearly. First, in the 1930s there were some really striking differences in the availability of leisure time, both between the classes and between the sexes. The middle classes, in general, did better than the working; women, with the exception of the middle classes, did worse than men in an equivalent position. By the 1970s the absolute size of both of these disparities had declined; the class difference has essentially disappeared, and the most important disparity is now between employed men and employed women. And, unlike the domestic work example (and with the exception of middle-class women), the disappearance of the class differences has resulted from an increase in working-class leisure time rather than a decrease in middle-class leisure.

Second, the mode of provision of leisure services has changed away from the 'serviced' towards the 'self-serviced' category – just as in the case of domestic services. This has happened, not just for spectator activities, where the spread of televisions makes the development unsur-

Table 2b   *Change in activities, minutes per day, 1937–1975*

	middle class			working class		
	self-serviced	service	total	self-serviced	service	total
employed men, with children						
spectator	+101	−23	+88	+ 75	+ 1	+ 76
sociable	− 49	− 6	−55	+ 42	+13	+ 65
other			−15			− 73
			+18			+ 68
employed men, no children						
spectator	+ 87	−45	+42	+135	−43	+ 92
sociable	+ 9	+ 9	+18	+ 44	−20	+ 24
other			−87			− 67
			−27			+ 49
non-employed women, with children						
spectator	+119	−50	+69	+143	−17	+126
sociable	+ 4	−93	−89	+ 60	+ 8	+ 68
other			−10			− 15
			−30			+179

prising, but also among sociable activities. Since 1961, a very large part of the growth in leisure activities has been accounted for by the self-serviced part of the sociable category – visiting friends and going to parties. We cannot explain all of the growth of 'self-serviced' leisure to the consumer durables distributed as a result of the overall economic expansion. But nevertheless, televisions, record players, motor cars to increase the ease and convenience of visiting friends, cannot be ignored as contributors to these leisure trends.

Just showing that overall leisure time has been increasing does not really dispose of the possibility of Hirschian congestion. Hirsch was really writing about the *quality* of leisure time, not its quantity. The evidence I have presented does not tell us anything about the state of crowding, the intensity, of recreational activity. My suspicion is that the arguments relating to this phenomenon in the book are quite valid. But the evidence does demonstrate empirically what I previously argued on theoretical grounds – a set of consequences of economic growth ignored by Hirsch.

The evidence demonstrates technical and organizational change in the mode of provision of final service functions to households *enabled by the diffusion of consumer durables*, which has the effect of equalizing access to services between the rich and the poor. This is not brought about by the slow march mechanism whereby the poor follow the consumption patterns of the rich – after all, doing your own housework, watching television, are, historically speaking, somewhat plebeian activities. Cross-sectional comparisons between the behaviour of the rich and the poor at one point in time seem, on the evidence I have presented, to be a rather poor basis for predicting change over time. The poor do not necessarily ape the past behaviour of the rich; rather, social congestion as a result of economic growth may well force the rich to imitate the activity patterns of the poor.

How should we evaluate the relative weight of Hirschian degradation of traditional services and the spread of new patterns of service delivery? There can be no single answer. I could never have told Professor Hirsch that my benefits objectively outweighed his costs. But similarly there is no way that he could have argued the opposite. He could certainly suggest that the very existence of costs and benefits distributed differentially to different people means that economic growth does not lead to a social improvement, in the Paretian sense of positive benefits to all affected parties. But the very imposition of the Pareto criterion would involve a political judgement; social change would be rare indeed if it could only happen when benefits to some involve no costs whatsoever to others.

A personal reaction

So where does this leave *Social Limits*? Unquestionably Hirsch identifies a clear set of *costs* of economic growth. But, in addition to their place in the (ultimately fruitless) competition for positional advantage, the goods that growth gives us access to have also intrinsic characteristics which may yield material benefits. So the question of whether these costs constitute *limits* is clearly a political one. It seems that, just as in the debate about the physical limits to growth, new forms of technology and social organization can enable expansion where traditional patterns would prevent it. To accept Hirsch's costs as limits would be to enshrine the standards of the upper middle class and exclude entirely the interests of absolutely everyone else.

The evidence in the previous section points to some categories of improvement in the life-styles of working-class people over the past few decades which may be reasonably directly attributed to economic growth. But it is not just the working classes who benefit.

Let me return to my veranda above the town of Aosta. In the pine woods around the hotel are a number of small, newly built chalets. I am told that they belong to families from Turin, no more than an hour and a half's travel away by car on the new motorway. They are weekend cottages. Is the economic growth that puts such luxuries within the grasp of the petty bourgeoisie of Turin entirely to be despised, even though it entails the breaking-up of the great estates which were the country homes of the Italian merchant aristocracy?

And I must finally consider my own presence here in these mountains. My grandparents arrived in England as penniless refugees from Eastern Europe. My family has become relatively well-off only because of the wealth generated by new demand for particular sorts of professional services. I can take a holiday like this only because of the wages I earn in a job in an institution that has doubled its size three times over in the last ten years, for which I have become qualified by academic degrees from three different universities, none of which was in existence a quarter of a century ago. For me, to accept Professor Hirsch's argument would be to reject my own class identity.

So this is my position: I accept the existence of Hirschian congestion in the pursuit of scarce positional commodities as a cost of economic growth; I reject, however, the suggestion that the pursuit of positional advantage is the only, or even the main, motive for the acquisition of material goods. Historically speaking, consumer durables have greatly extended the accessibility of a range of domestic, transport, and leisure services. In the future we might expect new commodities similarly to extend access to educational, medical, information, and communications services which are currently in restricted supply. In doing so, some of the extrinsic characteristics of the current pattern of provision of these services to their current privileged consumers may be degraded – this is a price which we may well wish to pay.

References

GERSHUNY, J. I. and MILES, I. D. (1983) *The New Service Economy*. London: Frances Pinter.

GERSHUNY, J. I. and THOMAS, G. S. (1981) Changement des modeles de loisirs, Royaume Uni, 1961–1974/75. *Temps Libres* **4**.

GERSHUNY, J. I. and THOMAS, G. S. (1983 forthcoming) *Changing Times*.

HIRSCH, F. (1977) *Social Limits to Growth*. London: Routledge and Kegan Paul.

LINDER, S. (1971) *The Harried Leisure Class*. New York: Columbia University Press.

MASS OBSERVATION LTD (1951) *The Housewives' Day*.

—— (1956) *The Housewives' Day*.

ROBINSON, J. P. and CONVERSE, P. E. (1972) Social Change Reflected in the Use of Time. In A. Campbell and P. E. Converse (eds) *The Human Meaning of Social Change*. New York: Russell Sage.

ROBINSON, J. P., CONVERSE, P. E., and SZALAI, A. (1972) *Everyday Life in Twelve Countries*. In A. Szalai (ed.) *The Use of Time*. The Hague: Mouton.

VANEK, J. (1974) Time Spent in Housework. *Scientific American* **231**: 116–20.

YOUNG, M. and WILLMOTT, P. (1973) *The Symmetrical Family*. London: Routledge and Kegan Paul.

3 Hirsch, Hayek, and Habermas: dilemmas of distribution

RAYMOND PLANT

'Capitalism's lack of a moral basis of its own and its reliance on the – weakening – morality of an earlier era, have of late been taken up in a remarkably similar fashion by both Marxists and economic liberals.'   *(Goldthorpe 1978: 213)*

This chapter will be concerned with the elaboration of John Gold-thorpe's very perceptive remark which is buried in a footnote in his recent contribution to *The Political Economy of Inflation* (Goldthorpe and Hirsch 1978). I shall try to show how recent work by Fred Hirsch on *The Social Limits to Growth* (1977), Friedrich Hayek on *The Mirage of Social Justice* (1976) (which forms volume II of *Law, Legislation and Liberty*), and Jürgen Habermas on *Legitimation Crisis* (1976) point to a rather similar diagnosis of the central problems of the liberal capitalist welfare state, and I shall investigate their divergent remedies for these problems and shall try to indicate some of the major lines of criticism which can be made of these different solutions.

One of the difficulties which these thinkers regard as central to the modern state is its lack of an agreed concrete morality, what Hegel would have called the lack of *Sittlichkeit*. I shall be less concerned with the historical validity of their strictures on the decline of an agreed morality in the process of capitalist development in this essay, than with the importance which the perceived lack of capitalist *Sittlichkeit* has to the capitalist state in the context of economic management, welfare, and distribution.

It might seem on the face to it to be rather implausible to suggest that issues of moral value could have any central importance for problems of economic management, and it is important to give some indication of what the connection is seen to be. It has become an important feature of the modern state that it should use the welfare system to counter some of the dysfunctional effects of the economic market and to pursue to a greater or lesser extent social justice, welfare, greater equality, and so on. In Habermas's view, the *legitimacy* of the modern state depends upon the possibility of securing welfare and raising living standards for its citizens. Until recently it has been a relatively painless matter to secure these conditions of legitimacy by utilizing the dividend of economic growth. Theories of both the left and the right have sought to utilize economic growth as a solution for distribution and welfare issues. Hayek (1960) argues the thesis that free markets increase wealth better than planned economies and that the benefits of economic growth will gradually be reaped by all through an 'echelon advance' or 'trickle-down' effect. People's living standards will improve as the result of the effects of growth and this will be the most efficient way of securing welfare:

> 'If today in the United States or Western Europe the relatively poor can have a car or refrigerator, or airplane trip or radio at the cost of a reasonable part of their income, this was made possible because in the past others with large incomes were able to spend on what was then a luxury. The path of advance is greatly eased by the fact that it has been trodden before. It is because scouts have found the goal that the road can be built for the less lucky and the less energetic . . . . Many of the improvements would indeed never have become a possibility for all if they had not long before been available for some. If all had to wait for better things until they could be provided for all, that day would, in many instances, never come. Even the poorest today owe their relative well being to the result of past inequalities.'   (Hayek 1960: 44)

As the final sentence of this passage makes clear, Hayek is not interested in social justice so much as the conditions necessary for raising living standards for all even though this will involve considerable inequalities. The capitalist state is legitimate in so far as it secures the necessary conditions, in terms of laws and procedures, for the successful pursuit of entrepreneurial activity, the success of which will secure higher living standards for all members of society. Obviously physical or social limitations on the possibility of growth would threaten the echelon advance which secures the allegiance of citizens to the system.

The echelon advance notion was also important for democratic socialists such as Anthony Crosland who were interested in the rate of economic growth not so much for securing increasing prosperity as such, but more for increasing equality and social justice. The reason for this is as follows: in a democratic society it is highly unlikely that consent will be secured from the electorate for redistributive taxation significantly to benefit the worst-off members of the community, taxation which is also going to hit the pockets of skilled manual workers, unless the better-off will be able to maintain their absolute living standards. This can only be secured in a situation of growth in which the dividends of growth can be used both to maintain the absolute living standards of the better-off and to raise the relative position of the worst-off. This argument is central to *The Future of Socialism* (Crosland 1956) and is repeated in *Social Democracy in Europe* (Crosland 1975). This argument was based upon an assumption about the limits of altruism of the electorate and also assumptions about the basis of the appeal to equalitarian ideals. Crosland was convinced of the non-cognitive basis of moral principles – that they are arbitrary and in the end depend upon the moral commitments and emotional attitudes of individuals. On this view of the nature of moral values, there are very definite limits to the extent to which it is possible to convince individuals rationally of the rightness of a particular act based on political principles. The solvent of economic growth bypasses this difficulty and the disputed basis of egalitarian distributive principles by demonstrating that social justice and equality can be achieved by levelling up rather than levelling down. Again the plausibility of this strategy depends upon the possibilities, both physical and social, of economic growth.

Crosland's argument is important because it focuses upon the main issue to be discussed in this essay. We are faced with moral pluralism and with no rational way of grounding a particular set of distributive values. Economic growth avoids the difficulties here by enabling a strategy for equality to be pursued while making no one (absolutely) worse-off. However, the strategy becomes very problematic once it is assumed that there are intractable physical and social limits to growth. It is of course no surprise in the light of this that as Secretary of State for the Environment from 1974–76 and previously as Shadow Minister, Crosland was a major scourge of what he saw as the no-growth Jeremiahs of the Club of Rome when they claimed that the limits to growth were physical rather than social. However, *Social Limits to Growth* poses a much more central challenge to this attitude and indeed to the more modest Hayekian attitude indicated earlier on. According to the view developed by Hirsch the limits to growth are not just physical but social and are linked to the idea of positional goods. On this view there are certain positional goods which cannot be distributed more widely or more equally by the echelon advance or trickle-down effect without altering their value as goods. The paradigm case of a positional good is standing on tiptoe in order to see something better. When one person stands on tiptoe he has a positional advantage over others. When all stand on tiptoe this advantage is lost and so the value of standing on tiptoe diminishes as more people indulge in the practice. A good example of Hirsch's thesis would be education, which on a purely instrumental economic view loses its value as a commodity to the extent to which more people possess it, as graduates over the past few years have found out. Power too, is a precise example of a positional good: its value to any individual who possesses it declines progressively the more widely it is distributed, and indeed if it is distributed equally its value disappears entirely. Positional goods are unlike washing machines and electric fires in that they cannot be distributed more widely without altering their economic value. Competition for them is a zero-sum game and this is bound to raise questions about the basis of distribution. In a situation of rising living standards for all it is not necessary to bring into sharp focus the theoretical or philosophical basis of distribution principles. Only when growth stops and we are faced with a static or diminishing national cake does it become important to discuss the principles on which the distribution of resources should proceed. Issues of this sort cannot be bypassed by the incremental dividend of economic growth. Limitations to growth give a major impetus to what Hirsch calls the 'distributional compulsion' – the desire of individuals and groups to gain advantage over others in the distribution of scarce resources.

Granted that the limits to growth pose problems about distribution, the question then arises whether this distributive compulsion can be principled – that is, based upon values which are grounded either in the sense of being widely accepted and established in society or in the sense of being open to some rational defence. If the form of distribution lacks a moral basis then the limits to growth are likely to lead to anarchical struggles between groups seeking to secure advantages over one another in the zero-sum game of distribution. Here we reach the centre of the issue to be addressed in this paper – the relation between economic management and the values which could provide a basis for making distribution principled. Samuel Brittan has pointed out the central problem here:

'If it is true that people do have an . . . emotional yearning for some quasi theological justification for differences in position, power and well being; if the rational arguments for accepting a system which does not aim at complete distributive justice are too abstract or sophisticated to command assent; and even if there is an emotional void that cannot be met merely by rising incomes and humanitarian redistribution unrelated to merit then the outlook for liberal democracy is a poor one.'   (Brittan 1978: 272)

Are there moral resources within liberal democratic welfare capitalism for tackling the question of distribution, and if not how are distributive problems to be handled?

To reiterate, it is central to the argument of Hirsch, and the argument is paralleled in the work of Habermas in *Legitimation Crisis* (Habermas 1976), that there are no established values, in the sense of widely accepted internalized values within capitalism, for rendering distributive issues principled. There is no *Sittlichkeit* – no concrete ethical life – within liberal capitalist society which can be appealed to in order to constrain attitudes to distribution. Nor do they believe this an accidental feature of capitalism. In the view of both of these thinkers capitalism *itself* is reponsible for the decline of an established *Sittlichkeit*. The success of capitalism hitherto has presupposed a set of internalized moral *restraints*, the source of which lie in pre-capitalist world views and which have become undermined by the very development of capitalism. As Habermas sees it the problem has been caused by 'the long term erosion of the cultural tradition which had regulated conduct, and which until now, could be presupposed as a tacit boundary condition of the political system. Because of this a chronic need for legitimation is developing today' (Habermas 1974: 5). In Habermas's interpretation of this problem we can clearly see the influence of Hegel; Habermas wants to argue that capitalism will exhibit crisis tendencies when the state seeks to steer the economy in the absence of a shared concrete morality which will reinforce attitudes of restraint in the pursuit of economic demands. Hegel argues in *The Philosophy of Right* that the system of needs is devoid of this concrete morality, that it is the 'realm of otherness' dominated by the pursuit of self-interest; and at the same time, the state as the universal – the collective whole – has to act through public authority to regulate the economy. In Hegel's view, in wider civil society there are mediating links – the family, corporations, class identities and solidarities – between the particular and the universal, between politics and the economy. In Habermas's view, however, these links have become fragmented by the subsequent development of capitalist society.

Habermas sees the pre-capitalist cultural tradition as fulfilling a number of functions in securing social integration and building up a sense of moral identity among individuals. The first general point is that capitalist economic activity rests upon certain moral expectations such as trust, truth, honesty, fair dealing and promise keeping, without which the economic system cannot operate. The moral basis of exchange cannot become part of the process of exchange and trade-off. This idea was perhaps most succinctly put by Durkheim's dictum that 'all in the contract is not contractual'. Economic activity depends upon agreement about this range of values to work effectively. Without such a *Gemeinsamkeit* to contribute what Habermas calls the 'socio-cultural life world' there would be no basis for economic exchange. However, in his view these social virtues were originally grounded in religious belief but the development of capitalism has itself eroded the religious basis of these beliefs and has replaced them with a form of moral individualism. To trace this theme in detail is beyond the scope of this chapter and in Habermas it seems more a piece of speculative cultural history than an empirical claim. Nevertheless some points might be made. The growth of free economic activity has led to the development of moral individualism, the acids of which, in Habermas's view, have eaten away the lineaments of traditional beliefs. Moral individualism has brought with it moral subjectivism and non-cognitivism and this is an unstable basis for the moral values which are central to market activity. If we lack a convincing account of how norms of action can be validated, those norms will be at the mercy of individual interest and interpretation. This is the position we are currently in, as Habermas sees it, although as we shall see it is central to his argument that it is possible to develop a theory about how norms may be inter-subjectively validated, and this he attempts in his ideas on undistorted communication.

Habermas also discusses the cultural role of several specific attitudes although he does not really go into any detail. His arguments are listed here in summary form:

1. *Restraint.* The internalization of religious attitudes encouraged restraint in the early periods of capitalist development and certainly some of the early defenders of liberal capitalist society saw self-interest and its pursuit as hedged around with all sorts of social and religious restraints. In some respects this brings up the disputed relationship between Adam Smith's *Wealth of Nations* and his *Theory of Moral Sentiments* in which Smith clearly argues that the pursuit of self-interest is subject to internalized constraints derived from morals, religion, custom, and education. The extent to which these have been stripped away by the very action of capitalism makes any appeal to restraint by government very difficult for it to justify. With the removal of inner restraints on demand and consumption the economic system will become very unstable and at

the political level is going to produce severe problems of co-ordination in seeking to meet the conflicting demands made upon it. (For a view of this from a different perspective see Brittan (1978).)

2. *Achievement and fatalism.* In Habermas's view these two attitudes have been central to the establishment and maintenance of the liberal capitalist economic and political system, and both sets of attitudes have been sustained by religious beliefs. The ideal of achievement and the belief that the market rewards effort have been central to maintaining the incentive motivation of the system, whereas fatalism was necessary to secure a docile and stable work-force. These attitudes were grounded in religion and mediated by child-rearing and family life in ways which Habermas regards as class specific: 'The repressive authority of conscience and an individual achievement orientation among the bourgeoisie and external super ego structures and conventional work morality among the lower classes' (Habermas 1976: 77). Here we see the dual nature of these attitudes: they secure relationships to an economic system and they generate a sense of personal identity and worth among individuals. Identity and legitimation go together in Habermas's mind.

3. *The work ethic.* Again the same argument is put to work here. The Protestant ethic gives individuals a sense of dignity and value in their working lives and at the same time produces integration with and provides work motives for the prevailing economic system. However, as the designation 'Protestant ethic' implies, it is Habermas's view that this kind of work orientation is sustained by religious belief and that this belief system has been eroded, so that the work motivations derived from it cannot be renewed. Again the thesis is that bourgeois culture is unable to reproduce itself from itself. It has always been dependent upon motivationally effective supplementation by traditional world views.

4. *Civil privatization.* The orientation to private norms is characteristic of capitalist society. Citizens are encouraged to look for fulfilment in private pursuits, particularly in Habermas's view in the areas of career, leisure and consumption. Along with this privatization has gone a general decline in political activity. Although capitalist societies usually embody at a political level formal democratic rights, the net effect of this, allowing political participation only at periodic elections and not through active participation in the public realm, elicits mass loyalty but avoids mass involvement. Any further politicization of the public realm would bring into the open the contradictions between the various demands the political system seeks to meet – the most basic of which, according to Habermas, is between socialized production and the appropriation and use of surplus value. Civil privatism again allows for a sense of personal

worth – giving one dignity in terms of private pursuits and family life – and it sustains the economic system just because of its restriction on political demands. From the point of view of classical political thought and of Marxism, however, this sense of dignity is illusory because it is based upon an attenuated conception of human powers.

Again civil privatism is sustained by the range of cultural attitudes which have been mentioned, and with the erosion of these attitudes and the attenuated view of the nature of man associated with them, we are likely to see greater demands for participation and self-determination which are likely to provoke more severe problems in the administration of the politicized economy. Indeed Habermas's debate with Luhmann (1975) is precisely on this issue.

All of this is rather speculative, and it must be remembered that *Legitimation Crisis* is a research programme rather than a final report; obviously the cultural history here is rather sketchy and one would want to see much more work done in this area of Habermas's thinking. However, despite this the thesis is provoking and gains in plausibility by being supported by the right as much as by the left. It is one more example of the pattern noted by Robert Paul Wolff in *The Poverty of Liberalism* (Wolff 1968), that both conservatives and those of the left are convinced that liberal bourgeois society cannot sustain itself because it possesses no *Sittlichkeit*. The demand for *Sittlichkeit* is likely to be seen on the right as a need for authority and the crisis of bourgeois society as a crisis of moral authority caused by the decline in the range of supportive values discussed by Habermas, while on the left the crisis is seen as a crisis of community or social integration. The phenomenon seen as producing the crisis – the collapse of the moral legacy by which capitalism has been sustained – is the same in both cases. At the same time this point detracts to some extent from the originality of Habermas's thesis because we seem to be back with the claim, common in the history of the social and political thought of the past 150 years, that liberal society has no substantive normative resources of its own.

To put the issue in this way, however, neglects one solution to the problem which, at least in terms of practical politics, seems to have gained the most ground. If the legitimation problem is exacerbated, or brought into the open by the growing coupling of the economic and the political, with the state being concerned with steering the economy and with distribution rather than with merely securing the general conditions of production, then the most obvious solution would seem to be to try to uncouple them, to attempt to bring the state back to securing the procedural setting for the pursuit of capitalist enterprise. This of course is the view which has been taken by Hayek in *Law, Legislation and Liberty* (Hayek 1982). We have to abandon state intervention in the economy in terms of the search for social justice and endorse the naturalistic outcomes of the market as being in principle unprincipled. This seems to solve the problem in a number of ways: the state is removed from the distributive arena and ceases to be a source of resentment to those whose distributive share does not fit their subjective notion of merit or desert, and it avoids the so-called depleting moral legacy upon which capitalism is based by abandoning the view that the market is constrained by any particular substantive moral principles. This general point about the moral pluralism of liberal society is coupled with a direct attack on distributive justice as a legitimate moral claim. Hayek argues that the disadvantaged do not suffer from injustice. Justice and injustice result only from deliberate action and Hayek wants to argue that this deliberate action is absent from the overall outcomes of an economic market. He argues as follows:

> 'It has of course to be admitted that the manner in which the benefits and burdens are apportioned by the market mechanism would, in many instances, have to be regarded as very unjust if it were the result of a deliberate allocation to particular people. But this is not the case. These shares are the outcome of a process, the effect of which on particular people was neither intended or foreseen by anyone when the institutions first appeared . . . . Society has become the new deity to which we complain and clamour for redress if it does not fulfil the expectations it has raised.'   (Hayek 1976: 64)

On this view, therefore, there is no basis for a legitimate moral claim to a particular distributive share in terms of rights and justice. The lack of an agreed moral basis for distribution means that the state will lack legitimacy and create tensions which it cannot resolve if it remains in the arena of seeking distributive justice. The only solution is to uncouple the state from distributive processes, and confine its role to securing the general legal and procedural rules for capitalist enterprise.

On the face of it this attempt to depoliticize the economy and withdraw from distributive activity looks to be a promising answer to the legitimation problem and it is certainly one which has had some political popularity in the last few years. However, there are difficulties with the Hayekian view which are recognized even by those who seek to defend the market and, I shall argue, Hayek himself. The central point which Hayek is making in this debate is that we should abandon the view that the market is constrained by any *particular* substantive principles to guide distributive outcomes. In his well-known essay 'When Virtue Loses All

Her Loveliness' Irving Kristol points out the extent to which Hayek's argument differs from traditional justification of the market and he doubts whether citizen loyalty can be linked to a system which detaches differences in wealth and income from considerations of principle based upon merit, desert, achievement, need, or whatever moral values citizens hold dear.

> 'The distribution of power, privilege and property must be seen as in some profound sense expressive of the values that govern the lives of individuals. An idea of self government, if it is to be viable, must encompass both the public and private sectors, if it does not you have alienation and anomie.'
> (Kristol 1978: 250–51)

Oddly enough Hayek seems to recognize the issues at stake here and he regrets the fact that a good many popular views about the justification of a liberal capitalist society have falsely stressed the role that the idea of rewarding merit plays in arguments in favour of the market, and he comments that it bodes ill for the future of the market mechanism that this seems to be the only defence of it which is understood by the general public (Hayek 1976: 74). However, he does confess to puzzlement about whether 'without such erroneous beliefs the large numbers will tolerate actual differences in rewards which will be based only partly on achievement and partly on mere chance'. A Great Society (Hayek's phrase) in which luck plays such a large part may well be unstable because it lacks a reference to an integrated moral basis and Hayek recognizes this in the suggestion that false beliefs about the market and about principled distribution according to merit may be functionally necessary. However, this is hardly satisfactory and Hayek implicitly allows that such a society would have a legitimation problem and might well depend for its survival on a legacy of outmoded beliefs about the nature of rewards which unconstrained markets produce. So even in this extreme case in which an attempt is made to detach the market from distributional principles the moral issue re-emerges as central to securing the loyalty of individuals to a market order. Hayek recognizes that the distributional beliefs in question may be outmoded and without an objective foundation but thinks that nevertheless they are functionally necessary.

Habermas discusses something like the Hayekian view from a rather different perspective in *Legitimation Crisis* (Habermas 1976). He takes the view that markets unconstrained by distributive principles will reveal too clearly the exercise of social power by those who own the means of production for such a system to be able to secure the loyalty of citizens who do not own them and have become accustomed to a state which does seek some redistribution. In an earlier phase of capitalist development a Hayekian view might have worked, securing loyalty by an appeal to a notion of fair exchange, but this is really no longer plausible:

'The precondition for this is equal opportunity to participate in a competition that is regulated so as to neutralise external influences. The market was such an allocation mechanism. Since it has been recognised even among the population at large that social force is exercised in the form of economic exchange, the market has lost its credibility as a fair (from the perspective of achievement) mechanism for the distribution of life opportunities.'   (Habermas 1976: 81)

On his view, therefore, a justification of the market which trades on contingency and luck and in which, without some redistribution of property rights amounting to an illegitimate exercise in social justice, the realities of social power will be revealed, cannot provide individuals with a sense of their identity and worth and will undermine the relationship between individual identity – particularly individuals' value systems – and the form of social life in question.

The other alternative form of depoliticizing the distributive issue is an attempt to turn it into a purely *technical* matter. The Hayekian view is to remove the state from the distributive arena; the alternative is to leave the state with a distributive role but instead of basing this role upon values and principles, the force of which has become disputed and the rational basis of which is obscure, we should rather attempt to turn the issue into a technical matter to be solved by administrative and technical proce- dures. An attempt to turn distributive questions into technical matters would insulate the distributive outcomes produced by such techniques from a value-based political critique (Habermas 1976: 134). So for example there would be a tendency to turn issues of distribution over to pay boards, relativities commissions, Royal Commissions, etc. This is the type of response which Habermas discusses in his critique of the work of Niklas Luhmann in *Legitimation Crisis*. The claim to technique and expertise and the authority which would go with it would insulate distributive decisions from the collapsing and contested *Sittlich* world of politics. However, it is very difficult to see how this can avoid normative problems. If administrative decisions can be regularly implemented against the interests of those affected by them, then this *must* be considered as the fulfilment of recognized norms and if this is so, Habermas argues, it raises the possibility that these norms could be defended against critique. That is to say, it depends upon a world view which legitimizes the authority of the administrative system so that we are left with the central issue: What are these forms of technique? How expensive are they? And how are they to be validated? (There is a very good account of the development of managerialism and technique in the light of a collapse of moral agreement in A. MacIntyre's *After Virtue* (MacIntyre 1981).)

We seem therefore to be in an impasse. On the one hand the limits to growth lead to the distributional compulsion. Hirsch and Habermas point out the way in which this is unmanageable without agreed, established and internalized values, and these have been undermined by capitalism. The solution proposed by Hayek – getting the state out of the distributive arena – looks as though it will not work and Hayek seems in some respects to see this. The attempts to depoliticize the economy by making distribution a matter of technical management seems to be unable to avoid normative difficulties. The only solution therefore would seem to be a search for a new *Sittlichkeit.*

It is at this point that Habermas's commitment to critical theory becomes more central. He is convinced that it is possible to secure normative agreement on an inter-subjective basis by appealing to the notion of undistorted communication. This theory allows the assumption that we can establish some normative agreement in terms of which state activities can be seen as legitimate, though this is not in itself likely to establish the legitimacy of the liberal capitalist state as a whole. Rather, the needs and interests which would be the basis of normative agreement, and which could be established in a situation of undistorted communication, would point the way to a transformation of capitalist society, whose present patterns of domination tend to lead individuals to systematically mistake their own needs. Habermas's point here is both ethical and meta-ethical. The ethical point is that he believes that he has shown that social life does depend upon some kind of moral agreement to provide not only a basis for personal identity, dignity, worth, and purpose, but also a basis on which inter-subjective economic and political activity can be conducted. Traditional morality fulfilled this role in the past but liberal capitalism now faces a crisis of authority because it has brought about a breakdown of community values. We need a new *Sittlichkeit*, an agreement on norms and values, to secure social integration. However, modern moral thinking is highly subjective and non-cognitivist and reflects an individualism which is itself the product of capitalism, and Habermas is forced to deploy a meta-ethical theory to demonstrate how a new *Sittlichkeit* could be formed. He does this by introducing the idea of undistorted communication. The basis of the new normative agreement would be the needs and interests which human beings would come to believe that they have in common *if* they were able to reason about their lives and their aims in a situation free of social power and domination. Such reasoning must be about aims or ends because needs are fundamentally means to ends. The normative claims which would emerge from such a discursive consensus would be valid. Such an account could generate norms which could be accepted by all. The problem posed in *Legitimation Crisis* becomes therefore for Habermas the question:

'How would the members of a social system, at a given stage in the development of productive forces, have collectively and bindingly interpreted their needs (and which norms would they have accepted as justified) if they could and would have decided on the organisation of social intercourse through discursive will formation, with adequate knowledge of the limiting conditions and functional imperatives of society?'   (Habermas 1976: 113)

It is Habermas's conclusion that if the distributive norms of capitalist society could come up for rational domination-free consideration, they would not be endorsed by those who are currently committed to such norms. The problems of legitimation, as we have seen, cannot be solved without a new *Sittlichkeit*, a development which can only be secured by the kind of rational consensus which Habermas points to. If we cannot do this we are left with some kind of non-cognitivist view of moral discourse based upon persuasion and propaganda, with the basis of normative agreement not being discursive dialogue and a commitment to truth, but rather a non-rational process which opens up the possibility of the exercise of power in the crucial area of normative agreement. Power relations thus become involved in the basis for personal identity, social integration, and legitimation. Practical politics, ethics, and meta-ethical issues are all closely related in Habermas's mind.

'Our excursion into the contemporary discussion of ethics was intended to support the assertion that practical questions admit of truth. If this is so, justifiable norms can be distinguished from norms that merely stabilise relations of force. In so far as norms express generalisable interests, they are based on a *rational consensus* (or they would find such a consensus if practical discourse could take place). In so far as norms do not regulate generalisable interests, they are based upon force.'   (Habermas 1976: 111)

Habermas's rational consensus theory of morality is highly suggestive and ought to be considered very seriously by moral philosophers in the analytical tradition. It seems to show a way out of what might be seen as the formalism and subjectivism of a good deal of modern moral philosophy and at the same time it is a theory developed with practical considerations in mind and claims to generalize certain presuppositions which are already present in our language. Indeed, some philosophers within the analytical tradition have shown some awareness of these features. Strawson (1963), Findlay (1964), Peters (1966), and Ackermann (1981) have all emphasized the ways in which speech and dialogue involve commitments of the sort which Habermas discusses and these philosophers have recognized that speech presupposes certain implicit moral requirements.

However, there are difficulties with Habermas's notion, not the least of which is explaining how his undistorted speech situation could be brought about. However, apart from this there is a more deep-seated difficulty. In a situation of undistorted speech citizens will be concerned with reasoning about norms which can then become the basis of a new *Sittlichkeit*, and they will be guided in this activity by the implicit values in speaking which I have mentioned. The difficulty however is that as the dialogue will be about the identification of needs, interests, the common good, community, etc., it is arguable that such complex concepts are always going to be controversial and will be influenced by different views of human nature and circumstances of human life. The terms in which dialogue is to be conducted may therefore embody radically different perspectives on human life. It may well be, as Habermas argues, that in a society marked by the unconstrained use of social power one interpretation of these notions becomes dominant and becomes an 'ideology',[1] but this is not to say that if the sources of domination and power were to be removed we would be able to reason our way to a single and ideologically neutral set of values which would define a new *Sittlichkeit*. There may be a number of ways in which a set of social and political terms may be understood and it may be that a coherence rather than a consensus view of truth does more justice to this complexity and essential contestability than Habermas's views.

On this view therefore the possibility of grounding a set of rational values on a basis of undistorted communication looks unpromising, but this does not exhaust the alternatives and in the remaining pages of this essay I want to explore the other main possibilities of grounding a new and perhaps rather modest *Sittlichkeit*. One is utilitarianism, and the other is developed by what might be thought of as either a dialectical or reflexive critique of the minimal morality of capitalist society.

The case for utilitarian morality as a way of avoiding the problems discussed so far seems quite powerful and appears to have been neglected by both Hirsch and Habermas. While they have concentrated upon the ways in which the secular progress of capitalist development has undermined the legacy of pre-capitalist restraints they have failed to pay sufficient attention to the ways in which utilitarianism might be regarded as the morality distinctive of capitalist society. Commentators have frequently pointed out the ways in which Bentham conceived utilitarian morality as meeting the needs of a society of strangers in which the springs of traditional morality were drying up (Manning 1964). Others have pointed out the way in which utilitarianism provides us with a second-order way of making defensible moral decisions in a situation of first-order moral pluralism. Individuals may define their good in their own way, but utilitarianism encourages a state of affairs in which as many people as possible will be able to gain as much as possible of whatever good it is that they happen to want. Why could not utilitarianism therefore be seen as the distinctive morality of a liberal capitalist society? On this view, far from capitalist society being entrenched in legitimation problems because it has no agreed morality to guide the outcomes of the 'distributional compulsion', it does indeed have such a morality, namely utilitarianism. However, the mention of the distributional compulsion should alert us to the main criticism which could be made of utilitarianism as a plausible response to the problems which have been at the centre of discussion, namely that utilitarianism has very little to say about principles of distribution as opposed to the *maximization* of goods, whereas of course the whole point of the argument so far is that the social limits to growth are bound to concentrate our attention on distribution rather than maximization. However, the extent to which utilitarianism is able to provide principles of distribution is debatable. Some commentators – Bernard Williams would be a good example – want to argue that the theory does not provide us with an adequate account of principles such as need, merit, desert, equality, etc., and cannot therefore address the distributional problems at the heart of the argument presented here (Williams and Smart 1976). Others however, such as Quinton (1976) and Nicholas Rescher (1966), argue that the principles of utilitarian ethics can, if combined with assumptions about diminishing marginal utility, provide adequate renderings of otherwise disputed notions of need, merit, justice, equality, etc. This seems to me to be an open question at the moment and I must say that such an approach seems to be *as* plausible as Habermas's much more convoluted approach to the question above.

The other strategy for looking for a moral basis to constrain the distributive compulsion within a liberal society would be to adopt an internal or reflexive critique of the assumptions of a liberal political order, and the first move in such a strategy would be to show that such a critique is actually compatible with a liberal political order. I think it can be argued that the search for reasoned principles is not merely compatible with the idea of a liberal democratic society but in some sense reveals the very essence of such a society. This point runs through the whole of Bruce Ackermann's recent and brilliant *Social Justice in the Liberal State*. The possibility of defending a pattern of distribution against a moral critique seems to be central to the democratic ideal, as Ackermann says: 'Whenever anybody questions the legitimacy of another's power, the power holder must respond not by suppressing the questioner but by giving a reason that explains why he is more entitled to the resource than the questioner' (Ackermann 1981: 4). In a liberal, democratic society the possession of a positional good such as power must be defended not by the exercise of that power but by reasoned argument about distributive principles. How might such reasoning proceed? It is often taken to be part of the constitutive assumptions of a liberal society that it should not hold fixed ideals regarding the government of a free society, but on the contrary must be agnostic about questions of the good life since citizens will differ in their conceptions of the good and the government does not treat them equally if it prefers one conception to another. This is certainly Hayek's view of a liberal society and it is endorsed by Dworkin (1978) as defining one of the basic constitutive principles of a liberal democratic order. Can we use this constitutive principle as a means of drawing out some principles of distribution? It could be argued that we can. A liberal society is concerned that each individual should be so far as possible free to pursue his own conception of the good, his own plan of life, and an equal right to do this is central to a free society. However, it could be argued[2] that this requires more than just a framework of law, as in Hayek's view, to facilitate his pursuit of life plans. Certain basic needs have to be satisfied before an individual can be in a position to pursue his conception of the good, whatever that might be. Values of whatever kind can only be pursued by agents who are capable of reflection, deliberation, and choice – that is to say able to choose between the diverse moral goals which they are likely to encounter in a liberal society. If this is so then it might be argued that physical survival and autonomy are the basic needs which have to be satisfied as necessary preconditions for the pursuit of a particular conception of the good life within a range of diverse alternatives, for unless individuals physically survive they cannot pursue values at all, and if they lack a capacity for autonomous agency they cannot rationally pursue their own plan of life. On this view, physical survival and autonomy are basic needs and the goods which satisfy them – food, health care, education, welfare – are basic, indispensable goods. So if the purpose of a liberal society is, as Hayek argues, to allow citizens to pursue their own good in their own way, the exercise of citizenship in a liberal state requires a certain set of basic needs and basic goods if this citizenship is to be exercised effectively. We can then say that the basic assumptions of a liberal society would point to an equal right to the provision of primary goods and that this is the only principle of distribution of these primary goods which is compatible with liberal values. An unequal right to these goods cannot be justified if a liberal society is to be agnostic about substantive moral questions, because if an equal right *were* to be denied it would have to be on the basis of one of two substantive principles:

1. The person who has an unequal right is in a disadvantaged position because we take the view that his particular plan of life lacks value – but this is inconsistent with supposed agnosticism about substantive moral questions.
2. We could say that a person has an unequal right because he lacks merit, but this judgement would depend upon a scale of values within which merit is assigned and again this would be inconsistent with the constitutive principles of a liberal society.

Equal access to primary goods then becomes the only principle consistent with treating citizens equally and not imposing on them substantive conceptions of the good. However, this does not exhaust the issue, because while each person has an equal right to the satisfaction of basic needs this does not mean that the resources required to meet these needs will therefore be distributed equally. The equal right to need satisfaction may require unequal treatment of persons because individual circumstances may differ and so what each person requires to pursue effectively his own conception of the good may differ. Some may be so crippled by circumstances for which they bear no responsibility – genetic handicap, unfortunate family background, and so on – that they require more resources than others to enable them to pursue their goals.

Of course the advantaged may well wish to object to this on the grounds that to burden them with this responsibility is unjust, because after all they merit or deserve their more fortunate position in society and so why should they be called upon to compensate the disadvantaged? It seems that there are perhaps two answers to this question, one of which is implicit in what I have already argued: that is that the recognition of this duty comes as a matter of moral conviction based upon the arguments about need. This takes us back to the starting point of the paper, that in this context agreement on principles is vital because problems of growth will mean that the advantaged may well not be able to keep their absolute standard of living if they respond to the claims of the poor. The second point takes us into very deep, not to say murky, philosophical water and concerns the basis of merit or desert. It is an argument developed by Rawls that merit is not a morally acceptable basis for a claim to a distributive share because it is morally arbitrary in the sense that it is usually based upon luck: a combination of natural talent (which depends upon a genetic lottery) and fortunate family background (Rawls 1972). In neither case can the individual claim to be responsible for his talent and the setting in which it was nurtured. In addition, in Rawls's view the qualities of character which enable us to utilize our talents are again arbitrarily determined by the very same features. Now as it stands this argument is much too extreme and needs some modification; there must be a place for an idea of merit in our thinking and Rawls's viewpoint does not do justice to this. However, a modified Rawlsian view will, I think, provide us with a way of thinking about the appropriate claims of desert and the needs of the disadvantaged. If we bear only some responsibility for our assets and talents then it is surely reasonable to ask those who possess these assets to better themselves within the constraints of a system where doing so will help those who are less well off and whose less fortunate position is, by parity of reasoning, not fully their responsibility.

This kind of attempt to secure some basic normative agreement for distribution is therefore pursued by means of an internal critique of the implications of the central principles of a liberal society. It is not, as for example in Rawls's *A Theory of Justice* (Rawls 1972) an attempt to produce an Archemedian point from which to judge justice and produce values which are valid for all persons in space and time. The aim is much more modest – to agree with Hirsch that in a situation in which growth is constrained, distribution is going to be a central problem. However, I have tried to show that there are moral resources within a liberal democratic state for dealing with this question and that the issue does not have to be turned over to the exercise of social power.

Notes

1. I have tried to take this further in 'Community: Concept, Conception and Ideology' (Plant 1978).
2. I have developed this argument at some length in Plant, Lesser, and Taylor-Gooby (1980). For similar versions see Finnis (1980) and Gewirth (1978).

References

ACKERMANN, B. (1981) *Social Justice in the Liberal State*. Cambridge: Cambridge University Press.

BRITTAN, S. (1978) *The Economic Consequences of Democracy*. London: Temple Smith.

CROSLAND, C. A. R. (1956) *The Future of Socialism*. London: Cape.

—— (1975) *Social Democracy in Europe*. London: Fabian Society.

DWORKIN, R. (1978) Liberalism. In S. N. Hampshire (ed.) *Public and Private Morality*. Cambridge: Cambridge University Press.

FINDLAY, J. N. (1964) Values in Speaking. In *Language, Mind and Value*. London: Allen and Unwin.

FINNIS, J. (1980) *Natural Law and Natural Rights*. Oxford: Clarendon Press.

GEWIRTH, A. (1978) *Reason and Morality*. Chicago: Chicago University Press.

GOLDTHORPE, J. (1978) The Current Inflation: Towards a Sociological Account. In J. Goldthorpe and F. Hirsch (eds) *The Political Economy of Inflation*. London: Martin Robertson.

HABERMAS, J. (1970) Towards a Theory of Communicative Competence. *Inquiry* 13.

—— (1974) *Theory and Practice*. London: Heinemann.

—— (1976) *Legitimation Crisis*. London: Heinemann.

HAYEK, F. (1960) *The Constitution of Liberty*. London: Routledge and Kegan Paul.

—— (1976) *The Mirage of Social Justice*. London: Routledge and Kegan Paul.

—— (1982) *Law, Legislation and Liberty* 3 vols. London: Routledge and Kegan Paul.

HIRSCH, F. (1977) *Social Limits to Growth*. London: Routledge and Kegan Paul.

KRISTOL, I. (1978) When Virtue Loses All Her Loveliness. In *Two Cheers for Capitalism*. New York: Mentor Books.

LUHMANN, N. (1975) *Theorie der Gessellschaft der Sozial Technologie*. Frankfurt: Suhrkamp.

MACINTYRE, A. (1981) *After Virtue*. London: Duckworth.

MANNING, D. (1964) *The Mind of Jeremy Bentham*. London: Longman.

PETERS, R. S. (1966) *Ethics and Education*. London: Allen and Unwin.

PLANT, R. (1978) Community: Concept, Conception and Ideology. In *Politics and Society* 8 (1): 79–107.

—— (1981) Democratic Socialism and Equality. In D. Leonard and D. Lipsey (eds) *The Socialist Agenda*. London: Cape.

PLANT, R., LESSER, H., and TAYLOR-GOOBY, P. (1980) (eds) *Political Philosophy and Social Welfare*. London: Routledge and Kegan Paul.

QUINTON, A. (1976) *Utilitarian Ethics*. Oxford: Clarendon Press.

RAWLS, J. (1972) *A Theory of Justice*. Oxford: Clarendon Press.

RESCHER, N. (1966) *Distributive Justice*. Indianapolis: Bobbs-Merrill.

STRAWSON, P. F. (1963) *An Introduction to Logical Theory*. London: Methuen.

WILLIAMS, B. and SMART, J. C. C. (1976) *Utilitarianism For and Against*. Cambridge: Cambridge University Press.

WOLFF, R. P. (1968) *Poverty of Liberalism*. Boston: Beacon.

4 The conscious relegitimation of liberal capitalism: problems of transition

JOHN HALL

The aims of this essay can be highlighted by counterposing it to an interpretation of *The Social Limits to Growth* given with characteristic brilliance by Ralf Dahrendorf in a lecture to the Royal Society of Arts in 1980. Hirsch's importance for Dahrendorf lay in the demonstration via the thesis of positional goods that growth cannot solve the social problems that now confront us, and perhaps for this reason there is a notable hostility to growth evidenced in Dahrendorf's comments. Broadly speaking, I would dub this interpretation of Hirsch *conservative*: the moral explicitly drawn by Dahrendorf is that life is hard, and it would be better for us to learn to accept our condition rather than vainly kicking against the pricks (Dahrendorf 1980). Now there is no doubt but that Hirsch himself lends support to this interpretation in varied passages in his work. At the end of the book, for example, he encapsulates his position thus: 'This book has suggested that the prime economic problem now facing the economically advanced societies is a structural need to pull back the bounds of economic self advancement' (Hirsch 1977: 190). But this exceptionally fertile book does not fit *entirely* within this schema. For there is a fundamental ambiguity about the concept of social limits to growth: does it mean that society has finally limited growth (and a good thing too) or could it mean that if we change some social institutions then (heaven be praised) the growth process can be restored? Dahrendorf's interpretation of Hirsch seems to me to have been typical in stressing the former of these, and I would guess that this derives from Hirsch's thesis being popularly associated with the concept of physical limits to growth. It is worth recalling that Hirsch was aware of the criticisms of the Club of Rome report, criticisms which can only be increased when we note that its author, Denis Meadows, now admits that he had only 0.1 per cent of the information necessary for his model (Gäbler 1982: 4). I shall argue that 'the second side' of Hirsch's thesis is interesting, and indeed that only the desire to restore growth should be taken seriously. The arguments to be advanced in support of this proposition are mostly banal, but the most important one stresses one factor about capitalism which rules out of court virtually any acceptance of the no-growth position.

My subject can be characterized as that of practice rather than of theory – that is, I ask about the mechanisms by which different theoretical traditions grappling with the problems raised by Hirsch expect their views to be realized. The chapter has three parts. In the first section, I analyse and dispute Hirsch's characterization of the problems that face our society. In so doing I present a rather different view of growth in general, and this leads to very heavy scepticism about the possibility of a no-growth society. The second section examines three approaches – those of the 'left', of the 'right', and of Hirsch himself – that seek social changes designed to allow once again the possibility of sustained economic growth. The third section introduces some consideration of the international character of capitalism. This factor is rarely considered by political strategists, to their very considerable loss, for it is this factor which undermines hopes of a no-growth society.

Liberal capitalism and social peace

The very brilliance of Hirsch's arguments combined with their having been taken from widely different disciplines has made it hard to unpack with exactness his principal theses. I believe that his account of the current crisis of liberal capitalism can be summed up in three points.

1. Some 'goods' are positional, i.e. they are positions that can only be occupied, or which gain their value from being occupied, only by a single person. Thus it has always been true that there can typically only be one prime minister or president or king. However, affluence is beginning to make it clear that social goods are of the same character. A single summer-house by a lake is a positional good destroyed when a second

dwelling is built. Thus Hirsch is led to argue that growth cannot, as it were, spread the goodies around. This is the first social limit to growth.

2. The political action of large groups of people is now being influenced by the frustration consequent on this first limit to growth. Hirsch's words are important here:

> 'But in the late 1960's the issue of who gets what returned in strength. *This reemergence could not be attributed to the collapse of economic growth – as had happened so abruptly in 1929 – or even to its decisive deceleration.* The inflationary crisis that pushed Western economies into their most severe postwar recession in the mid-1970's can itself be seen as, in part, a result of the surfacing of political and economic pressures of the poor to get what they saw as their fair share. In the quarter century following the end of World War II, the leading economies showed an exceptional performance in growth of national product. Why then did the intractable, divisive issue of economic equality return to centre stage?'   (Hirsch 1977: 174)

The sentence I have italicized highlights the crux of Hirsch's own answer to this question. The discovery that growth does not, as had been expected, bring satisfaction, breeds frustration. But instead of blaming this frustration on the inherent scarcity of positional goods, social actors continue, and in fact increase, their demands in the hope of being able to gain positional benefits. Hirsch sees this process as self-defeating, illusory, and the origin of our present crisis. Frustration was powerful enough, let it be noted once again, to start giving liberal capitalism problems even before growth had in fact collapsed.

3. There is a second limit to growth. Hirsch argues that liberal capitalism is also suffering from a declining moral legacy and he sees two aspects of this at work. In an accurate and striking chapter he argues that one of the central presuppositions of Keynesianism, and thus on this occasion at least of our own political economy, is that the élite will act in the interests of economic rationality. Keynes's Bloomsbury background gave him an unfettered contempt for the stupidity of capitalists who preferred, in the time-honoured Victorian manner, to save rather than to spend, and he believed that the enlightened behaviour of the mandarins could so adjust capitalism as to prevent its having dangerous troughs. This view Hirsch rightly insists is comprehensible only when we remember that the English mandarinate to which Keynes belonged was the world of Lord Reith, Oxbridge, Royal Commissions, and so on. This is to say that it was at once liberal, and in a position to exercise authority. The first of these factors disappeared, Hirsch argues, when the English

mandarinate/political establishment learned, if learning was necessary, that economic irresponsibility could help to buy votes. Thus only one English Chancellor of the Exchequer since Selwyn Lloyd has not overheated the economy before an election – and the fate of Mr Roy Jenkins within the Labour Party does not encourage emulation. And perhaps the behaviour of the mandarins is in any case in part a response to the second presupposition of Keynes's system, namely that the working class would be sufficiently deferential to accept the wise guidance of their leaders, secure in the knowledge that this guidance would lead to benefits for them as well. Hirsch believes that such deference has gone for good, and that capitalism has been all too successful in inculcating selfish motivations. Trade unionism, at least on its political side, is very much in this view just what Bernard Shaw believed it to be: 'the capitalism of the proletariat'.

One final point should be made about this analysis of our predicament. It is Hirsch's contention that the first and second limits to growth are connected. Frustration engendered by vainly trying to reach goods which can by their nature only be positional is responsible for people becoming more aggressive in their demands.

Some things in Hirsch's account seem to me much more true than others, and I think certain distinctions can enable us, first, to reject the total package deal we are offered, and second, to understand then more accurately the problems of liberal capitalism. For the sake of simplicity, I will comment in turn on each of Hirsch's points.

At first sight Hirsch's argument about positional goods has something of the quality of a logical proof. Personally, I follow Jonathan Gershuny's argument in this volume to the effect that a second, third, and even fourth house by a lake still leaves the original summer-house as a desirable enough good in itself. Perhaps it was once more pleasant to be rich, but I doubt we should overburden ourselves with the tribulations of our betters.

But there is a further, more important consideration that should make us sceptical of the salience of positional goods in Hirsch's argument. Hirsch's view of economic and social goods is often simple and absolute. The summer-house by the lake is a very typical example in this respect since it stresses how an absolute 'good' can be destroyed. But a look at some principal and well-founded theses in the sociology of fashion can demonstrate that his view is overstated, and indeed naive.

The foremost English writer on the sociology of fashion, Quentin Bell, describes its characteristic process thus:

'Novelty, audacity, and above all exclusiveness, the bright badge of social enterprise brings a fashion in, and when a hat or shoe has lost its social appeal, when everybody is wearing it, it dies of popularity. Such seems to be the fate of elitist art in our society, the social impulse that made it fashionable with the few ends by making it vulgar with the many where upon the elite must look for something else.'

(Bell 1976: 8)

Bell is a disciple of Veblen, whose book *The Theory of the Leisure Class* appeared, it should be noted, in 1899. And the same points have long been known in France. One of the most notable books on the subject was Edmond Goblot's *La Barrière et le niveau* (Goblot 1967) in which he demonstrated the exceptional ability of the rich to establish *new* positional areas in order to prevent themselves being swamped by the masses. This same thesis is neatly summed up in the title of Pierre Bourdieu's recent *La Distinction* (1979). But perhaps the clearest summary in the whole matter has been provided by a French sociologist of literature, Renée Balibar (1974). Her striking empirical work on the schoolbooks of French children in the later nineteenth and early twentieth centuries shows, for example, that just as soon as a broad spectrum of the population began to understand Zola, the élite changed its interests to symbolism and surrealism; that is, secondary schools began to teach these authors.

Now the point of this digression is to stress that if the crux of class is the business of distinction rather than the possession of absolutely scarce goods, then there is reason to doubt the full force of Hirsch's argument. Bluntly, Hirsch severely underestimates the capacity of the rich to dream up new goods and thereby to establish new scarcities. Some time ago a television programme explored the way in which very rich Japanese were able to spend their money. Notoriously Japan itself is short of summerhouses by deserted lakes, and perhaps it is for this reason that the wealthy choose to take their meals below the water in submersibles. These looked hot, cramped, and generally uncomfortable, but they doubtless serve the function of distinguishing the rich from the less well-off.

These cautionary words about the importance of the concept of positional goods to Hirsch's argument lead naturally to my major criticism. As argued above, Hirsch insists that the frustration engendered by conflict for absolutely limited positional goods became so great that it overflowed into politics before the ending of sustained economic growth in the early 1970s. I have already cast some doubt upon this proposition in arguing that the ability of the rich to 'move the frontier' of distinction meant that conflict was *not* suddenly exacerbated by any absolute limitation of desirable goods. Perhaps there was more frustration than hitherto, and perhaps there was a realization that *some* goods were positional and absolute; but Hirsch offers no evidence to suggest that this frustration boiled over in the 1960s, nor that it caused the disruptions to the political economy of the 1970s. Quite simply it seems to me that Hirsch is wrong in his historical account. Liberal capitalist societies were *not* coming to grief in the 1960s since sustained economic growth allowed the frustrating chasing of the Joneses to continue unabated. However, the current crisis of liberal capitalist societies *was* occasioned by the ending of sustained economic growth which turned competitive emulation into a zero-sum distributional struggle. The villain in the piece is not, as Hirsch suggests, economic growth, but its sudden failure. And that failure has most to do with OPEC and with the inability, at least in the British case, to integrate a powerful working class into the workings of society as a whole.

One final cautionary word may be offered on Hirsch's view of the declining moral legitimacy of liberal capitalist societies. Empirical work on the role of ideology in history, and particularly amongst the Western working classes, has thrown a great deal of doubt upon the view that capitalism was ever maintained by a shared or imposed consensus (Abercrombie and Turner 1979). Thus the Victorians, who had believed this, were very shocked by the census of 1851 which showed not only that the lower orders were areligious but that they could not have been religious, in the sense of attending church, for the simple reason that there were insufficient churches to accommodate them. Similarly the one liberal capitalist country which does sometimes look as if it rests upon some sort of moral consensus, modern Japan, apparently owes its success at least in part to hidden but effective social controls. It may be the case that Japanese organizations are womb-to-tomb in character, but apparently someone who once leaves such an organization is thereafter branded as 'not a company man', a dangerous reputation most wish to avoid. None of this means that Hirsch is wrong in claiming both that the mandarins are influenced by electoral pressures in ways Keynes did not expect and that working-class expectations have risen during the Keynesian post-war years.

We can now leave these criticisms of Hirsch and offer an alternative characterization of the current dilemma of liberal capitalist societies. Such societies are a combination of 'realistic' democracy (rights of opposition, the rule of law, the ability to change the élite) and social inequality. Such a combination scarcely deserves to be designated a social *system* since the very notion of giving equal rights to the unequal is inherently problematic. It is almost miraculous that this combination ever worked at all (Gellner 1975). Roughly speaking, it did manage to function in the nineteenth century when classical capitalism maintained a strong stick with which to discipline the work-force. But the risks of unemployment of the 1930s encouraged all liberal reformers to commit themselves to full employment, to welfare measures, and to growth, and on this basis (that of a carrot rather than a stick) liberal capitalism survived until 1973. The ending of economic growth in or about that year has meant that the inherently unstable combination described has finally become unstuck.

This is a problem of a social system formed from incompatible elements, and not of frustration being unleashed as the result of economic growth. In this connection it is worth insisting yet again that crisis followed, rather than preceded, the cessation of sustained economic growth. Indeed, the first and perhaps the worst affected liberal capitalist society was that of Britain. Had Hirsch's analysis been correct, one would have expected frustration to have led to crisis in Japan, America or Western Germany rather than in economically inefficient Britain. But the British case is not hard to explain in terms of the general contradiction of liberal capitalism described here: a failing economy meant that a powerful working class could no longer be bought off by means of growth. The stalemate in the political economy which was reached then is with us still. But even without growth, and the consequent frustrations Hirsch analyses, this combination would sooner or later have caused terrible problems. The evil days of reckoning now upon us were delayed by a period of economic growth, and the ability of this growth to create social peace seems to me to be something for which we should be profoundly grateful.

We can see this immediately we think of a society without growth. Consider a thought experiment. Clearly transition to a no-growth economy would require revolutionary changes in the economic structure. Not only the industrial sector, but the structure of jobs, education, and the regional structure of the economy would have to change. Investment goods industries would, of course, have to shrink very markedly, and their redundant workers would have to be absorbed elsewhere without a cushion of growth to make the process palatable. This sounds as if it would be very much a war of all against all, sufficiently powerful to undermine any supposed shared ideology. And things are really much worse than this. Zero growth would have to be enforced. This means that there could be no individual freedom to invest, nor could there be a free movement of labour. And if we did not want to keep present consumption patterns, as is likely, it would be necessary to compensate growth in one sector by a reduction in another. If we ask who, and with what standards, could oversee such processes, we must surely come to worrying conclusions. Analogously, the German Marxist thinker Wolfgang Harich has argued forcefully that the creation of a 'green economy' would require a highly authoritarian regime – a regime his critics have dubbed a kind of ecological neo-Stalinism (Harich 1975, cited in Gäbler 1982: 19).

This should draw our attention with great sympathy to the long tradition, briefly mentioned by Hirsch himself, which has always recognized that the great virtue of Western society lies in the relative softness of their social order, that is, more precisely, that they are not really command systems. Hirschman has recently traced the intellectual origins of this approach, which praised the emerging commercial order as one in which economic interests would rule over much more dangerous and unpredictable passions, both of rulers and subjects (Hirschman 1977). As Adam Smith realized in his magnificent Book III of the *Wealth of Nations*, commercial society would encourage the powerful to spend their money on goods rather than on retainers, and this would allow for the emergence of the rule of law – the characteristic he and others then and now have dubbed the crucial attribute of liberalism. And his discussion makes very clear how accidental it was that the combination of liberalism with industrial society emerged at all. Any reasonable understanding of the philosophy of history must recognize that the combination of forced industrialization with the creation of a modern national state is virtually such as to necessitate a command system.

But Hirsch is certainly not wrong to stress that liberal capitalism is now in terrible difficulties. Is there any possibility that some alternative strategy can make the economy function (and even grow) without resorting to a political power system?

Three strategies

In retrospect, it can clearly be seen that in the years between 1945 and 1973 politics were conducted without real stakes (Aron 1982). This was symbolized in the neologism invented in England at the time, namely 'Butskellism'. But the agreement about the retention of welfare policies and the regulated market economy has now definitely and decidedly gone, and seemingly real alternatives are now on offer. Obviously there are considerable and important national differences, but in discussing the right I shall have in mind the radical alternative promised by Margaret Thatcher and Ronald Reagan (but not by Helmut Kohl) whilst for the left some ideas of the Labour Party left will combine with the positions of President Mitterand to allow some general comments.

The right alternative often presents itself in the form of an abstract and technical economic theory, namely monetarism. Now it seems unlikely that politicians will follow this theory, and of course the experience of Mrs Thatcher's government evidences the relative speed with which the pure doctrine was abandoned. The central reason for this seems to me to have been most clearly demonstrated – against his own intentions – by Professor Hayek in his *The Mirage of Social Justice* (Hayek 1976). Hayek argues there that politicians must jettison Keynesian inspired powers to manage or fiddle with market mechanisms. I think it is exceptionally unlikely that politicians will willingly abandon their powers in this way. More generally, the electoral pressure to reflate the economy remains as strong as ever, and Mrs Thatcher's government, despite seeking public kudos for attempting to resist such pressure, is in fact succumbing to it. But perhaps such pressure may in the long run diminish. For if we wish to understand the right alternative, it must be seen in political and not economic terms. It is an attempt to restore the stick to capitalism by means of unemployment. As such, of course, it is deeply unpleasant. But it is also possessed of a certain machiavellian wisdom in that it takes on not so much 'organized labour' as those who are much more helpless; providing provisions are made for youth, older workers who become unemployed and thus lose their union cards are scarcely in a position to fight back (Bradley and Gelb 1980).

What assessment can be offered of this approach? I think that there is as yet every reason for scepticism. Most obviously, it does not comprise nearly as much of an alternative as promised. As noted, monetarist doctrine has been abandoned, whilst the electoral pressures on politicians remain. So too do the basic power structures of society, including that of union power; if the economy recovers so as to reduce unemployment there is every reason to expect as considerable a wages explosion as have hitherto followed the ending of periods of incomes policy. Moreover, one cannot help but note one large internal contradiction in the programme as a whole. A large part of the economics of the programme consists in the metaphysical hope that reductions in taxes will change the behaviour of economic actors; but can these taxes really be cut by parties simultaneously gaining their legitimacy from, and committed to, heavy increases in defence spending? But even if we presume that the diminishing of expectations was achieved so that the strategy was assured in this way, there remain very heavy reasons to doubt its success.

Most obviously, the strategy is designed to produce a cowed, nineteenth-century work-force. But it is entirely probable that the late twentieth century needs a sophisticated and self-motivated labour force. This is particularly true in matters of education. All industrial states are heavily involved in the provision of a basic social infrastructure, and to that extent the dream of freeing the government of all social commitments is the more illusory. Attempts in that direction may prove to be highly self-defeating. It seems likely that the secret to a sophisticated labour force lies in high levels of general education, as in America and Japan. If the creation of a compliant work-force means the destruction of education systems, then the price may well be bought at too high a price.

The most striking thing about the alternative left strategy is that a major objection to the strategy of the right can be made here just as appropriately. Current experience seems to indicate that, as was the case with social democracy, full-blooded democratic socialism is in fact not likely to be implemented. President Mitterand's change of course came in record time, and it is now possible to recognize him as a Clement Attlee in disguise. And we can see why this happened when we think of some of the factors that are likely to continue to disrupt this approach.

Bluntly, there is no evidence to suggest that full-scale planning of the economy by central government is likely to be successful. There are of course significant differences in different national traditions; one can note clearly the possibility of such a programme being run by a Colbertist industrially-trained French civil service, and the rank impossibility that an Oxbridge-trained English civil service without industrial experience could be expected to spot industrial winners. But in order even to allow this to happen much stronger controls would be necessary than have been envisaged in order to prevent 'investment strikes'; and it is at least doubtful whether such controls could actually engender economic success in the limited electoral period which places such pressures on the managers of the state. And it must be noted that there is a very soft centre to this supposedly 'tough-minded' left-wing theory. In order to revitalize the economy, it would prove necessary to have great flexibility in order to introduce new technology and so on. The theory suggests that such change would be accepted by trade unions since they would realize that the government was acting in their long-term interest. President Mitterand found that this sort of faith vastly underestimated the sectional interests of the groups involved, and there is no reason to believe that any other case would be different. It is very likely that a full-scale socialist economic programme would require a highly organized state, and there is little likelihood of this since there there is no sign that the working class is becoming increasingly motivated by socialist ideology, although its disruptive capacity, above all in bringing down British governments, is clearly evident.

Both left and right place great emphasis on the spread of a new moral consensus of some sort or another and Hirsch shares the same hopes.

There seems very little evidence of any such sea change in social values. It is for this reason that we should take seriously some other positive proposals suggested by Hirsch in the final chapter of his book. It is here that he seems to be suggesting that changes in our social organization may make it possible for growth to be re-established. The particular proposal he makes entails the uncoupling of the traditional linkage of status with reward. He suggests, in effect, that those with jobs with intrinsic rewards, that is, autonomy, greater leisure time, an inherent interest, may well be prepared to work for those reasons alone, and thus not insist upon the highest salaries. Such salaries could instead be used to integrate those with poorer quality jobs, as well, it can be added, as those with the negative power to disrupt the economy. We may characterize these proposals in two ways. First, they are concerned far more with power factors than with the spread of some new ideology, and convince accordingly, and second, they involve what we might call the creative use of the market. The market would be used by politicians in order, say, to see at what price it still proves possible to fill university posts – a price that might change at some future date.

Hirsch's proposal seems to me worthy of the highest praise since it shows a degree of imagination that left and right do not possess – not surprisingly considering they are in quite considerable part merely a rewriting of Adam Smith and Karl Marx. To some extent, moreover, his proposals have perhaps begun to be adopted – the status of the academic world is perhaps as high as ever, but its monetary rewards are now somewhat lower than they were a decade ago. But for all that sceptical points about Hirsch's strategy deserve to be made.

One suspects that his policy could only be implemented by a supremely intelligent élite in, as it were, the dead of night – that is, very widespread discussion of such a programme might well make it politically impossible to achieve. And perhaps ironically, such a programme would have a very much greater chance of success in a climate of some economic growth. Academics and others may well accept relatively less, but social protest would naturally arise if it were a question of taking something away from particular groups to give it to others. Finally, it is as well to note that Hirsch's strategy is in somewhat the same situation as, indeed perhaps in a potentially worse situation than, that faced by governments introducing incomes policies. As noted such policies take on organized power in a way in which right-wing economic policy does not. Hirsch's strategy entails taking on the most powerful sectors of the professional world, and it is easy to imagine difficulties here; we are thus returned to the first critical point, that such a programme would require a measure of secrecy.

The international dimension

One of the most unfortunate characteristics of contemporary social theory is the limited attention it gives to sources of power that extend beyond the boundaries of what has traditionally been seen as 'society', namely the European nation state of the late nineteenth and early twentieth century. There is no doubt but that the presence of such states is a vital matter in its own right since international military relations so often determine the internal form of the state. But it remains the case that, especially since 1945, it is proper to talk of an international capitalist system. We know all too little about this system, although we can obviously see that its leading institutions are IMF and GATT. Even more importantly, we know very little about the exact relationships between economic and military power in the modern world. Raymond Aron's brilliant analytic history of post-war American foreign policy demonstrates that post-war American foreign policy in Europe saw economic investment following by several years military consolidation through the establishment of NATO; but who can say if this is generally the case (Aron 1974)? What does seem clear, however, is that the international side of capitalism works best when the system as a whole can be guided by a single leading power capable of disciplining the system as a whole, not least through basing its action upon a reserve currency.

These general considerations are of exceptional importance for the subject of this essay. In one sense I have so far argued that inside Western societies, capitalism is dead – that is, I have argued that the separation of the economy from the power of politicians is now no longer feasible. (This is not to say, however, that I consider capitalism in the sense of the power of money to buy advantage has disappeared.) By contrast international capitalism witnesses the market principle at work in its fullest and strongest sense. Inside liberal capitalist states, corporatist links between governments, employers, and unions are powerful and probably irreversibly present, but they have no equivalent on the international scene. In international capitalism, especially now, given the presence of highly flexible multinationals capable of moving their operations to the scene of greatest advantage, the law of capitalism still prevails: the weakest go to the wall.

International capitalism makes it impossible to imagine a no-growth system, and thus places very considerable burdens and obstacles on what can be done inside single liberal capitalist states. Consider to begin with that the United Nations decided that there should be no growth at all in the world as a whole. How would this be possible? The Third World countries would not, of course, accept that the advanced societies continue to use so much energy and mineral resources, and it is enough to ask whether the advanced countries would voluntarily give up some of their standard of living to the Third World to know the answer. But we can get to the heart of our problem by asking whether it is possible for the developed world to have no growth, whilst the Third World does continue to have positive growth. In the competitive international economy this is simply not possible. One can consider Great Britain to be a case of a society which opted out of international economic competition for only a few years, with disastrous results. It is not possible to grow old gracefully in one part of the international capitalist economy if others continue to innovate. Standing still results in negative growth. Any policy that took the no-growth side of Hirsch's argument seriously would result in social catastrophe.

A few more points need to be made about this simple but vital matter. It may well be possible to have a no-growth society, should we think this desirable. But in order to have such a society in conditions of international capitalist competition it is absolutely vital to continue to innovate, to run, in other words, in order to stand on the same spot. Had Keynes's rule for the international capitalist system been adopted at Bretton Woods in 1945/46 this would not be quite so necessary since both failing and overly-successful economies would have been brought into line with a common norm; but such rules were defeated, and in any case could now only work if they included Third World countries. The future of Western society thus depends on continuing to innovate in high technology given that Third World countries are becoming ever more adept at dealing with the traditional staples. Obviously, the social flexibility required to innovate, and therefore to kill off dying traditional industries, would be greatly enhanced by the presence of some economic growth. All these considerations can be summed up by saying that the room within which a single liberal capitalist state can operate is extremely limited. And one final point can be added to this. There is more at work than simply internationalist market pressure; there is also the question of the way in which the international institutions mentioned actually work. In so far as any left-wing strategy depends upon borrowing large sums of money to ease its economic recovery or to finance its social experiments, it is correspondingly at risk (Mann 1983). This has been seen time and again in 'runs' on various currencies which have necessitated changes in planned programmes. But it can also be seen, as it was in Great Britain in 1976, in those visits by members of the IMF which result in terms for loans which undermine socialist strategies.

Conclusion

It is an historic fact that capitalism and liberalism arose in tandem. We know, however, that there is no necessary connection between the two since the former is capable of adapting itself to different political systems, provided that they can provide some form of dependent labour. I suspect that such linkage as there was in the European case ultimately depended upon the capacity of economic growth to sweeten the political process – something which has been true of European history as a whole, and not just of the Keynesian years from 1945–73. For this reason, my argument has as a background assumption the need to restore economic growth, if at all possible. I have dissented from Hirsch's argument that growth itself has caused the recent crises of liberal capitalist societies; exactly the opposite seems to me to be the case. However, I have warmly commended his attempt to try imaginatively to develop entirely new strategies to enable our complex political economy to work once again. Any such strategies must in future pay attention to international factors.

If there is a single conclusion to the chapter it is that growth remains necessary but that it is almost impossibly difficult to achieve. My argument as a whole suggests that two broad strategies are available. First, socialists might seek – or at least socialist governments might seek – to change the rules of international economic competition so as to allow them to undertake socialist experiments. On reflection, one must be pessimistic about this strategy being realized since it would entail an alliance of *weak* states, and there is no particular reason to believe that strong states would listen to them. Second, a strong nationalist strategy integrating the working class might allow a single state to participate effectively in the international arena. This has been the policy, above all, of Japan. But whilst one can see the logic of the policy it remains hard to know how national cohesion is to be created according, as it were, to plan. Perhaps it is not in fact possible.

References

ABERCROMBIE, N. and TURNER, B. S. (1979) The Dominant Ideology Thesis. *British Journal of Sociology* 29.

ARON, R. (1974) *The Imperial Republic.* London: Weidenfeld and Nicolson.

—— (1982) Alteration in Government in the Industrial Countries. *Government and Opposition* 17.

BALIBAR, R. (1974) *Les Francais fictifs.* Paris: Hachette.

BELL, Q. (1976) *A Demotic Art.* Southampton: University of Southampton.

BOURDIEU, P. (1979) *La Distinction.* Paris: Editions de Minuit.

BRADLEY, K. and GELB, A. (1980) The Radical Potential of Cash Nexus Breaks. *British Journal of Sociology* 31.

DAHRENDORF, R. (1980) The Limits of Equality: Some Comments on Fred Hirsch. *Journal of the Royal Society of Arts* June.

GÄBLER, J. (1982) Alternatives to Economic Growth? Paper presented to the Joint Seminar of the Universities of Frankfurt and Southampton.

GELLNER, E. (1975) A Social Contract in Search of an Idiom: The Demise of the Dangeld State? *Political Quarterly* **46**.

GOBLOT, E. (1967) *La Barrière et le niveau.* Paris: Presses Universitaries de France.

HARICH, E. (1975) *Kommunismus ohne Wachstum?* Frankfurt: Rowolt.

HAYEK, F. (1976) *The Mirage of Social Justice.* London: Routledge and Kegan Paul.

HIRSCH, F. (1977) *Social Limits to Growth.* London: Routledge and Kegan Paul.

HIRSCHMAN, A. (1977) *The Passions and the Interests.* Princeton: Princeton University Press.

MANN, M. (1983) Nationalism and Internationalism in Economic and Defence Issues. In J. A. G. Griffith (ed.) *Socialism in a Cold Climate.* London: Allen and Unwin.

VEBLEN, T. (1899) *The Theory of the Leisure Class.* New York: The Modern Library (1934).

5 Economic growth and political dilemmas: post-war policies in Britain

ANDREW GAMBLE

'It is now a possibility that the market oriented polyarchies cannot much longer reconcile the necessary privileged demands of business with the demands of strong unions and the welfare state . . . Britain has already succumbed to a fundamental problem in irreconcilable demands.'
(Lindblom 1977: 351)

In writings completed shortly before he died, Fred Hirsch developed a rich and suggestive analysis of the political dilemmas confronting the affluent consumer societies of the advanced capitalist world (Hirsch 1977; 1978). His work was part of a broad and pessimistic reassessment of the economic and political prospects of Western capitalism following upon the onset of new economic difficulties in the 1970s.

This mood contrasted sharply with the considerable optimism and complacency about the future of the capitalist economy and the legitimacy of its political institutions that existed in the 1950s and early 1960s. The principal threat faced by Western capitalism at that time was generally perceived as an external one – the militancy and economic challenge of the Soviet bloc. The internal problems appeared to have been overcome. No one expressed this mood better than Seymour Martin Lipset in a famous passage in *Political Man* (1963):

'The fundamental political problems of the industrial revolution have been solved: the workers have achieved industrial and political citizenship; the conservatives have accepted the welfare state; and the democratic Left has recognised that an increase in overall state power carries with it more dangers to freedom than solutions for economic problems.'   (Lipset 1963: 406)

These lines were written in the middle of the longest and most rapid period of expansion that the capitalist world economy had ever experienced. In the 1930s neither the friends nor the enemies of capitalism could envisage a new period of sustained expansion. The ideologies of left and right were starkly opposed. Even those like Keynes, who believed there were better ways to manage capitalism to avoid under-employment of resources, did not foresee any early return to economic growth. The key economic and political question was mass unemployment and whether it should be blamed on workers' resistance to wage cuts, on the capitalist organization of production, or on the mistaken policies of financial orthodoxy pursued by governments (Skidelsky 1967).

The issue was never resolved in Britain in the 1930s. There was economic recovery but little decline in the numbers unemployed. Keynesian remedies were proposed by Lloyd George and the Liberals, by Oswald Mosley, and by Harold Macmillan, but none were adopted (Liberal Party 1928, 1929; Mcleod 1978). Yet, following the transformation wrought by war, a new world economic order and domestic political order emerged; with the sudden quickening of growth in the 1950s, Keynesianism became formalized as a set of ideas justifying the increased economic role for the state that was visible everywhere. It was recognized as an integral part of the new social democratic consensus. For a time the achievement of this consensus appeared to ensure economic growth and political legitimacy, an easing of the problem of how the national income should be shared out, and a weakening of political ideologies and social conflict.

The reasons for the undermining of this consensus is one of Hirsch's central themes. He wrote in a post-Keynesian era at a time when the easy optimism of the 1950s had already been dispelled, when ideology and social conflict had burst out with new vigour, and when many of the problems that were thought to have been banished forever had begun to re-emerge. The clearest sign that the Keynesian era was at an end was shown by the return of mass unemployment to every Western capitalist economy after 1974, and the inability of governments to prevent it.

The discrediting of Keynesianism was already well under way, however, before it was clear that the long boom was over and that a new major slump had commenced. The challenge to Keynesian techniques of economic management, and the undermining of the social democratic consensus on such issues as the level of welfare spending and the need to protect trade union rights, arose because of the earlier failure to halt inflation. The gradual acceleration of inflation prompted many new analyses of the conditions which favoured economic progress and social stability. One major new perspective that grew in prominence was the revival of liberal political economy by Hayek and Friedman and its application to the problems of the public sector by the new school of public choice theorists (Mueller 1979; Hayek 1960; Friedman 1962).

Hirsch's work is especially interesting because while it shares the assumptions of an 'economic approach' with these theorists it is more aware than many of them are of its limitations. Hirsch has criticized much orthodox economic analysis of public policy for confining itself to a model of rationality appropriate only to private economic goods. This makes all the interesting questions 'residual categories', outside the scope of the analysis. What Hirsch is chiefly concerned with is precisely the relationship between economic and non-economic factors. In particular he seeks to develop the idea that the very manner in which economic behaviour is organized in a capitalist economy produces results which undermine the non-economic conditions which must be sustained if capitalism as a mode of economic organization is to persist. His analysis and conclusions are of general application and universal interest but they have a special relevance to British experience, since Britain has displayed in an acute form the contradictions and dilemmas which Hirsch describes.

He identifies three features of modern capitalism that are central to the way it works. The economic dynamism of the system arises from the organization of economic activity through a system of free markets. This enthrones the needs and wants of individuals as the spur for production and enlists the self-interest of each individual in producing the goods and services which are demanded or for which a demand can be created. Demand and supply are balanced through the adjustment of prices which signal changing wants and changing costs. This system of decentralized markets, which rests upon free exchange between independent, equal, and sovereign individuals, has its counterpart in a political system whose legitimacy is founded upon 'universal participation'. All individuals are citizens, equal members of the political community, with rights to join voluntary associations, to speak freely, and to vote. The sovereign power of the state derives from the people and, once properly constituted, its claims to authority over its citizens and their social arrangements are potentially unlimited. The third crucial aspect is that for all its affluence capitalism has not yet abolished scarcity. So the distribution of what is produced to different classes and groups remains highly contentious.

The problem as Hirsch sees it is that the organization of the economic system and the organization of the political system supply conflicting criteria for distributing the goods and services produced by the capitalist economy which may undermine its legitimacy. If distribution is organized through the market individuals will be rewarded according to the value of what they have to sell or, as Hirsch prefers to put it, according to their market power – derived from chance, heredity, talent, skill, and ownership of specific resources. This will create a highly unequal distribution of income. The heights of consumption and civilized living are in practice available only to a few, although formally open to all. Only abstinence from consumption and a dedication to accumulation by capitalists may make this inequality tolerable. Hirsch refers to the celebrated passage in *The Economic Consequences of the Peace* where Keynes reflects on the success of nineteenth-century capitalism:

> 'Europe was so organised socially and economically as to secure the maximum accumulation of capital. While there was some continuous improvement in the daily conditions of life of the mass of the population, society was so framed as to throw a great part of the increased income into the control of the class least likely to consume it. The new rich of the nineteenth century were not brought up to large expenditures, and preferred the power which investment gave them to the pleasures of immediate consumption. In fact it was precisely the inequality of the distribution of wealth which made possible those vast accumulations of fixed wealth and of capital improvements which distinguished that age from all others.'   (Keynes 1971)

The second criterion for distribution is political and derives from the egalitarian basis of the modern democratic state. Equal citizenship leads to demands for equal treatment and equal access to the necessities, the luxuries, and the opportunities of life. Markets too require equality, for if markets are to function successfully then exchange must be equal and fair and the rights of buyer and seller must be respected and enforced. But the political criterion of distribution goes far beyond legal equality at the point of exchange and introduces notions of equality of opportunity and equality of outcomes. The first means ensuring that all possible handicaps are removed in the competition for wealth and status; the second suggests that beyond this there should be rough equality between the goods, the wealth, and status individuals actually attain.

The results of the two principles of distribution are clearly very different in the amount of inequality that is aimed at and Hirsch is right to argue that each tends to subvert the other. This is because of the third aspect he identifies – scarcity. If goods and services are scarce their distribution according to market power will create such inequalities that it undermines the legitimacy of the political order which is based on the equality of all citizens. This may create political hostility to the principle of free markets. On the other hand if the political criterion is allowed to dominate, political legitimacy will be secured but economic efficiency may be lost, because material incentives may not be sufficient to encourage the performance of many essential economic functions. In time this will in turn undermine the basis of political legitimacy since the people will be denied the steady flow of goods and services which they have come to expect governments to guarantee.

In political terms Hirsch is describing the political options as many saw them in the 1920s and 1930s for the future development of capitalism. On the left there were those like Tawney who argued that the conflict between the two criteria should be resolved in favour of the political by relating the distribution of income to service and function rather than to market power (Tawney 1961). This would make the economy collectivist rather than individualistic and would mean the supersession of the acquisitive society. On the right there were those like Hayek and Schumpeter who argued that since the political criterion threatened economic efficiency and economic liberty the overriding need was to restrain universal participation and lessen the scope for democratic policy-making, and in particular its interference in the workings of the market economy (Schumpeter 1954; Hayek 1962). Marxists tended to agree with Hayek on the grounds that the distribution of the national product and the nature of state action were inseparable from the way in which the economy was organized. The state was a capitalist state and redistribution, they argued, would not be allowed to threaten the inequality in ownership of wealth that sustained private accumulation of capital (Strachey 1934).

The actual compromise that emerged in the 1940s was different from any of the options as they were perceived in the 1940s. Post-war reconstruction was initiated by the war-time coalition government which was presiding over the highly centralized and controlled war economy. The political price of a national war effort was a commitment to post-war reconstruction, the main aspects of which, as popularly perceived, were that there should be no return to mass unemployment and there should be much more generous and comprehensive social security provision. The two characteristic products of the reconstruction programme were, first, the Beveridge reports and, second, the 1944 White Paper on full employment (Addison 1975; Mcleod 1978). The experience of a war economy in which resources and labour were fully employed made it seem intolerable there should ever be a return to the conditions of the 1930s. As many of the leaders of the 'new conservatism' acknowledged, government must henceforward be conducted on new principles. Quintin Hogg exaggerated when he told the House of Commons in 1943 that 'if you do not give the people social reform they will give you social revolution' but there was a wide appreciation that the emergence of a new consensus between the political parties on domestic political issues would have to concede many of the long-standing demands of the Labour movement (Gamble 1974).

The real nature of the consensus between the parties did not emerge until the 1950s when the Conservatives returned to office and found themselves presiding over the British economy during the world economic boom. The period of reconstruction in the 1940s was a time of austerity and financial discipline, and only gradually were the controls on the economy relaxed. Labour implemented the plans of the coalition government and the Conservatives offered only mild criticism. There was much fiercer resistance, however, over Labour's plans to extend public ownership beyond the public utilities. The nationalization of iron and steel, followed by the proposals to nationalize sugar, chemicals, and cement, was taken as a clear sign that the thinking of the Labour leadership was still directed to the goal of a gradual socialization of the main centres of private capital and the replacement of private profit by public service throughout the economy. The general expectation was still that after the reconstruction boom the old problems of stagnation and unemployment would reappear. Tawney's views that redistribution was necessary to create equality and that public ownership was the best way to end unemployment had been reinforced by the experience in the 1930s of an economy that had apparently ceased to grow.

The social democratic consensus that blossomed in the 1950s was not initially because of a genuine consensus of view between the Labour and Conservative parties. Labour had not renounced its commitment to clause IV or the desirability of a progressive socialization of the economy; it had significantly enlarged the public sector both in terms of public enterprise and public spending on welfare, and it had brought the trade unions fully into the policy-making processes of the state. But it had failed to reduce very much the economic and financial power of private capital (the compensation for nationalized assets had been particularly generous), and through its support for NATO and acceptance of American leadership, the traditional international orientation of British economic policy and British business was consolidated, not challenged. There was an important change for policy, however, which has been well summarized by Hirsch: '[since 1945] organised labour has . . . exerted a counterforce to the extra-parliamentary influence traditionally commanded by business and financial interests through both their market responses and their informal contacts with government ministers and officials' (Hirsch 1978: 281).

This idea that there was a stalemate between labour and capital in post-war Britain rather than an active consensus is widely shared on right and left. But the stalemate, by defining the constraints on policy so tightly, contributed to rather than hindered the continuity of policy between different governments while the ideological argument about capitalism and socialism was bypassed by the new ideology of growth. For many social democrats a steady increase in the wealth of the community offered a means to effect redistribution without attempting to transfer ownership or risking massive social conflict. Many Conservatives, forced to relinquish the conception of Britain as the centre of an empire and a leading world power, found some compensation in their new role as successful managers of a welfare capitalism. If inequalities of wealth and power could no longer be outweighed in popular consciousness by the more potent experience of belonging to the imperial nation and participating in the story of Britain's expansion overseas, the constant and increasing flow of goods and services backed by universal welfare benefits might achieve the same. Conservatives were not disposed to be defensive in the 1950s or to 'appease' socialism. They believed they had won. The 'Middle Way' that Macmillan had written about in the 1930s was being substantially achieved. Macmillan had wanted to see an industrial society, the strategic control of which would rest with the state while the tactical management remained in private hands; public and private industry would work together in a mixed economy. *Laissez-faire*, Macmillan had argued,

> 'leads inevitably to socialism. The only anti-socialist programme that has any chance of success is the organisation of a social and industrial structure which shall be neither capitalist nor socialist but democratic; where the wage earner shall be neither slave nor tyrant but truly and in the widest sense partner.'   (Fisher 1981: 29)

Three general election victories in the 1950s convinced many Conservatives that capitalism could become popular again because of its evident success in creating wealth and distributing it (Eccles 1955: 5). The role of the state was to maintain a high level of demand in the economy, ironing out fluctuations, and ensuring that everyone was provided with a minimum standard of living. The government should be committed to managing the economy so that unemployment remained low, prices stable, expansion brisk, and the balance of payments in surplus. The main engine of wealth creation was to be the private sector but the public sector had an important supporting role and, after ritual denationalizing of steel and road haulage, the Conservative governments between 1951 and 1964 made no moves to contract the public sector. They made no serious attack on welfare spending or tried to cut the taxes necessary to sustain it. They brought forward no proposals for changing trade union law. They were content to preside over the *status quo* they inherited. Growth made other choices for a time unnecessary.

The counterpart of this new conservatism was the rethinking of the traditional socialist positions by leading Labour Party intellectuals such as Anthony Crosland and John Strachey. Strachey's argument was rooted in the preoccupations of the 1930s when he had been a prominent Marxist intellectual. In the 1950s he argued that capitalism might not have changed but its prospects had been transformed by democracy. If the people were sufficiently well organized politically then the power of the modern state could be deployed to counter the inherent tendency of capitalism to stagnation, mass unemployment, and growing inequality. Keynesian techniques of economic management could ensure prosperity, full employment, and growth, while public expenditure programmes could both assist in sustaining a high level of demand and in redistributing the wealth that the economy was creating. If democracy weakened, capitalism would again become a malign destructive system, but if the democracy remained strong and the popular forces vigilant, then the prospect opened up a successful capitalism purged of many of its former failings and serving the public welfare (Strachey 1956).

Crosland's position went beyond this in several respects (A. Crosland 1956, 1982). He argued, first, that the modern economy was no longer capitalist. Major institutional changes, such as the divorce of ownership from control, the changing class structure, the growth of the public sector, and the elimination of poverty, made the old socialist analysis based on class conflict and exploitation redundant. Second, he argued that socialist were often confused between means and ends. Equality was the ultimate end which all socialists were seeking. Nationalization was at best a means of realizing equality, sometimes an important one, but not to be mistaken for the goal of socialist activity itself. In modern circumstances, Crosland argued, equality could be secured better by other means. If economic growth could be maintained the transformation of society which socialists sought could be achieved far more painlessly than had previously been imagined. An expanding public spending programme, funded by progressive taxation, could ensure a gradual redistribution of wealth and power and a gradual approach to equality of opportunity.

What was central to Crosland's new political agenda for the Labour Party was growth. The engine of this growth, as for the new conservatism, was to be the private sector. This sector had to be organized through markets, it had to be competitive, and it had to be profitable. It was to be supported by a state using Keynesian regulatory techniques as well as fiscal and monetary policies to sustain growth and maintain high levels of employment.

Despite an underlying stalemate between the two leading political forces it did appear in the 1950s that the legitimacy of the modern capitalist order would not be challenged so long as growth was sustained. A greater and greater priority came to be attached to growth, reaching its climax in the 'growth mania' of the 1960s. This was the period when Britain's relatively slow rate of growth was pinpointed and became the focus for major political concern. Few politicians were prepared to question that governments could and should raise the rate of economic growth. Competition between the parties ensured that the 1964 election was fought on rival programmes to modernize British institutions and to raise economic efficiency and productivity by means of major new government initiatives and spending programmes – in fields such as planning, prices and incomes, technology, education, roads, and health.

The modernization strategy of the 1964 Labour Government built on measures already introduced by the Conservatives. At stake between the parties was not ideology, but which party could prove more competent managers of the national economy and which could raise the British economic performance at least to that of its European competitors. The parties were responding to the growing gap that was emerging between the expectations of the people for higher living standards and the sluggish economic performance. Perhaps that was understandable. With unemployment at such low levels and inflation a minor irritant, it was natural that the focus should have been on increasing wealth.

What is so striking about recent British politics and economic policy is how quickly the consensus on the need for growth collapsed and how complete was the failure to solve the problems of the economy within the constraints of post-war social democracy. Both parties competed to provide better economic management. But to the electorate each new attempt seemed worse than the one which preceded it; each new government more incompetent than its predecessor, and each in turn was rejected. Government changed hands in 1964, 1970, 1974, and 1979. The problems mounted and the political resources for dealing with them dwindled. Not surprisingly the result, especially after such a long period of technocratic rather than ideological politics, was to detach a growing part of the electorate from loyalty to either party, amidst signs of new political and ideological polarization of opinion amongst party activists.

The reason for Britain's turmoil in the 1960s and 1970s has sometimes been ascribed to a malignant tumour – the British disease – which has been eating away at the nation's vital parts. Observers, journalists, and politicians have recognized this illness in different symptoms. At times it has been the British balance of payments, at times pay, recently it has been public expenditure which, slipping its leash, has allegedly been dragging the whole nation towards a totalitarian future. This atmosphere of disquiet in British public life has contrasted with the much greater calm and confidence that has been observed amongst the people (Alt 1979). Yet there is a good reason for the anxiety. The failure of the modernization strategies of Macmillan, Wilson, and Heath has exposed the fragility of the consensus which has governed post-war policy and has reopened many of the unsettled questions concerning the special institutional character of British capitalism, the antique British state, and the manner of its integration in the world economy, as well as the institutions and goals of the British Labour movement (Nairn 1977). In Britain, growth came to be regarded as the solvent for the tensions that Britain's earlier political and industrial history had created. By the end of the 1970s it had become clear that there was little life left in the old political formulas of Macmillan and Crosland, though Crosland himself protested against this conclusion. In *Socialism Now*, published in 1974, he wrote:

> 'Extreme class inequalities remain, poverty is far from eliminated, the economy is in a state of semi-permanent crisis and inflation is rampant. All this undoubtedly belies the relative optimism of *The Future of Socialism* . . . Do these setbacks to our hopes demonstrate that the revisionist analysis of means and ends was wrong, and the Marxist analysis which it sought to rebut was right?'   (A. Crosland 1974: 26)

He thought not. The onset of economic problems was peculiarly British and the revival of Marxism was limited to Britain. 'If one examines the western world as a whole there are no clear signs of a new and fundamental crisis. . . . No long-term crisis comparable to that of the 1930s seems imminent' (Crosland 1974: 27). Many commentators said the same. Few were still denying the reality of the world slump eight years later.

The difficulty for Crosland in admitting that a new slump had begun was that it undercut the assumptions on which his politics had been based. It would have indicated that in certain fundamental respects capitalism had not changed and that all the questions about redistribution in a period of zero growth and the transfer of ownership that he had declared irrelevant might have to be reopened. Both liberal political economy and socialist political economy re-emerged as radical perspectives in the 1970s, while the social democrats of all parties looked temporarily disillusioned and bereft of ideas. But new ideas and new analyses have begun to flow again. One major concern has been to identify why the priorities of post-war policy have been abandoned and what needs to be done to restore a coherent social democratic programme, that is a programme which in the spirit of New Liberal and social democratic writings of the past seeks to sustain a capitalist organization of the economy, not by the subordination of the people to the disciplines of the market or by the coercion of the state, but by the fullest possible extension of democratic citizenship and participation that is compatible with an efficient and productive economy (Clarke 1978).

Hirsch has played an important part in this reorientation by showing how the process of growth in a modern capitalist economy is not the simple smooth process it is often taken to be. Instead it generates conflicts and instabilities which threaten its continuance. One expression of these tensions is inflation. What Hirsch offers is a non-monetary account of the causes of inflation and how it can be traced back to the competitive struggle for individual and group advancement. World recession makes the consequences of the growth failure devastating, because it heightens the struggle over distribution and potentially threatens the legitimacy of the entire social order for large parts of the population. But the importance of Hirsch's analysis is that he argues that growth has not halted because of some unfortunate external shock such as the quadrupling of oil prices in 1973. The process of growth itself created the tensions which destroyed it. This might seem to align Hirsch with Hayek who has also argued that the long boom was increasingly artificial, maintained by methods which seriously distorted the pattern of demand and the distribution of labour and made a slump inevitable (Hayek 1972). The methods, according to Hayek, were Keynesian monetary policy, which tolerated deficit financing and excessive credit creation, public expenditure programmes which restricted the scope of economic activities, and the political and legal tolerance afforded trade unions, which prevented many markets from functioning properly. The conclusions for policy which Hayek and new right opinion in the Conservative Party have drawn are that Keynesianism must be abandoned and the market order restored. This means severely curtailing the range of intervention which public agencies currently undertake, obliging governments to adopt a neutral policy stance renouncing responsibility for either full employment or economic growth (Gamble 1979).

The social market critique of British economic policy in the 1960s and 1970s focuses on the role played by the state in the economy. On this view the commitment to maintain high levels of employment and faster rates of growth meant that when these did not materialize the immediate response by government was to intervene still more in the market – by pumping in extra demand, by giving new incentives and subsidies, by setting up new public agencies to supplement and often supplant market forces (Brittan 1977). The social market critique of Keynesianism was never better stated than by James Callaghan at the Labour Party Conference in 1976:

> 'We used to think that you could just spend your way out of a recession and increase employment by cutting taxes and boosting government spending. I tell you in all candour that that option no longer exists, and that in so far as it ever did exist, it worked by injecting inflation into the economy. And each time that happened the average level of unemployment has risen. Higher inflation, followed by higher unemployment. That is the history of the last twenty years.'
>
> (Blackpool, 28 September 1976)

It is ironic that the only clear examples of such reflations are the 'Maudling boom' of 1963–64 and the 'Barber boom' of 1972–73. Both were in part prompted by an increase in unemployment (although in neither case had unemployment reached even one million). Both were also deliberate attempts to use the machinery of demand creation to stimulate a faster rate of growth in the economy, to break out of the depressing cycle of slow growth, low investment, and low productivity. In monetarist terms both made possible a sharp acceleration of inflation (Sewill and Harris 1975). These governments and their advisers were not blind to the inflationary risks of their policy. Their 'crime' was that they gave a lower priority to maintaining sound money than to full employment and economic growth. This meant that they were always inclined to deal with inflation not by introducing sound money policies but by attempting to suppress it by intervening still more in the market economy. The favourite device of the 1960s and 1970s was incomes policy.

Incomes policies have always been an anathema to monetarists and new right opinion. The reason is simple. As Hirsch explains, 'there is no doubt that the internal logic of a continuing incomes policy involves progressive departures from market principles in regulation of the economy' (Hirsch 1978: 279). This is because incomes policies invite political negotiation about many aspects of economic policy and the establishment of political criteria for determining relativities and rates of pay. For social market theorists the resort to incomes policy to suppress the inflation which the excessive creation of money has unleashed is a fateful step which can progressively lead to the destruction of the market order and to the establishment of a command economy. For they note that every incomes policy has eventually been sabotaged by both employers and unions. Accepted with varying degrees of reluctance at first every incomes policy in Britain was more and more resisted as time went on, until finally it collapsed (Brittan and Lilley 1977). Each succeeding incomes policy tended therefore to be wider in scope and more draconian in its proposed penalties. The logical outcome was plainly suspension of the market altogether in the determination of prices and wages.

The failure to control inflation was accompanied by mounting unemployment and a declining rate of growth. They naturally appeared to be linked together. Certainly the failure to evolve a permanent framework for the regulation of prices and incomes was one of the most important aspects of the failure of the modernization programme. The pay explosions in 1969–70, 1974–75, and 1978–79 which followed periods of severe restraint undermined faith in social democracy and in political methods of resolving economic problems, and raised fears that the country was becoming 'ungovernable' (Douglas 1976). The new wage militancy which inflation and the frustration of hopes for higher living standards generated was directed as much at the social democratic order as at the capitalist order and this aroused forebodings not just on the centre but on the left of British politics also. For the industrial militancy was often aggressively sectional, it was focused primarily on questions of pay and there was little wider sense of class solidarity or a general working-class political interest beyond the competitive struggle for higher pay. In retrospect it has been argued this made such militancy extremely fragile and transient (Hobsbawm 1981). It played its part in undermining the credibility of social democracy and opened the way to deflation and the rigours of monetarism.

As inflation accelerated and the modernization strategy in all its different forms fell apart, so the polarization of political opinion proceeded apace and so new ideologies and doctrines emerged to shape the debate. The stark contrast between capitalism and socialism was once more openly posed, the social market strategy of the Conservative new right confronted the alternative economic strategy of the Labour left. Since 1975 the new right has been in the ascendancy and a prolonged assault on the institutions and policies of social democracy has begun. But social democracy, precisely because it was embedded in specific institutions and did arise on the basis of a particular balance of political forces is not proving as easy to dislodge as if it had been simply a set of policies, ideas, and ideals. The social democrats of all parties have been regrouping not just politically (the most dramatic instance being the formation of the SDP in 1981 and the establishment of an alliance with the Liberals) (Bradley 1981), but also intellectually, searching for an analysis of what went wrong with British economic policy which does not lead to monetarist and social market conclusions.

Hirsch is an important signpost in this search since he draws quite different lessons from Britain's recent experience of inflation, rising unemployment, and stuttering growth than does Hayek. This is because he rejects the naive faith in markets which is widespread, although not universal, among monetarists. The failure of capitalism to maintain high employment and a high rate of growth is blamed by new right opinion on social democracy – on external interference with the workings of markets. Hence their programme: establish sound money by squeezing inflation out of the economy, no matter what the short-term consequences are for employment and output; at the same time improve the long-term prospects for employment and output by reducing public expenditure as a proportion of GDP, and therefore the burden of taxation, by curtailing all government interference in the market economy, except the essential upholding of the rules under which markets operate; and end the power of trade unions to oppose managers' 'right to manage', and their political power to commit governments to Keynesian techniques for managing the economy, interventionist policies, and high public spending programmes.

In Hirsch's view what all this fails to see is that Keynesianism is not a matter of bad economics, as Milton Friedman thinks (Friedman 1977), or of wrong policy advice which can be corrected by the exercise of political will, however indomitable; nor is the power of trade unions something that can be combated by dreaming about a sudden resurgence of faith in the values of a market order. As Hirsch notes, the importance of Keynesianism, quite apart from its status as technical economics, was that in the circumstances of mass democracy and universal political participation it provided the missing legitimacy for a predominantly capitalist system. It held out the prospect of an economy that was so managed that every citizen could look forward to reasonable security of employment and income, to an improving standard of living, and to widening opportunities. Keynesianism as an economic doctrine proclaimed that these outcomes were within the technical competence of governments to provide and should become its responsibility to ensure. Success in achieving these outcomes became the criterion by which political parties were to be judged by the electorate. If governments now disclaim responsibility for growth and for jobs on the grounds that they cannot guarantee them, how is social order in the widest sense to be maintained?

Sound money policies guarantee one kind of social order by defusing the explosive effects which inflation can have upon a market economy, but at the cost of prolonging and intensifying the slump. It defends existing concentrations of wealth and privilege by increasing inequality and consigning ever larger numbers into long-term unemployment, hence poverty. The plight of this growing surplus population cannot be relieved either by emigration – that avenue has long been closed – or by public spending, for it is an essential part of the doctrine of sound money that public spending should be curtailed and reduced. The grim cycle of monetary squeezes to halt inflation, rising unemployment, falling government revenue, and cuts in public spending, leading to renewed deflation of demand, causes disproportionate damage and hardship to some parts of the economy and some social groups, notably the populations of the inner cities (Friend and Metcalfe 1981). The more such a cycle is repeated the greater the risk of breakdowns in social order, hence the greater the resources given to security forces to contain them. There is a drift towards a heavily policed democracy; social order for those with jobs and property increasingly entails the repression of those without. In an economy in which competition is increasing for positional goods, the long-term effects of denying access to them, by denying the opportunity to compete for them to an increasing part of the population, must have explosive effects. Liberty in these circumstances can have a high price.

Those who value democracy more than liberty are uneasily aware, however, that there is much resentment against many public agencies, against the remote bureaucracies that administer welfare programmes, and the nationalized industries. There is resentment against the burden of taxation and considerable resentment towards those who are unemployed, particularly if they are black. There is also little confidence that orthodox Keynesian policies will create growth again.

One solution to this problem has come from the Liberals who have argued over a very long period that the institutional basis of the economy has to be recast if legitimacy is to be restored. In particular they advocate radical measures of industrial democracy based on co-ownership schemes (Gamble 1983). Many similar ideas for workers' co-operatives have been put forward in recent years (Jay 1976). In Hirsch's terms the value of such reforms would be to give individuals a stake in industrial society not just as consumers of its products but as producers as well. This might moderate at least some of the competitive pressures which the present division between employers and employees, managers and workers, creates.

The main defect of this solution is that it signals a retreat to individualism, even if the individual units are now co-operatives. Leaving aside the enormous practical difficulties of transforming the present economy and its giant enterprises in that direction, such an approach is unlikely to deal with the problem that Hirsch outlined. Western economies suffer from too much individualism rather than too little. According to Hirsch, the political direction in which Western capitalist states will have to move if they wish to avoid the dangers of a lurch towards authoritarianism is towards regulation of individual wants, the placing of limits upon individual competition, and the removal of certain goods from competition altogether.

Hirsch does not spell out the implications of this in any detail. But it seems clear that he favoured not a contraction of the present public sector but its extension. Nothing could be more disastrous for social cohesion in Hirsch's model than the present steady drift towards the privatization of health care and education, since both these goods embody in his terms significant 'positional' aspects. Though he does not state it openly the logic of his position would appear to favour a significant widening not contraction in the number of goods provided publicly and the winning of political consent for the payment of minimum incomes to all irrespective of work performed. This might have the effect of restricting the scope for individual economic striving, at the same time countering the estrangement of those without jobs and property from the political and social order, as well as building in most powerful automatic stabilizers of demand for the products of increasingly automated industries.

Such a programme would mean a more egalitarian society than exists at present and a much larger transfer of income through the state fiscal apparatus than currently exists. The obstacles to it are obvious enough. But a more immediate objection is that it is unnecessary. The doubling of unemployment three times in twenty years has not had the catastrophic effects many prophesied and politicians used to fear. The division and hostility between employed and unemployed has been one of the central supports for monetarist policies. The frustration of expectations about jobs and growth was accepted in the 1970s and early 1980s with remarkable calm. Electoral opinion became highly volatile, but, apart from the 1981 inner-city riots, there was relatively little overt protest about what was happening to the economy. It became common to speak of a politics of declining expectations (Alt 1979). Under the Thatcher government industrial militancy weakened and extra-parliamentary protest was considerably less than it had been under the Heath government ten years before. Might not the problem of growth breeding inflation simply be solved by a long period of no growth or even declining real output?

The problem however is not so easily disposed of. Capitalism has always been an expansionist system, constantly seeking out new technologies, new markets, and new needs. As the division of labour has widened and deepened, the whole of industrial society has become a vast interlocking inderdependent mechanism, the need for political and social equality of all members of the community has become both a requirement for further expansion and a demand pressed fiercely by the disadvantaged and the organizations representing them. The slump of the 1930s in Britain was also a period of relative quiescence and the continuation of the routines of customary life, but it was succeeded by war and the far-reaching social and political changes of the 1940s which made possible the boom. In periods of slump, restructuring to permit accumulation to proceed extends beyond the economy to social and political institutions as well. From this perspective egalitarian policies which redistribute wealth and enlarge the public sector, though not in themselves sufficient, are nevertheless necessary conditions for recovery to start and for the legitimacy of the market order to be maintained. This was the truth which Fred Hirsch saw so clearly and analysed with such precision.

References

ADDISON, P. (1975) *The Road to 1945*. London: Cape.
ALT, J. (1979) *The Politics of Economic Decline*. Cambridge: Cambridge University Press.
BRADLEY, I. (1981) *Breaking the Mould*. Oxford: Martin Robertson.
BRITTAN, S. (1977) *The Economic Consequences of Democracy*. London: Temple Smith.
BRITTAN, S. and LILLEY, P. (1977) *The Delusion of Incomes Policy*. London: Temple Smith.
CLARKE, P. (1978) *The New Liberalism*. Cambridge: Cambridge University Press.
CROSLAND, A. (1956) *The Future of Socialism*. London: Cape.
—— (1974) *Socialism Now*. London: Cape.
CROSLAND, S. (1982) *Tony Crosland*. London: Cape.
DOUGLAS, J. (1976) The Overloaded Crown. *British Journal of Political Science* 6 (4): 483–506.
ECCLES, D. (1955) Popular Capitalism. *Objective* 20.
FISHER, N. (1981) *Harold Macmillan*. London: Macmillan.
FRIEDMAN, M. (1962) *Capitalism and Freedom*. Chicago: Chicago University Press.
—— (1977) *Inflation and Unemployment*. London: Institute of Economic Affairs.
FRIEND, A. and METCALFE, A. (1981) *Slump City*. London: Pluto.

GAMBLE, A. M. (1974) *The Conservative Nation*. London: Routledge and Kegan Paul.
—— (1979) The Free Economy and the Strong State. In R. Miliband and J. Saville (eds) *Socialist Register*. London: Merlin.
—— (1983) Liberals and the Economy. In Vernon Bogdanor (ed.) *Liberal Party Politics*. Oxford: Oxford University Press.
HAYEK, F. (1960) *The Constitution of Liberty*. London: Routledge and Kegan Paul.
—— (1962) *The Road to Serfdom*. London: Routledge and Kegan Paul.
—— (1972) *A Tiger by the Tail*. London: Institute of Economic Affairs.
HIRSCH, F. (1977) *Social Limits to Growth*. London: Routledge and Kegan Paul.
—— (1978) The Ideological Underlay of Inflation. In Fred Hirsch and John Goldthorpe (eds) *The Political Economy of Inflation*. Oxford: Martin Robertson.
HOBSBAWM, E. J. (1981) *The Forward March of Labour Halted*. London: Verso.
JAY, P. (1976) *Inflation, Employment, and Politics*. London: Institute of Economic Affairs.
KEYNES, J. M. (1971) *The Economic Consequences of the Peace*. London: Macmillan.
LIBERAL PARTY (1928) *Britain's Industrial Future*. London: Benn.
—— (1929) *We Can Conquer Unemployment*. London.
LINDBLOM, C. (1977) *Politics and Markets*. New York: Basic Books.
LIPSET, S. M. (1963) *Political Man*. London: Mercury.
MCLEOD, R. J. (1978) *The Development of Full Employment Policy, 1939–45*. Oxford: unpublished D. Phil. thesis.
MUELLER, D. C. (1979) *Public Choice*. Cambridge: Cambridge University Press.
NAIRN, T. (1977) *The Breakup of Britain*. London: New Left Books.
SCHUMPETER, J. A. (1954) *Capitalism, Socialism, and Democracy*. London: Allen and Unwin.
SEWILL, B. and HARRIS, R. (1975) *British Economic Policy*. London: Institute of Economic Affairs.
SKIDELSKY, R. (1967) *Politicians and the Slump*. London: Macmillan.
STRACHEY, J. (1934) *The Nature of Capitalist Crisis*. London: Gollancz.
—— (1956) *Contemporary Capitalism*. London: Gollancz.
TAWNEY, R. H. (1961) *The Acquisitive Society*. London: Collins.

6 The distributional compulsion and the moral order of the welfare state

PETER TAYLOR-GOOBY

At first sight, the development of the welfare state enacts in microcosm the three puzzles of modern society that Hirsch identifies on the first page of *Social Limits to Growth*. Social expenditure increased in real terms at an average rate of just under 4 per cent a year between 1950 and 1978. It expanded from under 15 to over 25 per cent of state expenditure (Gould and Roweth 1980: 347–8). Measured by staffing ratios in the NHS, personal social services and education, proportion of students gaining qualifications, housing standards and real value, and coverage of state benefits, the standard of provision far exceeded that of earlier periods by the mid-1970s. Yet the paradox of affluence is readily apparent in the dissatisfaction with improved welfare evident in the writings of academics (e.g. Hadley and Hatch 1981; Legrande 1982); in public opinion survey (Harris and Seldon 1978); in the activities of pressure groups and welfare state trade unions; and most importantly in the land-slide election of a party that put the restoration of 'self-reliance and self-confidence which are the basis of personal responsibility and national success' (Conservative Party 1979: 7) at the heart of its mani-festo presentation of social policy.

It seems plausible to contend that the distributional compulsion underlies the growth of a welfare state which is commonly understood to restructure the distribution of resources and life chances; and that popular concern about bureaucracy, red tape, social security snoopers, high-handed professionals and officials, coupled with the evident resonance of the theme of 'rolling back the frontiers of the welfare state' to liberate the individual in the market, reflect the wistful reluctance in modern collectivism.

The object of this paper is to use empirical evidence about welfare policy to examine Hirsch's two main themes: that the increasing importance of social scarcity in an affluent society aggravates distributional competition at the expense of collective struggle for growth; and that the expansion of the market in which self-interested struggle rules depletes the moral legacy that is a necessary bulwark to Hobbesian disorder. It will be argued that despite the obvious changes in the recent history of the welfare state from Butskellism to the new right certain threads endure: among them is a remarkable constancy in the fact of the inequality of wealth and income distribution, whatever the rhetoric of politicians and reformers; and a continuing dominance of the moral principles of family and work ethic. Principles such as these provide a consistent foundation for social integration, despite the passing of a cohesive pre-industrial value system. There is no evidence of enhanced distributional compulsion or of a progressive weakening in the contribution to moral order from policy, although the normative principles evident in policy may differ from the values of altruism and obligation advanced by the protagonists of welfare. If anything, social policy has increased inequality, because different social groups differ markedly in their capacity to use universally provided services in kind. This moral tradition remains remarkably resilient despite social changes in the family and in employment opportunities that make it increasingly inappropriate.

The forces sustaining consistency in policy display considerable power. This supports the view that Hirsch places too great a weight on the idealist assumption that human affairs are determined ultimately by human ideas. The appeal of his analysis lies in the fact that it appears to give an account of recent developments which walks the tightrope between two perils. On the one hand it avoids the crude determinism evident in the Club of Rome's physicalist model-building which admits that 'neither this book nor our world model . . . can deal explicitly with . . . social factors' (Meadows *et al.* 1975: 46). This leads to the gloomy conclusion that uncertainty about human capacity for moral restraint makes the viability of a no-growth utopia precarious (1975: 178–79). This limitation is also evident in the positivism of the systems theory of the *Ecologist*'s 'Blue-print for Survival': 'nor is there any reason why sociology should be anything but a branch of natural science which deals with a particular type of natural system: human society' (1972: 32). On the other hand, Hirsch escapes the descent into individualism which renders psychoanalytic accounts of the human predicament – from Freud's analysis of civilization and its discontents through Fromm's escape from freedom and in large measure Marcuse's penetration of one-dimensional culture – unsatisfactory to many social scientists.

Hirsch's account roots human discontent in a social science framework. The force of the argument against idealism is that he does not go far enough in doing so. Materialists stress the importance of the social and material environment in influencing not only people's ideas but also the scope and limitations of the pursuit of particular values in society. Hirsch sees individual aspirations as moulded in the market: the problem is one of aggregation. 'What individuals want and what individually they can get, society cannot get' (Hirsch 1977: 106). A materialist approach might give a similar account of conscious expectation, although rooting the genesis of ideas more firmly in an account of the relation of social life to social production. It would differ in its understanding of the possibility of realizing life plans. A pattern of structural power is determined by the relations of production which are necessary to enable people in society (at a particular stage of development) to appropriate external nature and so survive. This poses additional barriers to people's capacity to change the organization of their social life. From this viewpoint, Hirsch's solution of moral restraint to allow the fair distribution of socially scarce resources, with perhaps a little progressive taxation of the superrich (Hirsch 1977: 184) is likely to be inadequate in the face of the structural power distribution that is part and parcel of capitalism.

In addition, idealism pays insufficient attention to the structures of power that influence the formation of policy over time and act as a brake to the distributional compulsion, and as a reservoir to refresh the moral legacy. Materialist approaches, broadly speaking, claim that the enduring features of social relations are founded on a structure of power that derives ultimately from consistent basic features of society (the capitalist mode of production and the family system) rather than from individual consciousness. To the extent that income distribution and the moral principles of welfare display rigidities over time, despite the pressure of popular demands in the case of the first, and social change in that of the second, this view becomes more plausible.

This essay will provide a brief account of the development of the welfare state, and review evidence of its impact on income distribution and its moral framework in more depth.

The development of the welfare state

The story of the welfare state is often produced as a drama in three acts: this version lends some support to the view that policy changes are sufficiently radical to embody the far-reaching transformation of ideas that Hirsch identifies. First in the immediate post-war period, the characters are established by the 1944 Education and Family Allowances Acts, the 1946 National Health Service and National Insurance Acts, and the 1948 National Assistance Act. From then up to the early 1960s the dominant theme is of political consensus on state responsibility for the provision of welfare services and an underpinning of economic management to ensure full employment. Consensus was neither achieved nor sustained without effort. Conservative support for Keynesian management did not emerge until the approval of the Industrial Charter at the 1947 party conference, and for social services until the acceptance of the Guillebrand Report on the NHS in 1955 and the Phillips Report on provisions for the elderly in 1954. On the Labour side, the imposition of NHS charges in 1951 led to the resignation of Wilson and Bevan. Through this period welfare expanded in step with relatively secure economic growth, so that government expenditure did not compete with rising personal living standards for resources.

The second act develops character through the intrusion of situation and the emergence of conflict. The worsening economic climate (highlighted by devaluation in 1967), uncertain growth, rising unemployment, the increase in dependent groups, such as school children, pensioners, and some single-parent families, put a greater strain on the welfare state. The programmes of the major parties diverge: the introduction of earnings-related pensions, comprehensive education, the control of private landlords, council house subsidies, university expansion and the institution of polytechnics, family allowance rates, prescription charges, means testing, NHS and personal social service reorganization, all became issues of controversy. This period marks the genesis of pressure groups – Child Poverty Action Group in 1965, Shelter in 1967. The welfare state is squeezed between enhanced service demand and the rising cost of provision. Public expenditure, fuelled mainly by social expenditure rises from about a third of GDP in 1960 to a peak of nearly a half in 1975. The state digs deeper into the pockets of the citizens to fund its activities: the income tax threshold for a married man with two children fell from just over average male manual earnings in 1960 to about 60 per cent of that level by 1975 (CSO 1982a: 88).

In the third act conflict reaches the crisis point. Party struggle intensifies with the 1972 Housing Finance Act, its repeal in 1975, and the current virtual moratorium on council house building; the rescinding of the 1965 comprehensive schools circular in 1970, its reimposition in the 1976 Act, and the repeal of the Act in 1979; the restrictions on private landlords in the 1965, 1969, and 1975 housing Acts and the introduction of fresh categories of tenure that escape control in 1979; the contradictions between 1969 and 1971 pension White Papers, the 1975 Act and current deindexation and real cuts in short-term benefits and proposals to deindex pensions. From 1975 onwards both Labour and Conservative governments have sought to contain welfare expenditure. However the approach of the 1979 Conservative Government displays a distinctive commitment to privatization in the sale of council housing, and support for pay-beds and private medicine, assisted places in public schools, occupational sick pay, and voluntary personal social services. In the long run experiments with voucher-assisted private education, the denationalization of universities, private insurance health care, the extension of occupational pension provision, and further sale of council housing seem possible.

The scale of the cuts should not be exaggerated. At the time of writing, government savings on housing and education have been outweighed by the increased cost of defence and unemployment benefits. The future of policy is uncertain.

The pattern of consensus, controversy, and crisis offers a rich basis for interpretation in terms of distributional compulsion and depleted moral legacy. The one could plausibly enhance the competition that underlies conflict and the other remove the moral fetters that restrain conflict from reaching a critical point. We now examine these two themes in more detail to see whether facts about the impact of policy on distribution and the moral principles it embodies – as opposed to rhetoric and the surface level of party politics – bear out this interpretation.

The distributional compulsion

Hirsch poses the question of why modern society has become so concerned with distribution, when it is clear that the great majority of the population can raise their living standards only through enhanced production. His discussion of the issue (Hirsch 1977: 152–58 and ch. 11) focuses mainly on trade union bargaining. However, the recent history of the welfare state provides, at first sight, an apt illustration of the puzzle. Commentators of all shades of political opinion have seen the welfare state as about redistribution in the direction of equality (see Marshall 1970: ch. 12; Townsend 1975: 28; Robson 1976: ch. 2; Gough 1979: 110–14; Joseph and Sumption 1979: 111; Sleeman 1979:

2, 101; M. and R. Friedman 1981: 176–8). Politicians have stressed the goal of equality (Crosland 1974: 15; Field 1981: 16). Egalitarian redistribution figures largely among 'the explicit aims enshrined in statute or in the speeches of those responsible for inaugurating or restricting the services' at the close of the Second World War (George and Wilding 1976: 106–17).

Official pronouncements reinforce this impression. In 1972 the Inland Revenue concluded that 'the broad picture of the last twenty years is of a tendency for variations between incomes to diminish' (Inland Revenue 1972: 4). A more recent analysis that includes the services provided by the welfare state as well as the tax it levies states that 'taken together, taxes and benefits reduce inequality' (CSO 1982b: 97).

The welfare state also embodies the trend toward 'defensive unionization, to protect differentials *vis-à-vis* traditionally organized occupations' associated by Hirsch with the distributional obsession (Hirsch 1977: 172). Between 1961 and 1979 union membership among NHS workers doubled from 37 to 74 per cent and increased by nearly a quarter among local government and education workers, from 66 to 81 per cent. Among the work-force as a whole the increase was much slower, from 45 to 55 per cent (CSO 1979: 195). The tendency to increased militancy among welfare state workers, from the first teachers' strikes in 1971 and nurses' strikes in 1974 culminated in the 'winter of discontent' preceding the 1979 election. Several commentators suggest that this was an important factor in the Conservative victory (Butler and Kavanagh 1980: 337–40). However, welfare state unionization is only a particular expression of a general trend among labour. Here we focus on the distributional compulsion in relation to the redistribution of command over resources through the provision of tax-financed social services. Detailed examination of what is known in this area produces a rather different picture from that painted above.

Evidence on the redistributive impact of the welfare state comes from two main sources which have been reworked and modified in many ways. First, the survey of personal incomes carried out by the Inland Revenue on the basis of tax returns. This provides information on the relative amounts paid in income tax by tax-payers. The data refers to a relatively long time period and is extensively discussed (see Atkinson 1975: 51; Sleeman 1979: 106; Townsend 1979: 125). The extent of redistribution through direct taxation may be gauged from this source, slightly modified with reference to other official survey data and presented by the Royal Commission on the Distribution of Income and Wealth (1979: Tables A1 and A2).

Table 3 shows the proportions of all income received by particular

Table 3

	top 1%		top 10%		bottom 50%	
	before tax	after tax	before tax	after tax	before tax	after tax
1948/49	11.2	6.4	33.2	27.1	23.7	26.5
1976/77	5.5	3.9	26.2	23.1	24.1	26.9

groups in the population arranged in order of pre-tax income. It can be seen that despite the real advance in living standards over the period (real income roughly doubled) and despite the real growth in the proportion of national resources commanded by government (public expenditure rose from about 34 to about 43 per cent of the GDP) the extent of redistribution has been limited. The share of the poorer half of the distribution was enhanced by less than an eighth in both years. The fact that the amount lost by the rich exceeds that gained by the bottom 50 per cent indicates that to a considerable extent redistribution is towards middle-income groups rather than the poor.

The Inland Revenue statistics are likely to give a misleading impression for a number of reasons: first, income is likely to be incorrectly reported. Sir William Pyle, Chairman of the Board of Inland Revenue, recently estimated that unreported income constituted about 7.5 per cent of the domestic product in 1979. Work by Macafee (1980: 86) and O'Higgins (1981: 378) indicates that this figure may be something of an exaggeration. In any case since the better-off have greater opportunities for tax evasion this factor is likely to lead to an over-estimate of redistribution (Atkinson 1975: 58). Second, capital gains are omitted from the figures. Estimates of the incidence of these gains by Prest and Stark (1967) indicate that they increase inequality markedly. Third, the imputed rental value of owner-occupied homes has been omitted since the abolition of Schedule A taxation in 1964. This amounted to about 3 per cent of total personal income in that year and is likely to enhance inequality. Fourth, fringe benefits, which have become steadily more important as the incomes policies of successive governments bite harder on cash income, are not included. These tend to benefit the better-off. The average value of benefits in kind exceeded a third of salary for managers but was less than a fifth for a factory superintendent and proportionately less for a shop floor worker in 1978 (HMSO 1980: 16). Fifth, the estimates ignore the value of home production. This is likely to be considerable in farm communities but less elsewhere and raises problems about the assessment of the value of leisure. Finally, the statistics are based on tax units, which may be individuals or households. This means that the distribution of command over resources within households is ignored. Recent work by Pahl (1980: 316–18) indicates that this is gender biased. Further, they are vulnerable to changes in the labour force. In particular, the tendency for increased participation in paid work by women within households which are presented by the Inland Revenue as one tax unit may increase the pre-tax income of those households and stretch the original distribution. Similarly, rising unemployment may lead to the omission of a greater proportion of the population.

Overall, it is hard to conclude from the Inland Revenue estimates that forty years of the welfare state have led to any marked redistribution through direct taxation. The unsatisfactory nature of the statistics has led to the use of the second source of data – the Family Expenditure Survey – as a basis for calculation. Before we consider this, we will briefly mention the distribution of wealth.

Estimates of wealth distribution are uncertain due to the power of the wealthy and their consequent capacity to conceal their good fortune from the prying eyes of officialdom. The calculations made by the Royal Commission on the Distribution of Income and Wealth derive from estate duty returns modified in various ways. Two points from these analyses are of interest. First government activities seem to have had very little effect on the gross inequalities in the distribution of wealth conceived of as marketable assets. The top 5 per cent of the wealth distribution owned far more than the bottom 90 per cent – the mass of the population – throughout the period (HMSO 1980: 21–2). Second, the introduction of an important form of non-marketable asset – pension rights – into the calculation modifies the distribution to a considerable extent. The addition of assumed capital values for occupational and state pensions nearly doubles the total amount of personally held wealth. Occupational pension rights effect a slight net shift from the rich to the mass of the population. State pension rights substantially enhance this effect, increasing the proportion of wealth controlled by the bottom four-fifths from 23 to 45 per cent. Wealth is as unequal as between a Kalahari bushman and President Reagan. However, the occupational pension sector (which is heavily subsidized by the state, as we shall show below) and welfare state pensions (which are far and away the largest single component in social expenditure, and the most rapidly expanding (Judge 1981: 509)) have had a modest redistributive effect.

The Family Expenditure Survey calculations are based on a large sample continuous survey of income and expenditure patterns among households established in 1957 to provide a secure basis for the calculation of the retail price index. Calculations of the incidence of social policy, understood as affecting the citizen through taxation and service provision may be based on the study. The overall conclusions have varied little over the twenty-three years for which information is currently available. A convenient summary is provided by Nicholson (1974: 77–8). Direct taxes such as income tax are progressive in that they take proportionately more from the better-off than the poor. Similarly cash benefits give more to the poor and to larger households. However, this pattern of horizontal and vertical redistribution is disturbed by indirect taxation and benefits in kind. Indirect taxation and rates are regressive, bearing heaviest on the second to bottom quintile of the income distribution (i.e. the fifth of households who fall between the 60 and 80 per cent points of a ranking by income). Benefits in kind (education, housing, the NHS) provide more in absolute terms to the better-off. 'However, expressed as a proportion of final income, the benefit is largest for low income groups' according to the official calculations (CSO 1982b: 99). These services also benefit larger households more. Thus the welfare state as a whole can be said to be mildly progressive, assuring that lower income households get rather more. The extent of redistribution should not be exaggerated: in 1980 the share of the bottom fifth was increased from 0.5 to 7.0 per cent of all income and the top fifth reduced from 43 to 39 per cent, once taxes and services are taken into account in these calculations. The redistribution on a horizontal level, between those without and those with children seems more marked. A worrying finding of recent work is that 'unemployment makes household incomes before taxes and benefits more unequally distributed. . . . Taxes and benefits substantially reduce, but do not eliminate this increase in inequality' (CSO 1982b: 97). Welfare state redistribution is a fragile benison.

The findings of the CSO studies have been called into question for a number of reasons. First, the amount of government expenditure and income that can be conveniently allocated to households is limited. In 1968 only about a third of expenditure and half of tax revenues were allocated (Peacock and Shannon 1968: 30–46), and by 1980 refinements in the calculations had increased this to just 46 and 58 per cent (CSO 1982b: 97). This is because much government income derives from sources (such as taxes on corporations and excise duty) and much expenditure is on programmes (such as employment programmes, road building, agricultural subsidy, and defence) whose incidence is difficult to attribute. However, this state activity certainly does have distributional effects in relation to the price of commodities and the benefits from subsidized facilities such as roads which apply differently to different groups. Attempts to reallocate the missing expenditure by Nicholson and Britton (1979: 325) and Peretz (1973) indicate that the CSO studies tend to exaggerate both vertical and horizontal redistribution. In addition, work by Nissel, which attempts to develop adequate methods for comparing the needs of households with and without children concludes that 'for the average household with children . . . cash benefits . . . were small and substantially outweighed by taxes' (1978: 4). This work indicates that the extent of redistribution through the welfare state is even less than official estimates imply.

Second, there are a number of problems with the data available. The results suffer from the margin of error common to all data gleaned from probability samples. It is known that expenditure on luxury items is under-recorded, as is investment income, which may bias the estimates disproportionately for higher income groups (Nicholson 1974: 74). The response rate is between 70 and 75 per cent: it is likely that the group of non-respondents contains a greater proportion of better-off households.

The third problem with the use of this data to provide evidence of egalitarian redistribution concerns the attribution of benefits from the state services in kind. The recent work of Legrande (1982) has radically undermined the assumptions about service use. CSO attribute the benefit of social services by dividing total expenditure on the NHS, primary, secondary, further and higher education, and council housing subsidies between the population, taking into account the different utilization of services by different age groups. Thus the average cost to the NHS and personal social services of someone over 65 in 1979 was more than twice the average for all age groups (CSO 1982a: 142). This approach ignores the fact that the privileges of class tend to extend into the area of state-provided services. Higher social classes are better able to get the best out of the NHS and the education system and have the biggest mortgages which command the most tax relief. Legrande applies an exhaustive survey of available evidence to class differences in the use of state-subsidized private services in health care, housing, and transport. He concludes in health care: 'the evidence suggests that the top socio-economic group receives 40 per cent more NHS expenditure per person reporting illness than the bottom one. This almost certainly underestimates the overall inequality' (Legrande 1982: 46). In education: 'the richest fifth of the income distribution receives nearly three times as much expenditure per household as the poorest fifth' (1982: 75). In housing (taking the effect of mortgage interest subsidy, exemption from capital gains taxation on owner-occupiers, improvement grants, council housing subsidies, and rent rebates and allowances into account) 'the net result is that the richest [fifth] receives nearly twice as much public subsidy per household as the poorest group' (1982: 101). In transport 'it seems reasonable to assert that public expenditures . . . have not promoted greater equality in final income' (1982: 117). Overall:

> 'almost all expenditure on the social services in Britain benefits the better off to a greater extent than the poor. This . . . is . . . true for services whose aims are at least in part egalitarian, such as the National Health Service, higher education, public transport and the aggregate complex of housing policies.'   (Legrande 1982: 4)

This detailed review of services in kind indicates that it is the middle classes, with their superior knowledge and ability to negotiate with welfare gatekeepers, their determination to realize their aspirations and, as Donnison puts it, their 'sharper elbows', who have benefited from the welfare state. Legrande's point is that the official data analyses lack a class dimension. It seems likely that an application of a gender dimension to the data would produce a similar outcome. Women achieve less well in the state education system and are under-represented in the most expensive advanced sector (Byrne 1978: 128–32). Differences in the utilization of the education system accounted for almost all the differences in utilization of state services by different income groups noted in the CSO analysis (CSO 1982b: 97).

It is possible to paint an even more inegalitarian picture of the impact of the welfare state than that offered by Legrande. This emerges if state support to the private sector is taken into account. Field (1981: 172–75) demonstrates that independent schools received state subsidies (through local education authority and Ministry of Defence purchase of places, charitable status rates and tax exemption, state training of teachers, and tax concessions to insurance-based fee payment schemes) of between £350 and £500 million in 1979. To this may be added the further subsidy of between £9 and £90 million a year promised in the 1982 assisted places scheme. The users of private schools are overwhelmingly middle and upper class (Halsey, Heath, and Ridge 1980: 203) and these subsidies are provided out of state revenues which derive from taxes of net proportional impact. The redistributive effect, which is not included in Legrande's calculations, is inegalitarian. Similar arguments may be developed about the impact of private health care, and the provision of cars for private use as an occupational fringe benefit.

A striking feature of Legrande's analysis is that transfer payments which make up the biggest single item in the welfare state are not included. All reanalysis of the Family Expenditure Survey concurs that the progressive effects of direct tax are cancelled out by the regressive effects of indirect tax: 'for each type of family, direct and indirect taxes combined form a remarkably stable proportion of income' (Nicholson 1974: 77). Benefits are mildly progressive, means tested and flat-rate benefits rather more so, earnings-related benefits rather less so. This, combined with the evidence from the wealth studies that the most noticeable (although modest) step in the direction of redistribution results from the spread of state pension rights, suggests that it is in the area of cash benefits if anywhere that we should look for evidence of welfare state redistribution. The evidence that we have indicates that the egalitarian dreams of post-war reformers have been rudely shattered by reality. Redistribution is largely horizontal to periods of need in the family life-cycle. For the most part this is from working life to retirement pension. There is a strong suggestion that the rest of the welfare state benefits the better-off at the expense of the worst-off. The distributional compulsion is evident at the level of rhetoric and, more modestly, in official commentary. At the level of reality the distribution of power embodied in the old law of 'to him that hath shall be given . . .' is the stronger. This implies that while the experience of seeking satisfaction within a positional economy may be a growing force in the shaping of ideas, there is a consistent structure of countervailing powers underlying the level of ideas which exerts a determining influence on the course of social development.

Pensions form the largest single item in social expenditure and, arguably, the social programme with the greatest contribution to such egalitarian redistribution as does take place in the welfare state. Recent developments in pension policy provide a clear illustration of the appeal and limitations of egalitarian rhetoric.

Beveridge's plan made no promises about equality: indeed the third basic principle stated:

> 'The state in organising security should not stifle incentive, opportunity, responsibility; in establishing a national minimum, it should leave room and encouragement for voluntary action by each individual to provide more than the minimum for himself and his family.'
>
> (1942: para. 9)

The assumptions about the dependency of the family on a male bread-winner and the role of the private sector in providing privileged welfare for those who choose (and can afford) it have determined all subsequent policy.

The goal set out in Beveridge's plan was freedom from want through a framework of flat-rate benefits designed to meet the contingencies of everyday life and assure a national minimum income: most needs would be met by social insurance benefits, and a system of means-tested tax-financed national assistance would fill in the holes in the safety net for anyone whose circumstances were out of the common run. Flat-rate benefits were to be paid for by flat-rate contributions – the same for everyone in each category of membership – so that everyone got the same rights and the redistributive possibilities of the scheme in an unequal society were limited to a pooling of risks, rather than a pooling of available resources.

Beveridge had envisaged that contributions would be paid at full rate immediately while benefits would be built up over a twenty-year period, so that an actuarially sound fund could accumulate. However the post-war government decided to blanket-in all pension scheme contributors in 1948 when the scheme started. This meant that the scheme could only finance pensions at a level below that of the minimum subsistence poverty line established by means-tested assistance.

By 1965, when the first accurate survey of pensioners' living standards was carried out, 47 per cent of retirement pensioners were shown to have incomes below the means test level. Of these just under half were failing to claim their entitlement (Ministry of Pensions 1966: 19). The failure to pay adequate insurance benefits had been long apparent and had earlier led Beveridge himself to disown the scheme in the House of Lords: 'either the Government will have to raise the benefit rates to adequacy for subsistence, or to say . . . that they have . . . abandoned security against want without a means-test: and declare that they drop the Beveridge Report . . .' (Hansard, House of Lords, 1953, vol. 182, col. 677).

The uncertain financial basis of the scheme and the steady increase in the pensionable proportion of the population through the 1950s made growing Treasury subventions essential. The decision to abandon the Beveridge principle and political responses to concern about the size of pensions seem plausibly explained in terms of traditional plural politics and recognition of the size of the pensioner vote (about a fifth of the electorate were receiving pensions in 1951, rising to more than a quarter by 1971) rather than any distributional compulsion rooted in an increasingly positional political economy.

In 1957, the Labour Party presented a radically revised pension scheme at the national conference. This would provide the cash to raise pensions to a level where the average male manual wage-earner would command a pension equivalent to half-pay through the introduction of earnings-related contributions, which could raise proportionately more cash from the better-off. The scandal of retirement on stop-gap means-tested assistance would be ended and a modest step towards redistribution would be made. The egalitarian impact of the scheme was weakened by the fact that earnings-related contributions were only levied up to an income ceiling of about four times average manual earnings, so that the managing director of ICI paid no more than his best-paid foreman; and by the provision of earnings-related pensions to sugar the pill of higher contributions.

The Conservative response was to uprate pensions by 22 per cent in real terms in 1958 (the largest uprating ever) a decision probably influenced also by the army of half a million late entrants to national insurance who were to become entitled to state pensions within a few months. Legislation was passed in 1959 to add a hastily cobbled earnings-related scheme to flat-rate pensions in 1961. However this provided supplementary payments worth very little in comparison to the contributions it demanded, and was essentially a device to increase the income of the national insurance scheme. The expansion of social security was a major theme in Labour's 1959 election platform and formed the mainstay in 'the ending of economic privilege, the abolition of poverty in the midst of plenty, and the creation of real equality of opportunity' that were the 'immediate targets of political action' of the 1964 manifesto (Labour Party 1964: 5). Wilson shrewdly seized on the proposal for an income guarantee and promised 'a guaranteed income beneath which no one will be allowed to fall' in the first weeks of a Labour Government in an election broadcast (Kincaid 1973: 64).

The fate of these egalitarian promises was unsurprising. The income guarantee was dismissed in the 1965 National Plan on the grounds that it would not contribute to national growth. A wide-ranging reform of means-tested assistance was diluted to restyling the operation Supplementary Benefits: the number of recipients continued to grow due to demographic trends (especially the increase in the numbers of single parents) and the failure to reform insurance benefits such as pensions, so that their recipients no longer needed means-tested supplementation. It was not until 1969 – a curious lacuna – that pension proposals were again unveiled in a White Paper. The new scheme differed from the previous one in two important respects. First, while pension levels were roughly the same, the method of finance was modified. The ceiling for earnings-related contributions was lowered to one and a half times average earnings (rather than four times) and the size of Treasury subsidy was cut from 24 per cent of the cost to 18 per cent. Since this came from general taxation which, as we have seen, is roughly proportional in effect and since it pays for pensions which benefit the poor rather than the rich it is mildly redistributive. The net effect of these changes was to radically reduce the possibility of redistribution through social insurance.

Second, the scheme was markedly more generous to the private sector. The abatement of state contributions for members of private schemes was set at 33 per cent rather than the 20 per cent originally proposed. More important, the state took full responsibility for maintaining pensions against the ravages of inflation once in payment. Life expectation at retirement age was about thirteen years for men and twenty years for women by the late 1960s. Inflation at only 5 per cent annually would demand a state subvention equivalent to about 90 per cent of the private sector payment in the first case and 165 per cent in the second by the end of the period.

The scheme was lost in the 1970 election defeat (where it formed the central theme of the discussion of welfare in the manifesto (Labour Party 1970: 19–20)). The Conservative Government presented a scheme that was markedly more inegalitarian and generous to the private sector. The Labour proposal finally passed into law in the 1975 Social Security Act, no doubt aided by the fact that the levying of earnings-related contributions now in return for a slow increase of pensions over the next twenty years has provided a real surplus to the Exchequer in recent years.

This brief summary of developments in the most important single area of social policy indicates how difficult it is to demonstrate that a distributional concern centred on competition to gain access to socially scarce resources is the mainspring of events – or that this compulsion has grown in importance over recent years. Equality has played a major role in the rhetoric of politicians and the pronouncements of officials about pensions just as it has in relation to the welfare state as a whole. In both areas, policy has made no great strides in this direction. The inequalities of 1948 are embodied in the pensions of 1982. The simple struggle of interest groups provides a convenient account of the general structure of pension scheme developments, governments competing to attract the pensioner vote without alienating the interest of today's contributors. The enhanced respect for the private sector, especially evident in the expanded concessions of Labour's plans from 1957 to 1969, is perhaps best explained by two factors: first, the growth in membership of occupational schemes (from 30 to 62 per cent of the male work-force and 12 to 26 per cent of women workers between 1951 and 1967 (CSO 1982a: 56)). Wilson's promise of 'the white heat of the scientific and technological revolution', designed to appeal to the new middle class beyond Labour's traditional manual constituency meant that such developments demanded attention. Second, the power of the private sector: the neighbourly face of the man from the Pru takes on a different expression in the City, where the assets of long-term insurance companies totalled about one-fifth of all domestic fixed capital investment in

1969, of which the greater part is accounted for by pension funds (CIS 1974: 1, 26). The expansion of private sector pensions makes them a formidable component in the interests of capital as well as those of the electorate, and one which governments of any political complexion cannot afford to damage without risking palpitations in political economy as well as psephology. The ground rules of the capitalist system constitute the framework within which the game of plural interest negotiation is played out. In the case of pensions, the entrenched power of the funds enables capital also to enter as a powerful and articulate interest in the political arena. As Crossman admitted on presenting the 1969 scheme to the House of Commons: 'I always knew [the pension interest] comprised a powerful group, but their influence has been brought home to me more than ever' (Hansard, House of Commons, 19 January 1970).

In general, it seems that the development of pension policy displays the same rigidities as the distribution of income and wealth over the mature years of the welfare state. The pattern can be accounted for in terms of the organization of political groups to advance self-interest within a framework determined by the power of capital. Appeal to a distributional compulsion is unnecessary. We now move on to consider how far Hirsch's second major theme, the depletion of the moral legacy, is borne out in the development of the welfare state.

The depletion of the moral legacy

The market system offers the promise of the co-ordination of myriad individual self-centred productive activities through the operation of a hidden hand. However, market individualism offers no normative restraints to the exaltation of personal interest against that of society. Why should not the stronger in the market organize to take all and society disintegrate in a self-stultifying Hobbesian conflict? Hirsch quotes Smith and Mill to show that the original ideologues of *laissez-faire* realized that a framework of overarching morality was essential to the system (1977: 137). However the market cannot itself guarantee such values and the individualist culture of capitalism is itself corrosive of its moral legacy. The results are twofold: first, the Keynesian system of the managed market is undermined:

> 'central guidance of the invisible hand . . . wilts under the legitimized standard that covers the heartland of the market economy, the maximization of private interests. . . . Individual maximization can be held to its social purpose . . . so long as it operates on the basis of properly

> designed . . . rules; yet individual maximization means manipulating
> these rules too.'   (Hirsch 1977: 131)

Second:

> 'the internal forces released by liberal capitalism have exerted pressure
> for conscious justification of the distribution of economic rewards, a
> pressure that undermines the system's drive, and equipoise. That is
> the current crisis.'   (Hirsch 1977: 177)

Here we focus on the second point. It follows from the analysis of the distributional compulsion. The social nature of consumption generates an obsession with status in the pecking order. The individualist and libertarian ethos of capitalism means that no ultimate justification of the order is available. Under the ideology of *laissez-faire*, the market assumes the character of a natural force – one might as well complain about the way the wind blows as about the fact that the market values the skills of a Harold Robbins at a rate a thousand times those of a William Golding.

The entry of the state into the market twists the screw: if people's market interests can be advanced through political organization, the lack of any agreed morality to bar holds in interest group conflict or to make the outcome palatable to the aggrieved is likely to lead to a loss of legitimacy for the system as a whole. The essay by Plant in this volume explores various treatments of this theme in depth.

Recent strikes by welfare state workers and the tussles of government and unions over the social contract indicate that the moral value of concern for the interests of the needy is not advanced against pure self-interest when this is organized to achieve its object. A well-publicized example of the near-victory of expediency over commitment lies in the child benefit scandal of 1977. Despite a manifesto pledge in 1974, and the passing of an Act in 1975 that did not give a starting date for the scheme, the Labour Cabinet wished to postpone child benefits indefinitely. It was prompted by concern that the abolition of child tax allowance, which, for the most part, reduces the tax liability of fathers in order to increase cash child support to mothers, would affect the interests of male trade unionists and might endanger the social contract. A spectacular leak of Cabinet minutes to *New Society* compelled the Labour Government to honour their commitment (MacGregor 1981: 142). The unusual feature of this case seems to be that the cynicism of government was undermined by journalism: the normal course of social policy-making is likely to display a congruent, but better-concealed disregard of conventional moral norms.

It is unlikely that such developments represent a modern tendency to depletion of the moral legacy, at any rate since the Second World War. Established interest groups have always acted to influence state policy to suit themselves. Perhaps the most celebrated example of interest group politics is the British Medical Association campaign against the salarying of GPs and the provision of a front-line health service through local authority-owned health centres after the passing of the 1946 NHS Act. An amending Act scotched the one and a circular the other in 1947 before the service came into operation. The independence of GPs and their right to lucrative private practice was preserved (Thane 1982: 235–36). Similarly, the Wilson government's egalitarian attack on public schools through the Newsom/Donnison Commission of 1965 was successfully weathered by the interests involved. The Commission's reports strengthened the provisions whereby local authorities could subsidize the private sector by paying for a small number of nominated pupils and ultimately resulted in the withdrawal of the direct grant in 1976, and the conversion of the majority of direct grant schools into independent schools. The success of the private sector in resisting recent intrusions by the state parallels the achievement of the Endowed Schools Act (1869) which followed the Clarendon and Taunton Commissions and enabled private schools to break the terms of endowments and direct their resources into the most privileged areas of the private market; and the arrangements whereby the schools first extensively tapped the local education authority market following the Fleming Report of 1944. The power of pension fund interests has already been discussed. It is not clear that the post-war development of the welfare state represents any tendency to the conquest of a valiant morality by grim self-interest. Political organization to secure group interest can plausibly be detected throughout the period of the modern state.

As Hirsch points out, any politico-economic system requires a foundation of morality to enable it to cohere over time. Pure interest group competition conjures the spectre of Hobbesian anarchy. The quick-lime of market individualism corrodes the communitarian value system of pre-industrial society. However, the argument that this undermines any possibility of the long-term legitimation of economic intervention and guidance by government ignores an important fact, at least as far as evidence on the development of social policy goes: a rather different normative order is implicit in the practice of state welfare. This order enacts a moral tradition entirely adequate for social cohesion, and one that shows no sign of depletion. The assumption that women are and should be dependent on male bread-winners will be considered here. Themes of racism (implicit in the arrangement of policy so that blacks in general achieve lower standards of health care, education, state housing, and access to social work resources than whites); the legitimacy of class inequality and respect for private property embodied in the account of differential access to welfare services and the failure of redistribution given earlier; the morality of equivalent exchange framed in the institutional stigmatizing of those without appropriate contribution records; and the work ethic implicit in much harsh treatment of the able-bodied unemployed: all these could also be advanced in a celebration of the enduring strength of the welfare state's moral legacy.

The dependency of married women on their husbands was a central feature of Beveridge's scheme, as the third principle quoted above and the organization of contributions and benefits demonstrate. Married men paid higher contributions than women on the grounds that 'men are contributing for themselves and their wives as a team' (Beveridge 1942: 50). Married women were permitted to pay much lower contributions than single women, waive their rights to most insurance benefits and rely on the dependent's allowance attached to their husband's benefit. About three-quarters choose to do so, since the married woman's rate of sickness and unemployment benefit was much lower than her single sister's and she had to satisfy tougher conditions to be entitled to pension in her own right. No dependent's allowance similar to her husband's was attached to her benefit if she paid full rate.

The legislation that introduced a fully earnings-related scheme in 1975 removed the disparity between men and women's contributions and provided for the phasing out of the married women's option to pay at a reduced rate. However, despite the fact that that year (International Women's Year) saw the passing of the Sex Discrimination Act, the assumption of dependency still remains. Married women are entitled to the same benefits for the same contributions as their husbands for themselves. However, they are not normally entitled to additional dependent's benefits for their children and there is no dependent's benefit for the husband unless it can be proved that he is incapable of paid employment. The man simply has to satisfy the weaker test of showing that his wife is not working to gain the dependent's benefit for her.

The assumption that married women are dependent on a male bread-winner and do not normally work contradicts all evidence. The Central Policy Review Staff concluded that by 1976 'almost two out of three married women between 35 and 59 years of age were working or seeking jobs . . . compared with one in ten in pre-war years' (Central Policy Review Staff 1980: 101). This in fact accounts for all the increase in the labour force in recent years: the number of men in the labour force fell by 0.2 million and the number of single women by 0.6 million between 1961 and 1976, whereas the number of married women workers increased by 2.8 million. Married women's earnings are important to the family budget, contributing on average over a quarter of it in 1974 (Hamill 1977). A DHSS report in 1971 showed that the number of families with fathers in full-time employment living at a standard below the official poverty line would have trebled without the mother's pay (DHSS 1971: 14). In that year one in six of all non-pensioner households were exclusively dependent on a women's earnings (Land 1976).

However the myth of the housewife and the male bread-winner is as sprightly as ever. A DHSS Minister of State wrote in an official letter in 1975: 'it is normal for a married woman in this country to be primarily supported by her husband, and she looks to him for support when not actually working rather than to a social security benefit' (quoted in Land and Parker 1978: 338). The same value influences the decisions of commissioners on benefit appeal cases (Land and Parker 1978: 340–41), and is embodied in the organization of new benefits. A married woman is debarred from claiming the non-contributory invalid care allowance introduced in 1975 and payable to other categories of men and women who give up paid employment to care for an infirm relative. Similarly married women have to undergo an additional test to claim the non-contributory invalidity pension introduced at the same time for those whose insurance record is inadequate to claim other non-means-tested benefits. Whereas men and single women only need a simple statement from a GP that they are incapable of paid employment, married women must pass the harsher test of satisfying DHSS that they are incapable of normal housework. Tribunals have held that women so severely disabled that they can only move from room to room with difficulty are ineligible. Family income supplement, a means-tested addition to low pay dating from 1971, is not available to married women workers whose husbands are unemployed. Instead the husband must claim supplementary benefit. State social security is channelled through him.

The counterfactual assumption that the social security system can cater for the needs of married women by treating them as dependents of male bread-winners runs consistently through social security policy. It also affects the treatment of the unmarried. The rapid increase in the number of one-parent families (from about 9 to 15 per cent of all families with children between 1961 and 1978 – Study Commission on the Family 1980: 17) led the government to establish the Finer Committee. The Committee recommended a special guaranteed maintenance allowance to meet the social security needs of these families, roughly half of whom are dependent on means-tested social security at any one time.

The failure of the last four governments to implement this led one commentator to remark that: 'in Britain the problem of lone mothers is perceived more in terms of how best to remove barriers to their remarriage rather than to overcome obstacles to their increased participation in the labour market' (Land and Parker 1978: 336).

The other side of the coin of dependency for income on the breadwinner is assumed availability to carry out unwaged domestic tasks. Here, evidence is patchy. The assumption that daughters (usually themselves middle-aged married women) will provide care was the most common reason for refusal of an application for home help found in an official study in 1967 (Hunt 1970: 338–39; see also Rees 1976: 89). Recent policy has emphasized community care and resulted in provision for fewer elderly, mentally handicapped, and mentally ill in state institutions. However, the support services that are necessary to supplement care by the family are inadequate even by official standards. By March 1979 only 2 out of 107 local authorities had achieved the target figure of 60 per 100,000 population day care places for the mentally ill laid down by government (DHSS 1975). Over a quarter had no places at all. Provision of domiciliary services such as home helps, meals on wheels, and aids was at about half the DHSS recommended level in 1976 (DHSS 1976). Inevitably, the burden of filling the gap falls on families, and especially on women. It is hardly surprising that two recent writers conclude that without adequate support for community care 'equal opportunities legislation represents nothing more than pious hypocrisy' (Finch and Groves 1980: 511).

The view that the development of a positional economy in recent years has led to a depletion of the moral legacy seems open to question, at least in the sphere of welfare. Only by wistful reference to a dimly glimpsed Golden Age of Enlightenment, Altruism, Solidarity, and Titmuss is it possible to see current politics as the Fall. Moral rules can be detected in the organization of welfare, but they are not the rules of ultra-obligation, community, and egalitarianism. Rather they represent family and work ethics and they are consistently enduring over time. Indeed the most striking feature of the principle of married women's dependency is its resilience in the face of social change, a resilience that undermines any claim to reflect the facts of people's lives.

Conclusion

Hirsch's twin themes – the distributional compulsion and the depletion of the moral legacy – provide concise accounts of much of the surface politics of the past forty years of state welfare. In particular, they summarize neatly the major currents in popular ideas that appear to have been dominant, where increased concern with the distribution of provision (and of the incidence of taxation) and an erosion of the legitimacy of the state are central issues. A more detailed analysis, however, of such evidence as is available indicates that the distribution of resources and the moral framework imposed by state welfare are more striking in their permanence than their erosion.

Empirical evidence is always subject to rectification and reinterpretation, especially in an area where the involvement of powerful interests ensures that the data are at best incomplete and at worst corrupt. However, the balance of fact suggests that the trajectory of welfare statism is best accounted for by a materialism that throws the emphasis on the relative durability of the basic features of society that mould human affairs than by an idealism that stresses the possibility of change through the development of human consciousness. Hirsch's account of contemporary ideology is compelling because it forms part of and sustains ideology. It represents an account of currents in ideas as an account of society. The truth is other, the same tired truth about the persistence of gender inequality, poverty, and injustice despite the welfare state that is rediscovered afresh every decade; and has to be rediscovered precisely because it conflicts with ideology and is overlain, obscured, and defeated by it.

References

ATKINSON, A. (1975) *The Economics of Inequality*. Oxford: Clarendon Press.

BEVERIDGE, W. (1942) *Social Insurance and Allied Services*. Cmnd 6404. London: HMSO.

BLUE-PRINT FOR SURVIVAL (1972) *Ecologist* 2 (1).

BUTLER, D. and KAVANAGH, D. (ASO) (1980) *The General Election of 1979*. London: Macmillan.

BYRNE, E. (1978) *Women and Education*. London: Tavistock.

CENTRAL POLICY REVIEW STAFF (1980) *People and Their Families*. London: HMSO.

CIS (1974) *Your Money and Your Life*. London: Counter Information Services.

CONSERVATIVE PARTY (1979) *Conservative Manifesto, 1979*. London.

CROSLAND, A. (1974) *Socialism Now*. London: Cape.

CSO (1979) *Social Trends No. 9*. London: HMSO.

—— (1982a) *Social Trends No. 12*. London: HMSO.

—— (1982b) *Economic Trends No. 339*. London: HMSO.

DHSS (1971) *Two Parent Families*. London: HMSO.

—— (1975) *Better Services for the Mentally Ill*. Cmnd 6233. London: HMSO.

—— (1976) *Priorities for Health and Personal Social Services*. London: HMSO.

FIELD, F. (1981) *Inequality in Britain.* London: Fontana.

FINCH, J. and GROVES, D. (1980) Community Care and the Family. *Journal of Social Policy* 9(4): 487–511.

FRIEDMAN, M. and R. (1981) *Free to Choose.* Harmondsworth: Penguin.

GEORGE, V. and WILDING, P. (1976) *Ideology and Social Welfare.* London: Routledge and Kegan Paul.

GOUGH, I. (1979) *The Political Economy of the Welfare State.* London: Macmillan.

GOULD, F. and ROWETH, B. (1980) Public Spending and Social Policy. *Journal of Social Policy* 9 (3): 337–59.

HADLEY, R. and HATCH, S. (1981) *Social Welfare and the Failure of the State.* London: Allen and Unwin.

HALSEY, A., HEATH A., and RIDGE, J. (1980) *Origins and Destinations.* Oxford: Clarendon Press.

HAMILL, L. (1977) *Wives as Sole and Joint Breadwinners.* Mimeo, SSRC Social Security Workshop.

HARRIS, R. and SELDON, A. (1978) *Over-ruled on Welfare.* London: Institute of Economic Affairs.

HIRSCH, F. (1977) *Social Limits to Growth.* London: Routledge and Kegan Paul.

HMSO (1980) *An A to Z of Income and Wealth.* London: HMSO.

HUNT, A. (1970) *The Home Help Service in England and Wales: A Survey Carried Out in 1967.* London: HMSO.

INLAND REVENUE (1972) *Survey of Personal Income, 1969–70.* London: HMSO.

JOSEPH, K. and SUMPTION, J. (1979) *Equality.* London: John Murray.

JUDGE, K. (1981) State Pensions and the Growth of Social Welfare Expenditure. *Journal of Social Policy* 10 (4): 503–30.

KINCAID, J. (1973) *Poverty and Inequality in Britain.* Harmondsworth: Penguin.

LABOUR PARTY (1964) *Let's Go with Labour.* London.

—— (1970) *1970 Election Manifesto.* London.

LAND, H. (1976) Women: Supporters or Supported? In D. Barker and S. Allen (eds) *Sexual Divisions and Society.* London: Tavistock.

LAND, H. and PARKER, R. (1978) Family Policy. In S. Kamerman and A. Kahn (eds) *Family Policy.* New York: Columbia University Press.

LEGRANDE, J. (1982) *The Strategy of Equality.* London: Allen and Unwin.

MACAFEE, A. (1980) A Glimpse of the Black Economy in the National Accounts Statistics. *Economic Trends* 316: 81–7.

MACGREGOR, S. (1981) *The Politics of Poverty.* London: Longman.

MARSHALL, T. (1970) *Social Policy.* London: Hutchinson.

MEADOWS, D. and D., RANDERS, J., and BERHENS, W. (1975) *The Limits to Growth.* London: Pan.

MINISTRY OF PENSIONS (1966) *Financial and Other Circumstances of Retirement Pensioners.* London: HMSO.

NICHOLSON, J. (1974) Distribution and Redistribution of Income in the UK. In D. Wedderburn (ed.) *Poverty Inequality and Class Structure.* Cambridge: Cambridge University Press.

NICHOLSON, J. and BRITTON, A. (1979) The Redistribution of Income. In A. Atkinson (ed.) *The Personal Distribution of Income.* London: Allen and Unwin.

NISSEL, M. (1978) *Taxes and Benefits.* London: Policy Studies Institute.

O'HIGGINS, M. (1981) Tax Evasion and the Self-Employed. *British Tax Review* no. 6.

PAHL, J. (1980) Patterns of Money Management within Marriage. *Journal of Social Policy* **9** (3): 313–36.

PEACOCK, A. and SHANNON, R. (1968) The Welfare State and the Redistribution of Incomes. *Westminster Bank Review* no. 1: 30–46.

PERETZ, J. (1973) *Beneficiaries of Public Expenditure*, mimeo.

PREST, A. and STARK, T. (1967) Some Aspects of Income Distribution in the UK. *Manchester School* **35**.

REES, A. (1976) *Old People and the Social Services.* Southampton: Southampton University Press.

ROBSON, W. (1976) *Welfare State and Welfare Society.* London: Allen and Unwin.

ROYAL COMMISSION ON THE DISTRIBUTION OF INCOME AND WEALTH (1979) *Fourth Report.* Cmnd 7595. London: HMSO.

SLEEMAN, J. (1979) *Resources for the Welfare State.* London: Longman.

STUDY COMMISSION ON THE FAMILY (1980) *Happy Families.* London.

THANE, P. (1982) *The Foundations of the Welfare State.* London: Longman.

TOWNSEND, P. (1975) *Sociology and Social Policy.* London: Allen Lane.

—— (1979) *Poverty in the United Kingdom.* London: Allen Lane.

7 Market thinking and political thinking

ROBERT E. LANE

'God . . . stands in no need of general ideas . . . .
Such, however, is not the case with man.'
                                        (Alexis de Tocqueville)

'The human understanding when it has once adopted an opinion
draws all things else to support and agree with it. And though there
be a greater number and weight of instances to be found on the other
side, yet these it either neglects and despises, or else by some
distinction sets aside and rejects, in order that by this great and
pernicious predetermination the authority of its former conclusion
may remain involate.'   *(Francis Bacon)*

If, as Aristotle believes, 'a state is good in virtue of the goodness of the
citizens who share in its government', might it not be true that an
economy is good in virtue of the goodness of its producers and consumers? The proposition is ambiguous, as well as revolutionary. Better to
state the proposition in John Stuart Mill's way: 'a state which dwarfs its
men, in order that they may be more docile instruments in its hands, even
for beneficial purposes, will find that with small men no great thing can
really be accomplished.' Similarly, an economy that fails to develop
its producers and consumers as human beings, rather than merely
as 'human capital', will never achieve maximum efficiency. But that
is to look at the matter as an economist might, with the assumption that maximum production, at least cost distributed on market
principles, best serves society. Why not say it outright? Social institutions are to be evaluated principally on the basis of their contribution to the human personality; all other considerations are secondary.

We go through life engaged in a variety of experiences structured in
part by governments and markets, learning as we go. Each of these
experiences shapes our moods, our concept of self, our moral reasoning
and practices, our ways of thinking; in short, our personalities. John

Rawls thought our self-esteem might be determined by our political rights. Fred Hirsch's analysis of social scarcity implies that we are increasingly required to compare ourselves with others, learning invidious social comparison in the process. Perhaps neither is right, but these authors raise the right issues: the shaping of personality by political and economic experiences.

In the following analysis we focus on the effects of political and market experiences on cognition, the way we think (not what we think about). In my opinion, no facet of personality is more important, for cognitive abilities affect our moral reasoning, our capacities to cope, and hence our self-esteem, our interpretations of the world. Claiming that 'it is a fundamental human right' to develop one's information-processing capacities, Luis A. Machado, the Minister of Intelligence of Venezuela, has launched a programme to implement that right. 'We think that our [true] riches are not in oil', he said, 'but in our brains.' Unguided by a Minister of Intelligence, how do our politics and economies develop or fail to develop our cognitive capacities? This chapter offers an analysis of the cognitive training stimulated by the demands of markets and electoral politics.

Concrete and abstract

Concrete thinking is dependent upon a particular stimulus; it is iconic, tied to perception of some kind. Abstract thinking on the other hand employs concepts to enable a person to see and use the similarities of varied stimuli, to recombine them, 'going beyond the information given' (Bruner 1957). It is characterized by symbolic thinking, which gives people the ability to deal with 'the non-present, with things remote in space, qualitative similarity, and time from the present situation' (Bruner 1964: 13). In agreement with Piaget, Bruner, and others, psychologists often 'assume that development represents progression toward abstractness on the concrete-abstract dimension' (Harvey, Hunt, and Schroder 1961: 4).

The distinction between concrete thinking and abstract thinking is not to be found by simple reference to the use of concrete or abstract terms. There are tendencies in everyone to employ both; the distinction lies in how they are used. On the one hand, people tend to remember concrete words more easily than abstract ones (Paivio 1971); they are likely to notice, remember, and use single, vivid concrete cases instead of the general (and colourless) statements giving probabilities, principles, or appropriate base-line data – all much more important for correct inference or generalization (Nisbett and Ross 1980: 47–9, 159–60). On the other hand, there is a quite widespread tendency to generalize from concrete instances poorly sampled and selected – a phenomenon Abelson once called 'sweeping concretization' (Abelson 1976). These generalizations or inferences are often based on concrete cases whose representativeness is not well established (the representativeness bias); people categorize with a careless label, and select 'theories' without bothering to test them (Nisbett and Ross 1980: chs 5 and 6). Once achieved, a theory may prove almost invulnerable to falsification, as Bacon suggested in the quotation at the head of this chapter. The distinction, then, may be summarized as follows: (1) concrete thinking is easier and therefore available to more people with less error than may be seen in these people's abstract thinking; (2) the use of abstractions is very easy but especially prone to error; and (3) abstract *thinking*, as contrasted to the mere use of abstractions, is difficult and rare.

One can get along quite well in the consumer market with concrete thinking, making sequential decisions on this item and that item for this amount and that amount. Nothing is more concrete than a fetish: the fetishism of commodities is a disease of concreteness. This interpretation must (and will be) qualified by the concept of choice among alternatives, implying an abstract standard of reference, but if this standard is something as inchoate as preference, the concreteness of market choices prevails.

In politics one must supplement concrete observations (this candidate, that party) by the use of abstract terms, such as justice, freedom, democracy. But I think it will be agreed that to do well in politics, to understand the concrete items in the news, to sort out rhetoric from factual messages, requires abstract thinking. On the concrete-abstract dimension, the competent consumer need not travel far to master the market medium but the competent citizen must travel further towards abstract thinking.

While the idea of concreteness seems to imply some meanings cognate to the philosophers' 'thing in itself', the methodologists' 'ideographic' (contrasted to 'nomothetic') and the sociologists' 'particularism' – meaning immanence as contrasted to transcendence – these implications lead one astray. Yet there is one meaning of particularism which is usefully related to the concrete: seeing individuals (or other objects) primarily in their relationship to a particular, specified situation, as contrasted to seeing their relationship to a general function or a standard. (This is my interpretation of Parson's particularistic-universalistic dimension which forms one of his five pattern variables (Parsons and Shils 1962: 76–83).) Particularistic justice, for example, depends on kinship or friendship –

who the person is; universalistic justice requires the treating of all offenders of a certain kind alike, e.g. 'justice is no respecter of persons'. In its idealized version, the labour market is universalistic, 'abstracting' from the individual functional qualities which alone are relevant to firms. Civil services are universalistic, as well, but politics tends to be particularistic: the individual is favoured for his past and future services to a particular party or candidate. If the parallels between concreteness and particularism, and between abstractness and universalism are correct, in this sense the market encourages abstractness, politics concreteness.

Yet the individuals engaged in these sytems are not to be characterized by the system properties – the fallacy of division. For the ordinary citizen, very little of national politics turns on particular rewards, most of it deals with general issues. Indeed, people base their voting decisions more on their perception of the state of the nation than on their perception of any particular rewards or expected rewards benefiting themselves.[1] More people, more of the time, are engaged in the consumer market than in the labour market, and in the consumer market the concrete dominates: this good for this price. Nothing could be more iconic, more dominated by what is before the eyes than a supermarket, as packaging experts well know. So, setting aside the labour market, it seems to be the case that for most experiences in these two domains, the market encourages concreteness, politics abstractness.

Throughout this discussion we turn from time to time to the transfer of learning from one domain to the other; John Stuart Mill gives us a case in point. Speaking of political life, Mill says, 'interests by which they [human beings] will be led when they are thinking only of self-interest will be almost exclusively those which are obvious at first sight, and which operate on their present condition' (Mill 1910: 253). What is 'obvious at first sight' is iconic; what is 'limited to their present condition' forecloses, to repeat Bruner, 'things remote . . . from the present situation'. The market's enlistment of such short-term self-interest reinforces concreteness which, when applied to politics, does damage to political thinking.

We may summarize this discussion as follows: (1) The apparent abstractness of the market system conceals the concreteness of consumer experience in dealing with commodities. (2) Concreteness in politics serves the citizen less well than market concreteness serves the consumer. (3) More than markets, politics invites the use of abstract terms, especially in the form of charged symbols to organize meaning, but this falls far short of abstract thinking and does not lead to understanding.

Differentiation and integration

The core of cognitive complexity is the dual process of differentiation and integration. 'Differentiation refers to the breaking of a novel, more undifferentiated, situation into more clearly defined and articulated parts. Integration is the relating or hooking of such parts to each other and to previous conceptual standards' (Harvey, Hunt, and Schroder 1961: 18). The processes bear a close relation to the more familiar analysis and synthesis. For differentiation (analysis) one must be able to see parts as well as wholes (field independence); for integration (synthesis) one must possess a set of heuristics or integrating rules governing the recombinations. One measure of the capacity to differentiate asks the respondent to evaluate a person (say, Nixon) along a number of dimensions: honest-dishonest, shrewd-obtuse, effective-ineffective, etc. In this measure of evaluate discrimination, if all the ratings are favourable or all are unfavourable, the respondent is scored low on differentiation (cognitive complexity) (Bieri *et al.* 1966). Such global judgements reveal a 'halo effect' subordinating differentiation. Clearly, tolerance for cognitive dissonance is a condition for this kind of differentiation. People can differentiate who cannot integrate, but is not possible to integrate without first differentiating.

The presentation of situations differentially elicits these two capacities, teaching the individual skills as these are. Homogeneous situations, look-alike stimuli, and aggregate decisions inhibit differentiation while heterogeneity, variety, and the presentation of discriminating choices encourage it. It has been argued that economies of scale and the advantages of mass production lead the market to produce standardized, undifferentiated products. These arrays of similar products in each category are stimuli to homogenized tastes which are rewarded by lower prices. The penalties, as Hirsch and Mishan have pointed out, are paid by an increasingly discriminating clientele.[2] While recognizing with some poignancy the force of this argument, especially as it refers to culture goods, we must conclude that for most classes of goods it is quite archaic, as any comparison between the Sears Roebuck catalogue of the current year and fifty years ago will show. The critics of the standardized, homogenized society have been driven from the field by the critics of stimulus overload, the plethora of choices in modern society (never quite the choices desired by the sophisticated, however) (Toffler 1970). In fact, free markets and affluence together tend to multiply market choices, permitting the individuation of bundles of commodities to suit individual, differentiated tastes. Differentiation is facilitated by the fact that decisions are multiple, frequent, and sequential. The concept of marginality permits, if it does not wholly embrace, differentiation: each item is considered for its individual, differentiated utility (or productivity). Like manufacturers, householders are thought to avoid aggregate decisions wherever possible because they impair differentiation at the margin.

Both markets and politics are said to suffer from the 'Hotelling effect', the tendency for any two producers or distributors to clump together along any single dimension in their struggle for the disputed ground between them (two drug stores in the same block; two parties with similar platforms). Anthony Downs, among many others, seeks to apply the Hotelling effect to politics (Downs 1957). But, because entry is usually easier for a firm in the market than for a party in politics (at least politics marked by single-member constituencies), politics is more often characterized by duopoly than the market – and once a third agent enters the scene the Hotelling effect no longer works.

Confining our attention to electoral choices (we will consider the interpretation of political news in a moment), few will disagree that political stimuli are more often homogenized, lacking in variety, and require more aggregate decisions than market stimuli. Historically, this has been especially true of American politics, Bryce characterizing the political parties at the turn of the century as Tweedle-Dum and Tweedle-Dee. That their policies often turn out to be significantly differentiated is not so much a product of their differentiated platforms (which, are, however, somewhat different from each other), as the result of their practices in office. But what is important is the electorate's perception of their differences and few people can explain these with any clarity or perception.[3] In local elections, moreover, the undifferentiated perceptions of the candidates are even more marked.

The aggregate character of electoral decisions might be thought to be an opportunity for integration, for summarizing and assessing the properties of the competing candidates and parties – an exercise in value integration requiring, among other things, the kind of integration demanded by Bieri's simple test mentioned above. But, as we said, integration must follow differentiation – the property which was reported missing in the electoral studies. There is no opportunity for marginal analysis in politics, no sequential utility maximization, no disaggregation of decisions. Because they are not required, they are not taught, and the field is left to global, undifferentiated decisions.

Anticipating our discussion of budgets and ideologies, let us note that the constraints on market decisions are tastes and budgets, calling for trade-offs in taste satisfaction, a form of value integration. The constraints on political opinions are tastes and ideologies, but there is nothing really equivalent to a budget; therefore the integration of policy opinions (as separate from electoral decisions) has less urgency and force. Tentatively, therefore, we might argue that the integration of policy opinions is less likely to be successful than integration of market decisions. Idea budgets or ideologies do not have the constraining power of cash budgets, in part because they are not marked by scarcity. With theoretically unlimited ideas to choose from a person may simply add a costless idea without dropping any other idea, or worrying about the compatibility of the ideas thus assembled, or integrating ideas in some coherent form, or suffering from the need to trade one preference for another. This is one reason why ideologies do not constrain opinions (Converse 1964).

Number of schema and their information density

The general rule is that a person can understand, and sometimes even perceive, only that for which he has some schema, concept, dimension, category, vignette, or script. In its active reconstruction of the world, the mind imposes upon sound, light, and movement a configuration which may be either rich or spare in 'meaning', that is, in information significant to the individual. One might use the term 'schema' for a static concept, 'scenario' or 'script' for a set of anticipated linked actions. In both cases, a single schema or script implies a given response, a form of stimulus boundedness, low levels of cognition, and, if emotionally charged, dogmatism. Two available schema are said to lead to oppositional thinking; tenacity in the face of challenge to the preferred schema (Schroder, Driver, and Streufert 1967: 17). Cognitive complexity is enhanced when multiple schema are held in solution in the mind, available for tentative fitting and matching, for assimilation and accommodation as the situation may require.

Both economic theory and market practice are saturated with the concept of alternatives, with choice; indeed, economics has been called the science of choice (Mises 1960: 61). The central idea of efficiency is the substitution of alternative factors of production at the margin, of utility maximization as rational consumer choice among alternatives. This implies that the job seeker or consumer holds constantly in mind a set of alternatives to what is present before him – narrowly defined schema perhaps, but concepts nevertheless, of alternative goods and services that might be procured. This is not necessarily a natural order of things; mothers must deliberately teach children to think in terms of alternatives to what is present (Ward, Wackman, and Wartella 1977: 127–35), and the giveness of traditional societies yields only slowly to the idea of choice. In a market society, these concepts of alternatives are likely to be relatively informed due to the dense, market-relevant information in the communication networks. Yet the mere fact that information is available does not tell us much about the fitting of that information to schema, nor much about the nature of the schema. Consider the case of breakfast cereals. A study provided a consumer sample with thirty-five different dimensions of information (nutritional value, unit price, etc.) on sixteen brands of breakfast cereals. If the brand-names are schema, or even if some preferred constellation of properties are schema, the consumer is confronted with a matrix of 16 × 35 bits of information or 560 items to analyse in matching schema with choice. It was found that a fifth of the subjects employed only the brand-names as guides to choice and that of the 560 bits of information the mean number employed was 11.2 (Jacoby 1976: 21–2). As in similar studies in other areas, including gambling, most people are found to ignore relevant information in making their decisions (Tversky and Kahneman 1974: 1124–131). Two things stand out: much consumer choice is, indeed, concrete and stimulus bound, partly for want of time, effort, and skill in processing information; and much is straining towards complexity, a rehearsal of complex decision-making which nevertheless cannot match the complexity of the environment.

Single-party systems, of course, limit choice and make it relatively meaningless, but plural party systems, as in any democracy, also offer choices, invoking competing schema and scenarios of the chain of events likely to follow the election of each candidate. In spite of the rich information on politics in the media, relatively little of this information is retained because its meaning for everyday life is obscure. The consequence may be a set of relatively empty schema, untested scenarios heavily impregnated with preference. Empty and hence undifferentiated schema may be called stereotypes; political thinking indeed tends to be stereotypical, often mere labelling.

Schema are useless unless the mind possesses sets of integrating rules, and the maximization rules of the market are among the easiest to employ. Maximization is more easily possible with much economic information which is given in money terms and permits comparability. But politics more often deals with unlike categories, made comparable only with difficulty. Efforts to convert models of political thinking to models of economic maximization, often with a single dimension, have not been very successful; they have contributed little to political predictability, for example (Downs 1957; Buchanan and Tullock 1962; Abrams 1980). If citizens habitually employed the multiple dimensions of politics in some optimizing fashion, they would, indeed, be learning important elements of cognitive complexity. But, in fact, neither the economic models nor the multi-dimensional optimization models seem to describe political thinking. Nor is there a set of 'capping abstractions' which permit the easy relation of separate schema to each other (Converse 1964).[4] Rather, some combination of the extension of personal experiences, a search for defining scenarios, *ad hoc* 'theories', stimulus-bound emotional reactions, and the strong force of habit better characterizes the process.[5]

The different presentation of stimuli and choice requirements in the two domains makes a difference. The market permits multiple decisions related to each other only by budgetary constraints and preference schedules. While politics has a day-to-day menu of news, the decision points are infrequent and necessitate aggregation of issues. The market's demand for syntheses is thus less than that of politics. Fragmented schema with fewer integration rules are thus more easily accommodated in the market than in politics. Here, as elsewhere, we must conclude that political thinking of the order demanded to make proper use of political machinery is simply more difficult than market thinking.

Cybernetic processes

The term 'cybernetic' is used in two different senses, a social sense referring to the way in which information is fed back to a decision point, and an individual sense, referring to the way in which decisions may be made. The market is a cybernetic instrument in the social sense, not only in the supply and demand, 'consumer sovereignty' meanings, but also in the way it provides the individual with information on the consequences of his acts: money for work, goods for money. But it is the individual sense that is of interest here. Puzzled at the ability of rather simple organisms (as well as humans) to make apparently complex calculations, Ashby observed his cat adjusting her comfort in front of a fire: when she was cold she moved closer, when she was too hot she moved further away (Ashby 1952). By behaving like a thermostat, the cat could achieve its purpose. When the purpose is simple, cybernetic decision-making is efficient because the rules and the purposes are joined; when the purpose is complex, so that the decision rules must be flexibly adjusted to the purposes they are intended to serve, cybernetic decision-making is likely to frustrate any large purpose (Steinbruner 1974).

In the larger societal sense, compared to politics the market is a better cybernetic machine for providing information on the consequences of an act, although the information, like a grade without comments on an exam, often conveys only the simple message that one did *something* wrong and not what to do better next time. But even that information is often missing in politics, for the connection between the act and governmental responses, not to mention information on what to do better next time, is obscure. Furthermore, since the purposes served by voting, as contrasted to buying, are complex, any simple cybernetic political rule (say, when the economy is down, vote against the incumbents), is unlikely to be fruitful. Finally, it is quite unimportant for the functioning of the economic system whether or not individuals understand the workings of the economy; consumer sovereignty is not an experience. But in politics, that kind of understanding is often crucial, for the consequences of votes affect the working of the system; people are voting on candidates who may reshape the constitution rights, the province of the courts, and so forth. So, following Deutsch, we see that people are voting on the basis of a second-order feedback system, the system that protects the workings of the first-order, direct gratification, system (Deutsch 1963: 91–3). Rule-bound, cybernetic decision-making in the market is simpler, more likely to satisfy; in politics, it is more complex, more demanding, and less likely to satisfy.

Transitivity and ideological constraint

While consumer cognition may involve more or less complex ends-means chains, the one form of logic which is required for the consumer choice is transitivity: if a person prefers A to B and B to C, he prefers A to C. Otherwise he is a 'money pump', vulnerable to trading C for B, and B for A, and then his recently acquired A for C, starting the sequence over again. And he must have relatively stable preferences, a characteristic rather than a logical attribute. These give him a map of preferences and a set of indifference curves (which, however, live more in texts than in people's minds). Beyond that, the consumer and job seeker may well be guided by private ideologies, but they are, so to speak, *obiter dicta* for the system.[6]

In politics the individual needs a more complex map to guide him – he needs a political ideology. In spite of their bad name, ideologies are socially necessary to permit a politics independent of religion and economics, and individually necessary to form a set of guiding values (like the consumer's preference map), a set of concepts, theories, and scripts showing likely causal sequences. Political decisions, unlike most consumer decisions, also imply assessment of personalities and their likely behaviour, and complex beliefs about the world. The disappointment over the nature of these ideologies and their constraining power is, given the tasks assigned to ideologies, quite misguided.

Living up to the simple requirements for transitivity and stability in consumer decisions is not hard, whereas meeting the requirements for an ideology *is* hard; one needs hierarchical thinking, logical inference from major value premises, inductive inference from observations, constrained thought in the sense that one idea is seen to imply its corollaries, and, as we shall see, plausible causal attributions. The very difficulty of the task, combined with its poor provisions for learning and its opaque consequences, discourages most people from a full engagement. Nevertheless, it would be wrong to say that political tasks do not, at least for some people, enlist, and contribute to the development of, more complex cognition. For example, few people carry in their heads indifference curves showing their relative preferences for efficiency and equality, but some do, and these trade-offs are fully as important as the indifference curves relating preferences for grapes to preferences for potatoes, or even leisure and work (see Okun 1975). The trade-off represents a central problem for Rawls (1971). One can over-estimate the rationality of consumers: most rarely search for pertinent information on the commodities they buy, and even those who say they want more information do not know what information they need. Nor is it merely the want of information that inhibits rational market behaviour, for, as we have seen, many do not use the information they have, and many do not even know how it might be used.[7] If Keynes is right, even management investment decisions reflect 'animal spirits', and if Knight is right, in economics as elsewhere 'human activity is largely impulsive, a relatively unthinking and undetermined (*sic*) response to stimulus and suggestion' (Keynes 1936: 161; Knight 1935: 50). But even if the absolute level of market cognition is low, preference schedules and budgetary constraints impose a kind of personal logic on market behaviour which is not found in political behaviour, constrained as it may be by idiosyncratic ideologies.

The open and closed mind

If the task of political ideology formation is both necessary and difficult, resulting in rather primitive and often excessively personal formulations, the ideologies thus formed can be put to two different uses. They can be used to interpret and explore the world (the open mind), or to defend against it (the closed mind). It has been said that the main cause of using ideologies defensively is anxiety, the fear of the unfamiliar, of change (Rokeach 1960; Vachiano, Strauss, and Hochman 1969: 261–73), but it seems likely that tolerance of dissonance, learned styles of cognition, attitudes toward authority and the authoritative, capacity for formal operations, and much more enter into the dogmatism of the closed mind. The closed mind rejects and impugns information challenging its cherished ideology; it is not necessarily more stupid than the open mind, but it is less analytical because it cannot recombine the parts of a protected ideological gestalt and so compromise is difficult for the closed mind for this reason. It suffers from the *einstellungen* effect (the inflexible perception of an object or an idea as fit only for its previously observed employment) (Luchins and Luchins 1968: 65–79) and from irreversibility; and like the field-dependent mind (Witkin *et al.* 1974), the closed mind accepts only undifferentiated wholes in their given contexts.

These closed-minded cognitive processes have reduced utility in market life, for the market (1) works through incremental adjustments, (2) looks at margins rather than at wholes, and (3) requires as a condition of good performance that the units it works with be as divisible as possible. Perhaps this analogy between market processes and cognitive processes is misleading, merely metaphoric, but let the reader consider whether American consumers were well served by their ideology of big cars which persisted well after the 1973 oil crisis, or whether the ideology of 'small is beautiful' helped the man searching for a profitable career in the 1980s, or what an ideological fixation on organic foods does to the time and effort of shopping in a metropolis (let alone a balanced diet and a balanced budget). We have seen that brand-name fixation is common; beyond that preference fixation, inability to compromise and experiment, and rejection of information incompatible with preferences also bring upon the closed-minded consumer real and substantial penalties. Of course in the labour market and the consumer market the ideologist is entitled to his values, but he pays for them when they are part of a closed-mind configuration,[8] that is, his values incur costs in other values given up. In markets, an ideology is put to the test.

As noted above, the function of an ideology in political thinking is much more substantial, apparently less costly to the individual if it is confused and misleading, and its values and beliefs are less clearly tested against the competing values and beliefs of other ideologies. All of this invites dogmatism for it fails to punish the rigidities and poor information processing or the closed mind. Without underrating the merits of speculative, even utopian thinking, tested by conversation and argument rather than by experience, one cannot help wondering (like those who fear the irrational in politics) whether the corrective experiences of the market do not encourage undogmatic thinking rather more than do the uncommitting conversations of the political domain.

Three caveats come to mind. First, over the long-run history has its own correctives for dogmatism: it is reported that today French communists are much less dogmatic than they were a generation ago (Lacorne 1977: 421–41). Second, comparing those most heavily engaged in the market – businessmen – with comparable others endowed with an alternative source of cognitive style – professionals – we may ask, which are the less dogmatic? Do we not rediscover here the domain specificity of dogmatism; undogmatic in their business engagements, businessmen (like others) are capable of extreme dogmatism in other areas (even discounting for the motivation to protect their economic interests)? Third, might it not be the case that market learning teaches open-mindedness in concepts of narrow width and special reference, while politics, dealing with large domains of general reference, invites a different kind of thinking, risking dogmatism but also rehearsing cognition of a more philosophical character, which we should sorely miss if all our thinking were even the most flexible kind of market thinking?

The elements of an ideology should be 'constrained' in the sense that they should cohere and should not contradict each other, but they should be separately open to correction. The open mind should not 'bolster' an idea because of its ideological value. Shils (1968) argues that it is the nature of emotionally charged ideological constructs to reject the threat of discrepant information and to impede pragmatic adjustment. But an empirical study of parliamentarians' thought reveals that there is no difference in levels of pragmatic adjustment between those who claim or reveal an ideology (i.e. by reference to an ideology or future utopia, a tendency towards generalized statements, and use of deductive inference from these statements) and those who do not (Putnam 1973: 63). It is quite unclear that these relationships would hold in the public at large, but if they did, then it follows that political thinking suffers as much from the lack of an ideology as from its presence.

Causal attribution

Because the human mind shuns uncertainty, it seeks explanation in order to foster a sense of control over the environment, a cognitive expression of the desire to be effective. Explanations, of course, require causal attribution, hence there is an 'attribution motive' within the more general 'cognitive motive'. But the accuracy and complexity of the resultant attributions vary greatly according to circumstances, field of endeavour, and practical requirements. Since Hume we have known how hard it is to discern and correctly attribute causation. As everyone knows, attribution implies a theory of causation, or a merely verbal substitute for a theory (such as Divine Providence, Fate, or Telos), or, more modestly, a script or scenario apparently 'explaining' a normal, expectable sequence of events. The reliability of these theories or scenarios, in turn, will be affected by (1) the intelligibility of the processes they interpret, (2) the degree of 'passion', partisanship, or ego-involvement in the outcome of the process, and (3) the corrective influence of experience, that is, the feedback effects mentioned above.

In various places Mannheim speaks of the 'calculability' of economic processes and of the effort of politics to make rational the irrationality of history (Mannheim 1948: 51–75). Although he believes that the calculability offered by market economies has declined, and there are many voices currently expressing concern for rising uncertainty in market processes (currency fluctuation, inflation, more rapid obsolescence, etc.), I know no evidence to support this belief – given the dampening of the business cycle after World War II. In any event, it seems clear that for the ordinary individual in a labour or, especially, in a consumer market, the calculability of economics is still greater than the calculability in politics. One reason is that the market is constrained by some more or less automatic forces while politics is a much more discretionary area. Markets have a degree of 'immanence' which politics does not have. Making rational the irrationality of politics is certainly a longer-term project. In this sense, then, theories and scenarios interpreting causal sequences in the market are more calculable and the field is more intelligible than are causal theories and scenarios in the field of politics.

While 'partisanship' does not accurately describe the cathexis (emotional charge) invested in market outcomes, 'ego-involvement' does. Self-definition and self-esteem both stem from success in the labour market, and utilities of all sorts (including the good opinion of others) flow from success in the consumer market. No doubt the weight of these considerations exacerbates a common form of biased attribution: the tendency to see oneself as responsible for success and as constrained by circumstances in failure (Nisbett and Ross 1980: 202–07). A second form of attributional bias is also exacerbated by the market: the desire to experience control fosters the illusion of control over events which are, in fact, beyond one's power to control (Langer 1975: 311–28), a tendency that might be called the 'internality bias'. Finally, it is common for the individual mentally to convert chance outcomes to skill outcomes (the 'skill bias'). The emphasis in market economies on self-reliance and individual responsibility seems to elicit both the internality bias and the skill bias.

In politics, democratic ideology exaggerates the causal influence of the public and sometimes (but decreasingly) this collective influence is interpreted by individuals as a reason for attributing political outcomes to their own actions. Nevertheless the circumstances are sufficiently varied and the chain of contingencies sufficiently attenuated as to relieve most individuals of a need or even desire to attribute political outcomes to themselves. Politics does not, therefore, reinforce internality to the same degree as does market behaviour, setting free attributions to find their most congenial targets. Conspiracy theories are thus encouraged by a combination of external attribution, the tendency to reject 'chance' explanations in favour of 'skill' attributions, and the need to put some construction upon the flow of events. Attributions pointing to capitalists, communists, Jews, foreign agents, and so forth are not easily corrected (Lane 1962: ch. 7). The opposition is conveniently blamed for defects it could not have caused, an extension of externality in the sense that 'we' are not the cause, 'they' are. Thus, if the characteristic attributional bias of the market is self-attribution, the characteristic attributional bias of politics is scapegoat or partisan attribution, reflecting projective styles of thought (see below).

Curiously, too, when people observe economic functioning, they attribute prosperity to the market and depression to the government (Katona and Strumpel 1978: 43). This may be compared to the tendency, mentioned above, for individuals to attribute success to themselves and failure to others, and, paradoxically, also to see themselves constrained by circumstances and others ruled by dispositions. It is as though the market represents 'us' and the government represents some other, external agency.

The social outcomes of these characteristic biases are quite different: market self-attribution leads to attempted individual remedies, useful to the economy for the effort enlisted, but often bad for the economy and the individual when the source of the difficulty lies in governmental inaction or misguided policy. Partisan political attributions, without diagnosis or understanding, lead to a cycle of voting which bears no relation to what the government is doing or what the opposition proposes: the unemployed will vote against the party which is the more likely to relieve their immediate condition. Scapegoat attribution makes no sense. And, finally, attributing success to the market and failure to government leads to chronic undervaluation of government programmes that work (as in the case of the neo-conservatives of the 1970s and 1980s).

The market's capacity to enlist self-attribution and teach the individual what he did wrong depends for its therapy on a set of circumstances which he can correct. Structural unemployment or general recessions, inflationary prices, a rise in the crime rate, environmental pollution, and many of the other ills of our time are quite beyond the powers of the individual to correct. Under these circumstances, self-attribution will teach him the wrong things, will frustrate him to despair, as in any other serious failure of contingency reinforcements over a period of time. If all he learns from the experience is to 'try harder', or to adapt more successfully to his fate, market experiences and the market theory have seriously misled him and he will do well to be guided by the characteristic attributional bias of politics: lay the blame at the door of the government that permits these evils to occur.

Counter-factuals and stimulus boundedness

Some students of cross-cultural cognition suggest that a salient deficiency of people in the less-developed countries is not their linguistic or their analytical inabilities but their inability to imagine situations contrary to fact, or to 'shuffle things around in their heads' (Goodnow 1970: 244–45). While this suggests problems with formal operations, reversibility, dominance of the iconic, stimulus boundedness, and so forth, let us focus on the problem of counter-factuals and the problem of 'going beyond the information given'. Both markets and politics stimulate these capacities, but in different ways. As mentioned above, any field of endeavour which presents individuals with choices takes them part way towards transcending the given; but binary choices, which can require a simple yes or no, are the least cognitively stimulating. It is true that negation is a separate cognitive step, but only a small one, for reactive thinking is as stimulus-bound as is simple affirmation.

Markets and politics both rely substantially on stimulus-bound, reactive thinking; it is their strength in dealing with the mass public. Like Ashby's cat behaving like a thermostat, the consumer may say simply, 'If the price is too high, don't buy', and the job seeker may say 'If the job is too far away, don't take it'. But in the market, although possibly not in politics, the individual is kept within the decisional field by his wants, and he is stimulated to go on and ask, 'If the price is high, where can I save to get the money? How can I earn more?' And, 'If the job is distant, should I move? Can I find a car pool?'

Similarly, in politics simple binary decision rules prevail: 'If the economy is in good shape, vote for the incumbent' (suitably rationalized). Or, even more simply, 'If there is a Democratic label, vote for it'. As Weber noted in discussing the forms of rationality, habit (the traditional mode) can become a substitute for thought (Weber 1947: 116). In politics the incentive to go beyond the stimulus-bound or binary thought patterns to imagining how things might be otherwise, to counter-factuals, is weakened by distance, ineffectiveness, and (in, for example, the United States) by a culture that dampens the political imagination.

To translate dissatisfaction in political reform is a sluggish process, with, for each individual, an uncertain pay-off. The dissatisfied stimulus-bound thinker is, therefore, led to a reactive posture. For him, indeed, negation is enough, but it comes all too easily.

Beyond these binary processes, however, counter-factual thinking may beckon. In markets, discretionary money is the key. As Simmel said, in contrast to physical possession (especially of land), wealth in money encourages the expression of idiosyncratic personality, freeing its owner from burdens of property management and location (Simmel 1900). Dreams of wealth are unconfined by probabilities, but they are only for the young; older people reminisce over what happened (Singer 1975: 149–79). Money income is a store of possibility for individuals, permitting an almost infinite combination of purchases within any budget. In a sense quite different from that intended by Marx, money buys the opportunity for thought, and its very neutrality and fungibility enhances thought about what one can do with it. Discretionary income, greatly increased in the past two decades, enriches constrained choices up to the point where choice becomes the mere expression of a preference, and then, one could imagine, the thinking and planning associated with choice are only indifferently performed. At the other end of the scale, the consequences are more certain. Poverty narrows choices, limiting thought to the bare facts, the given, the necessary, and imposing a present-time orientation, all considered in the miasma of anxiety (Lewis 1966: xlviii). The market's many alternatives, then, stimulate the imagination for the middle and working classes; they do so with less certainty for the upper class and cannot do so for the under-class. To serve this cognitive purpose, money must be sufficiently plentiful to offer choices, and sufficiently scarce to require planning in exercising these choices.

Utopian thinking, the essence of counter-factuals, is too rarely practised for it to have much effect (Lane 1962: ch. 13). But sentences beginning 'if only . . .' or 'why didn't he . . .' are not rare in politics, and there is no constraint of any kind on such projects or on thought about the courses history might have taken, but did not. American policy with regard to the hostages taken by Iran was rich in 'it might have beens'. But these are retrospective, prompted by an unfortunate event, and imaginative regret minimization is easier than prospective reconstruction of social policy. The stimulation of what C. Wright Mills called 'the sociological imagination', the transformation of problems or dissatisfactions into policies, is rare (Mills 1959: 177–94). Mills scolded the social scientists for its rarity, but how much less frequent and more difficult it is for the layman to find such an imagination in his repertoire.

Projection

One reason for the interpretation of economics as the domain of the rational and politics as the domain of the irrational is the exclusiveness of the economists' definition of their field: economists prefer to take wants or 'tastes' as given, devoting themselves to the study of the efficient satisfaction of given wants, while political scientists and political philosophers concern themselves with the formation of wants, tastes, and values, a process in which the 'irrational' unconscious is heavily involved. But it would be absurd to take these field definitions as determinative of the actual thought processes involved in the two types of activities. Is it true that unconscious processes, especially internal conflicts, somehow guide political thinking in a way not characteristic of economic thinking?

First let us examine similarities in the effects of personality traits upon behaviour in the two domains. For both domains high self-esteem facilitates effective participation, acceptance of responsibility, reception and processing of relevant information, acceptance of criticism, and so forth (Rosenberg 1965; Sniderman 1975). The only difference is that people with low self-esteem can choose not to participate in politics, but due to the exigencies of earning a living they cannot opt out of economics. The same kinds of need for achievement (combined with power needs) lead to success in politics as in business, while affiliation motives tend to inhibit success in each field in the same way (Browning and Jacob 1964: 75–90; McClelland and Winter 1971). The uses and sublimation of aggression in competition are said to be enlisted in similar, if not identical ways (Horney 1937: 284). Although it is politicians rather than businessmen who are accused of narcissism, the current allegation of a hedonistic, consumer culture marked by narcissism evokes some echoes of the political discussion. People as readily give to authority responsibility for their own acts (the 'agentic state') in firms as in bureaux or police stations (Milgram 1974). Allport once said 'the political nature of man is indistinguishable from his personality as a whole. . . . A man's political opinions reflect the characteristic modes of his adjustment to life' (Allport 1937: 238).

Nevertheless, in line with those who favour the explanatory power of situations over personality traits, there remains an important difference between our two domains that affects the manner in which persons enlist their experience of the self to interpret the world. That difference lies in the greater calculability and intelligibility of market as contrasted to political situations – at least as they confront the ordinary person.

When people try to explain the larger economic system, they engage in projective and ego-defensive thinking no less colourful than their political thinking (Ashby 1952). But the market does not invite them to explain economies; rather it invites them to understand and deal efficiently with the more or less comprehensible, immediate world of their environment. As we have said, political questions are different: they inevitably deal with the larger world, whose ambiguities and 'irrationalities' encourage projective thinking.

Conclusion

While it takes great intelligence to create or manage a business, the consumer market where one selects these business products can be negotiated with only modest cognitive capacity. The labour market is, in most cases, structured to help the individual match his talents with whatever opportunities are available. As we have seen, markets, especially consumer markets, call for relatively little abstract thinking; they present ready-made differentiations (integrated to the extent necessary), preference schedules, and budgets rather than ideologies. They do not require much in the way of self-made schemas; they impose their own penalties for response sets and for dispositions towards balanced sentences. The market does not require complex causal inferences, and since it is by and large taxic or concrete, it does not suffer from a consumer's limited capacity for counter-factual thinking. Because of its presentational, iconic forms and low moral content, the market does not invite projective thinking. In comparison to politics, the market is a domain where relatively simple cognitive processes are sufficient to master its routines and to take advantage of its many alternatives.

If it takes considerable intelligence to create and manage a firm, it surely takes even more to manage a country. While voting or even 'following the news' can be done with the guidance of very simple cognitive skills, to be a competent citizen is much more difficult than to be a competent consumer, or, in most occupational categories, to be a job seeker. It requires a creative approach: one must think abstractly, differentiate complex stimuli and integrate them, supply missing schema, and make complex causal inferences. The constraint on closedness of mind must be internal, for the use of an ideology to constrain thought where thoughts are cheap is a disciplined act of considerable difficulty. Because there are no external punishments for response sets or intolerance of dissonance the 'punishments' must be internal, while ambiguity makes coherence difficult and projection easy. Going beyond reciprocity, politics requires empathy. For the ordinary person democratic politics makes much greater demands on cognition than does market economics.

It follows that democracy is a much more difficult system to work well than is a market system – granted the presence of exceptional men to give leadership to both systems. Perhaps it is for that reason that in the close historical association between the two systems, the market came first. With considerable license, one might construct a cognitive theory of history. First there was the cognition required for hunting and gathering, which could not be routine and which characterized the periods of evolutionary cognitive development. The politics of these periods seems to have been in part participatory, calling for a relatively high order of cognitive skills (Berry 1976). Second came an agricultural period, marked by household economies, where routines were passed on in unchanging fashion and choices were relatively few. This period gave rise to a politics of obedience, cognitive simplicity itself. With the rise of the market, more complex choices made for more complex cognition, but still, as we have seen, relatively concrete, simple, iconic, even, at times, stimulus bound. Gradually the politics of the market period was associated with cognitive demands for choices, comparable in some ways to market choices, easily cued by patrons, parties, classes, slogans. As markets and politics developed, these cognitive skills remained sufficient for the market, but became increasingly insufficient for politics; hence democracy seemed inadequate for its tasks while the market, in so far as the decisions of ordinary persons were concerned, seemed to function well. Where markets had once taken the lead in demanding more of people, now politics took the lead. It is at that point where we now find ourselves.

The puzzle is made more complex by changing needs. Having discovered how to make a sufficiency of commodities (if not how to distribute them equitably), social needs have shifted to those which the market cannot satisfy: security, public health, higher levels of culture, more beautiful cities and less polluted water and air, and public safety in the sense that crime is not only penalized but is also neither necessary nor attractive to those who have, in the past, chosen it. The demands on politics have thus increased.

Posing a related set of problems dealing with increasing competition for positional goods, goods for which enjoyment by one is affected by the attainment of those goods by others, Fred Hirsch proposes a solution to his set of problems by demanding less from government. For Hirsch, the solution is in part the development of a social ethic that induces people to internalize the concept of the others' needs, to act out of self-interest 'as if' they were altruistic because their long-term interests are served by this posture. In line with the principles in this chapter, ethical behaviour would thus become internalized – learning by doing in a special sense. On the other hand, also in line with the principles set forth above, the solution confronts cognitive barriers. An 'as if' solution implies counter-factual thinking which is difficult to achieve for some. Behaving in ways for which the long-term pay-offs require short-term costs implies a longer time span than is common. Conformity is reinforced by the concrete images of others, but understanding a social ethic requires abstract thinking; before conformity can take over there must be enough idealists who understand the social ethic to initiate the process – and quite a lot of them. But they will have to grapple with the abstract values involved. The market works because no one has to understand the way it works. For the same reason externalities will likely remain externalities in any solution that relies on consciously adopted social ethics to improve the system. To realize the hope that somehow 'the functional need for a change in the social ethic can be expected, over time, to promote it' (Hirsch 1977: 179) we must take into account the cognitive limits and capacities of a mass public.

We now know that we are faced with bounded rationality, limited channel capacity, decision overload. The complexity of problems must somehow be fitted to these capacities, and this must be done just as our needs are changing from those readily provided by a market economy whose demands do, at the level of households, fit the capacities of consumers and job seekers. Consumer sovereignty, as we have pointed out (ignoring but not opposing the 'producer sovereignity' school), works reasonably well because no one needs to understand the system. Popular sovereignty demands more because it requires more system knowledge. Our interdependency can be solved in a market system (with such exceptions as Hirsch has pointed out) because the market is designed to treat each connection or dependency as a separate decision without requiring any knowledge of the larger system. But where the market fails, as it often does because of externalities, our interdependency requires central intelligence with a synoptic view, a central intelligence sensitive to the electorate. Under these circumstances, fitting the complexity of problems to our limited capacities is not easy.

What is required is a system design where individuals do what they are capable of doing, while the system to some extent protects them against the consequences of (but not from) cognitive failures. It must be a design which lifts each to the level of cognition of which he is capable. The commodity market and, with some adjustments, the labour market seem well designed to this requirement. Further, the system may not be so protective that it prevents errors, for, as Hayek pointed out about the market, its justification is not so much that the individual knows his own interests better than others, but rather that by pursuing what he imagines to be his interests he creates, invents, and opens up new possibilities for exploration (Hayek 1948). To some extent markets and democracies were always such systems: in so far as consumers were protected at all, it was by producers and distributors looking out for their own recurring interests more than by consumer wisdom; the fallible democratic public was usually presented with choices which were 'guided choices' or else were inconsequential; an informed bureaucracy protected the legislators from their own fallible reasoning. But the casualties were always high and to the extent that these protections worked at all in periods of simplicity, or so it now seems, they will not work today.

Failing sufficient cognitive powers to guide or rule, elect or legislate with wisdom, can we devise a system which makes fewer demands on these resources? George Miller has suggested that we must pool our talents, work as teams, forsake some of our individualism in the process (Miller 1967: 883–96). But these are counsels appropriate for an élite embedded in institutions, not for electorates. And even for élites they assume too much. Rather, might it not be the case that markets, fitted as they are to limited cognitive capacities, could teach politics a method? It is possible in political life to devise a product, offer it to the public, see how it is received and whether or not it works, and, if it does, market the product to the general public, filling the airwaves with information about it and its reception in genuine public debate.

This is the experimental method as well as the market method. Its advantages lie partly in the fact that it is inductive; it relies on experience rather than on deduction in fields where non-normative first principles or axioms are extremely shaky (Campbell 1969: 409–28). It can be participatory by enlisting the co-operation of those involved in the experiment. The precedents in the United States, especially in the agricultural experiment stations, the land grant colleges, the Wisconsin social security experiment of the early 1930s, the guaranteed income experiments in new Jersey, Denver, and Seattle, and various manpower training experiments, are encouraging. And, going beyond manipulation, we may also observe the world as a series of social experiments, borrowing (as we have) from the Japanese the concept of participatory quality control groups, and learning the consequences of fiscal, tax, and monetary policies in Europe. Ideologies are random assortments of instrumental means held together, if at all, by values and preferences. The values and preferences are indispensable;

the assorted means are better put to the test of a market-like series of experiments.

If people are not likely to transcend their concrete cognitions, their use of vivid examples as the basis of their generalizations, let us make policy concrete; let us give them genuine vivid examples to reason from. Let us match policy to cognition.

Notes

1. Donald Kinder, following some work by David O. Sears, has offered a series of persuasive papers documenting what he calls 'sociotropic politics': Kinder and Kiewiet (1979: 495–527); Kinder and Sears (1981: 414–31); Kinder and Kiewiet (forthcoming).
2. See Mishan (1969), Scitovsky (1976), and Hirsch (1977) who argue that relative to Europeans, Americans suffer from fewer discriminating demands in the market.
3. See, for example, Campbell, Converse, Miller, and Stokes (1960). On page 543 these authors state that the general electorate is 'almost completely unable to judge the rationality of government actions, knows little of particular policies and what has led to them. The mass electorate is not able to appraise either its goals or the appropriateness of the means chosen to serve these goals.'
4. As I have argued elsewhere (Lane 1973), such integration as political ideologies may have is not due to 'capping abstractions' but rather to the more or less integrated character of a person's experience.
5. Kinder, Abelson, and Fiske (1979) find that questions designed to discover 'affective responses to leaders' are superior to purely cognitive or evaluative ones in predicting outcomes. For a review of research on electoral decisions, see Kinder (1982).
6. I have, however, recently seen some preliminary work by William Salter of Yale University mapping the economic ideologies of ordinary people. They are much more coherent than one would have supposed. Nevertheless, this must be put in the context of the fact that of a national sample a quarter of the respondents could not say what the function of investment is, and almost half gave meaningless answers.
7. From studies cited in Marquez (1977: 483) I am indebted to Richard Merelman for this citation.
8. Rokeach provides information on occupational selection which only partially confirms the generalization stated in the text. Classifying a group (in a YMCA college intending to go into scouting) according to their open-mindedness, he found that the most open-minded changed to go into social work of a more intellectually demanding character, the middle group went into scouting as planned, and the closed-minded group tended to go into commercial or military occupations. The labour market, it seems, can accommodate people with open or closed minds. Rokeach's other data imply difficulties for the closed-minded approach to politics (Rokeach 1960: 342–45).

References

ABELSON, R. (1976) Script Processing in Attitude Formation and Decision Making. In J. S. Carrou and J. W. Payne (eds) *Cognition and Social Behaviour*. Hillsdale, N.Y.: Lawrence Erlbaum.

ABRAMS, R. (1980) *Foundations of Political Analysis*. New York: Columbia University Press.

ALLPORT, G. W. (1937) *Personality: A Psychological Interpretation*. New York: Henry Holt.

ASHBY, R. W. (1952) *A Design for a Brain*. New York: Wiley.

BERRY, J. W. (1976) *Human Ecology and Cognitive Style*. New York: Wiley/Sage.

BIERI, J. (1966) *Clinical and Social Judgment*. New York: Norton.

BROWNING, R. P. and JACOB, H. (1964) Power Motivation and the Political Personality. *Public Opinion Quarterly* **28** (spring): 75–90.

BRUNER, J. (1957) Going Beyond the Information Given. In J. Bruner *et al. Contemporary Approaches to Cognition*. Cambridge, Mass.: Harvard University Press.

—— (1964) The course of Cognitive Growth. *American Psychologist* **19**: 13.

BUCHANAN, J. M. and TULLOCK, G. (1962) *The Calculus of Consent*. Ann Arbor: University of Michigan Press.

CAMPBELL, A., CONVERSE, P. E., MILLER, W. E., and STOKES, D. E. (1960) *The American Voter*. New York: Wiley.

CAMPELL, D. T. (1969) Reforms as Experiments. *American Psychologist* **24**: 409–28.

COMPTOM ADVERTISING COMPANY (1975) *National Survey on the US Economic System*. New York: Compton, unpublished research report.

CONVERSE, P. E. (1964) The Nature of Belief Systems in Mass Publics. In D. Apter (ed.) *Ideology and Discontent*. New York: Free Press.

DEUTSCH, K. (1963) *The Nerves of Government*. New York: Free Press.

DOWNS, A. (1957) *An Economic Theory of Democracy*. New York: Harper and Brothers.

GOODNOW, J. (1970) Cultural Variation in Cognitive Skills. In Jerome Hellmuth (ed.) *Cognitive Studies* vol. 1. New York: Brunner/Mazel.

HARVEY, O. J., HUNT, D. E., and SCHRODER, H. M. (1961) *Conceptual Systems and Personality Organization*. New York: Wiley.

HAYEK, F. A. (1948) *Individualism and Economic Order*. Chicago: University of Chicago Press.

HIRSCH, F. (1977) *Social Limits to Growth*. London: Routledge and Kegan Paul.

HORNEY, K. (1937) *The Neurotic Personality of Our Time*. New York: Norton.

JACOBY, J. (1976) Perspective on a Consumer Information Processing Research Program. In M. L. Ray and S. Ward (eds) *Communicating with Consumers: The Information Processing Approach*. Beverley Hills: Sage.

KATONA, G. and STRUMPEL, B. (1978) *A New Economic Era*. New York: Elsevier North-Holland.

KEYNES, J. M. (1936) *A General Theory of Employment, Interest and Money*. London: Macmillan.

KINDER, D. R. (1982) Political Psychology. In G. Lindzey and E. Aronson (eds) *Handbook of Social Psychology* 3rd edn. Reading, Mass.: Addison-Wesley.

KINDER, D. R., ABELSON R. P., and FISKE, S. T. (1979) *Development Research on Candidate Instrumentation: Results and Recommendations* (typescript). New Haven: Yale University Press.

KINDER, D. R. and KIEWIET, D. R. (1979) Economic Discontent and Political Behaviour: The Role of Personal Grievances and Collective Economic Judgments in Congressional Voting. *American Journal of Political Science* **23**: 495–527.

KINDER, D. R. and KIEWIET, D. R. (in press) *Sociotropic Politics*.

KINDER, D. R. and SEARS, O. (1981) Prejudice and Politics: Symbolic Racism Versus threats to the Good Life. *Journal of Personality and Social Psychology* **40** (March): 414–31.

KNIGHT, F. (1935) *The Ethics of Competition and Other Essays*. New York: Kelly.

LACORNE, D. (1977) On the Fringe of the French Political System. *Comparative Politics* **9** (July): 421–41.

LANE, R. E. (1962) *Political Ideology*. New York: Free Press.

—— (1973) Patterns of Political Belief. In Jeanne N. Knutson (ed.) *Handbook of Political Psychology*. San Francisco: Jossey-Bass.

LANGER, E. J. (1975) The Illusion of Control. *Journal of Personality and Social Psychology* **32**: 331–28.

LEWIS, O. (1966) *La Vida: A Puerto Rican Family in the Culture of Poverty – San Juan and New York*. New York: Random House/Vintage.

LUCHINS, A. S. and LUCHINS, E. H. (1968) New Experimental Attempts at Preventing Mechanization in Problem-Solving. In P. C. Wason and P. N. Johnson-Laird (eds) *Thinking and Reasoning*. Harmondsworth: Penguin.

McCLELLAND, D. C. and WINTER, D. G. (1971) *Motivating Economic Achievement*. New York: Free Press.

MANNHEIM, K. (1948) *Man and Society in an Age of Reconstruction*. New York: Harcourt, Brace.

——— (1949) *Ideology and Utopia*. New York: Harcourt, Brace.

MARQUEZ, F. T. (1977) Advertising Content: Persuasion, Information or Intimidation. *Journalism Quarterly* **54** (Autumn): 483.

MILGRAM, S. (1974) *Obedience to Authority*. New York: Harper and Row.

MILL, J. S. (1910) *Utilitarianism, Liberty and Representative Government*. London: Dent.

MILLER, G. A. (1967) Some Perspectives on the Year 2000. *Daedalus* **93** (Summer): 883–96.

MILLS, C. W. (1959) *The Sociological Imagination*. New York: Oxford University Press.

MISES, L. VON (1960) *Epistemological Problems of Economics*. Trans. G. Riesman. Princeton, NJ: Van Nostrand.

MISHAN, E. J. (1969) *The Costs of Economic Growth*. Harmondsworth: Penguin.

NISBETT, R. and ROSS, L. (1980) *Human Inference: Strategies and*

Shortcomings of Social Judgment. Englewood Cliffs, NJ: Prentice-Hall.

OKUN, A. M. (1975) *Equality and Efficiency: The Big Tradeoff.* Washington, DC: Brookings Institution.

PAIVIO, A. (1971) *Imagery and Verbal Processes*. New York: Rinehart and Winston.

PARSONS, T. and SHILS, E. A. (eds) (1962) *Toward a General Theory of Action*. New York: Harper Torchbook. First published 1951.

PUTNAM, R. (1973) *The Beliefs of Politicians*. New Haven: Yale University Press.

RAWLS, J. (1971) *A Theory of Justice*. Cambridge, Mass.: Harvard University Press.

ROKEACH, M. (1960) *The Open and Closed Mind*. New York: Basic Books.

ROSENBERG, M. (1965) *Society and Adolescent Self-Image*. Princeton, NJ: Princeton University Press.

SCHRODER, H. M., DRIVER, M. J., and STREUFERT, S. (1967) *Human Information Processing*. New York: Holt, Rinehart and Winston.

SCITOVSKY, T. (1976) *The Joyless Economy*. New York: Oxford University Press.

SHILS, E. (1968) The concept and Function of Ideology. *International Encyclopaedia of the Social Sciences* 7: 66–76. New York: Macmillan/Free Press.

SIMMEL, G. (1900) *The Philosophy of Money*. Trans. T. Bottomore and D. Frisby (1978). London: Routledge and Kegan Paul.

SINGER, J. L. (1975) *The Inner World of Daydreaming*. New York: Harper/Colophon. First published 1966.

SNIDERMAN, P. M. (1975) *Personality and Democratic Politics*. Berkeley, Calif.: University of California Press.

STEINBRUNER, J. D. (1974) *The Cybernetic Theory of Decision*. Princeton, NJ: Princeton University Press.

TOFFLER, A. (1970) *Future Shock*. New York: Random House.

TVERSKY, A. and KAHNEMAN, D. (1974) Judgment under Uncertainty: Heuristics and Biases. *Science* 185: 1124–131.

VACHIANO, R. B., STRAUSS, P. S., and HOCHMAN, L. (1969) The Open and Closed Mind: A Review of Dogmatism. *Psychological Bulletin* 71: 261–73.

WARD, S., WACKMAN, D. B., and WARTELLA, E. (1977) *How Children Learn to Buy*. Beverly Hills, Calif.: Sage.

WEBER, M. (1947) In T. Parsons (ed.) *The Theory of Social and Economic Organization*. New York: Oxford University Press.

WITKIN, H. A. *et al.* (1974) *Psychological Differentiation*. New York: Wiley/Erlbaum. First published 1962.

8 Pre-capitalist and non-capitalist factors in the development of capitalism: Fred Hirsch and Joseph Schumpeter

KRISHAN KUMAR

'The habit of looking at the last ten thousand years as well as at the array of early societies as a mere prelude to the true history of our civilization which started approximately with the publication of the Wealth of Nations *in 1776 is, to say the least, out of date. It is this episode which has come to a close in our days, and in trying to gauge the alternatives of the future, we should subdue our natural proneness to follow the proclivities of our fathers.'*
(Karl Polanyi 1957: 45)

One

The question as to the long-term future of capitalist industrial society – whether or not so called – has been raised since its very beginning. Much of the speculation has turned on that society's capacity or otherwise for indefinite expansion and growth. Capitalism, all admitted, was a unique social formation. It had a dynamism and a self-propelling energy unprecedented in mankind's history. All other civilized societies – Egypt, China, Rome, Byzantium – had gone into stagnation or decline through the self-limiting principles of their economic systems. In these societies, nature had indeed 'audited her accounts with a red pencil'. Only Western capitalism seemed to have discovered the secret that would enable it to escape from the cosmic trap of hunger and poverty, inertia and decay.

Or had it? Fred Hirsch stands in a long line of critics and commentators who have cast doubt on this optimistic belief. In eighteenth-century England, in the very springtime of modern capitalism, an intense debate raged over the inherent 'progressiveness' of the new economic order (Low 1952). On one side were ranged the passionate opponents of mercantilist regulation and advocates of free trade, such as Adam Smith and Josiah Tucker. These argued that the capitalist nations could look forward to a future of more or less unlimited growth and prosperity. Freed of mercantilist rivalries and restrictions, they would maintain and increase their superiority over the rest of the world, turning the non-capitalist societies into peripheral and dependent provinces supplying raw materials for the capitalist core.

Against these were those who held that the very principle of the free market in goods and people would ultimately impoverish the capitalist nations. David Hume propounded a general law of economic decay:

'There seems to be a happy concurrence of causes in human affairs, which checks the growth of trade and riches and hinders them from being confined entirely to one people.... Where one nation has gotten the start of another in trade, it is very difficult for the latter to gain the ground it lost. . . . But these advantages are compensated . . . by the low price of labour in every nation which has not an extensive commerce, and does not much abound in gold and silver. Manufactures, therefore, gradually shift their places, leaving those countries which they have already enriched and flying to others, whither they are allured by the cheapness of provisions and labour, till they have enriched these also and are again banished by the same causes.'

(Hume 1903: 290–91)

Thus any nation embarked on the capitalist course will, in the long run, descend from the heights of prosperity to the depths of misery and unemployment for the mass of its population. It was this melancholy cycle that prompted Hume's friend, Lord Kames, to see 'chrematistic' society as 'Janus double-faced', and as providing a clear illustration of the general law that 'nations go round in a circle from weakness to strength and from strength to weakness' (Low 1952: 322).

The thinkers of the Scottish Enlightenment – notably Adam Ferguson – were indeed among the most sceptical about the glowing promise of the new commercial society (Forbes 1954, 1966). Smith's own admiration was, as we know, itself highly qualified. Vanity, the striving for the admiration of others, rather than the desire for utility or convenience, he saw as the irrational passion behind the ceaseless activity of the modern world. 'And thus place, that great object which divides the wives of aldermen, is the end of half the labours of human life' (Smith 1969: 122). All the 'toil and anxiety' bestowed upon the pursuit of wealth issued from the chimerical delusion that it would bring security and fulfilment. But 'it is well that nature imposes upon us in this manner. It is this deception which arouses and keeps in continual motion the industry of mankind. It is this which first prompted them to cultivate the ground, to build houses, to found cities and commonwealths, and to invent and improve all the sciences and arts' (Smith 1969: 303; Rosenberg 1968). Smith was, moreover, as is well known, fully alert to the spiritual and moral deficiences of capitalism; and in his later writings he came even to see an inevitable material decline, in which the 'cheerful and hearty' progressive state would be succeeded by a 'dull' stationary state and a 'melancholy' declining one (Smith 1910, I: 72). Thus, even in Adam Smith's case, we are faced with 'the deeply pessimistic prognosis of an evolutionary trend in which both decline and decay attend – material decline awaiting at the terminus of the economic journey, moral decay suffered by society in the course of its journeying' (Heilbroner 1973: 243).

At the very outset of the capitalist era, therefore, we find a fundamental ambivalence and anxiety about the capacity of the capitalist system to fulfil the goals variously set for it. The welcome generally given to the new commercial order was cautious and qualified. There was an inherent element of irrationality and arbitrariness about it that boded ill. Even those most fervent in their advocacy feared for its future. Hence it is not really surprising to find that the arguments in its favour that appeared most convincing were directed as much to the *past* as to the future of society. Hirschman has suggested that capitalism appealed to many thinkers and statesmen of the seventeenth and eighteenth centuries not because of any alleged positive virtues, since people of this kind were generally united in an aristocratic and intellectual disdain for commerce, but because, to an age frightened and exhausted by the continuous civil and international wars of the seventeenth century, the 'interest' of money-making appeared an altogether safer channel for the people's unruly energies than more exciting pursuits such as power and glory (Hirschman 1977). The appeal, in other words, was political rather than economic, and certainly never moral. 'In an age in which men were searching for ways of limiting the damage and horrors they are wont to inflict on each other, commercial and economic activities were . . . looked upon more kindly not because of any rise in the esteem in which they were held; on the contrary, any preference for them expressed a desire for a vacation from (disastrous) greatness, and thus reflected continuing contempt' (1977: 58–9). Dr Johnson's remark, that 'there are few ways in which a man can be more innocently employed than in getting money', captures both the basis of the appeal and the condescending manner in which it was often couched. Other writers, more deeply impressed by the point that commerce would restrain the passions not just of subjects but also of their rulers, were inclined to be less snobbish. Savary wrote of 'this commerce [that] makes for all the gentleness of life'. *Le doux commerce*, declared Montesquieu, 'polishes and softens barbarian ways, as we can see every day'. Capitalism triumphed, according to Hirschman, in part at least because it was dull and passionless. The features that were later to be most denounced by humanistic and romantic critics – those that made capitalism 'alienating' and 'one-dimensional' – were precisely those that made it so attractive in the earlier stages.

Hirschman's account, however debatable (Gellner 1979), has the particular merit of insisting on a point often overlooked: that the emergence of capitalism can only be understood by relating it directly to the (pre-capitalist) society out of which it came. What might seem an obvious banality becomes more interesting when we consider the usual method of dealing with this. In the standard Marxist accounts, for instance, capitalist society emerges out of feudalism on the basis of a principle – the market – and a class – the bourgeoisie – wholly antithetical to their feudal counterparts. Some of the liveliest passages of the *Communist Manifesto* dwell on the deep-seated differences between the heroic-chivalric feudal aristocracy and the prosaic bourgeoisie (the bourgeoisie 'has drowned the most heavenly ecstasies of religious fervour, of chivalrous enthusiasm, of philistine sentimentalism, in the icy water of egotistical calculation', etc.). Although the new society is said to mature in the womb of the old, the newborn infant is born with remarkably few parental characteristics. This is an oddity indeed, and it should be seen as such in society as much as in nature.

Max Weber, like Marx, also stresses discontinuity. His problem is to account for the emergence of 'the spirit of capitalism' in the modern West, a spirit totally at variance with the prevailing attitude to money-making in medieval Christendom, and to be found nowhere else in the world. Unlike Marx, however, Weber is driven by his comparative method and his *verstehen* principles to search more deeply in late medieval society for the roots of the capitalist outlook. He accepts that in a civilization permeated by religious belief, only religion can be the source of a new ethic that will be sufficiently strong and resilient to maintain itself against the hostility of the traditional culture. In *The Protestant Ethic and the Spirit of Capitalism* he sought to show how, through the beliefs and activities of certain Protestant sects, money-making was made respectable for its members and, to the extent that they became influential, for the particular society as a whole.

This is moving halfway to Hirschman. But it still leaves a problem. Weber has shown how certain social groups of relatively humble origin were able, by reforming and re-working traditional religious ideology, both to motivate themselves in an economic direction and to offer a justification of their practices to the wider society. Economic activity was thereby sanctified and promoted, even though of course with ultimate consequences – the capitalist system – that were quite unintended by sixteenth and seventeenth-century Protestants. Hirschman himself puts the pertinent question: Weber accounts plausibly for the motivation of the 'aspiring new élites', but what of the 'gatekeepers' of medieval society? His own discussion is intended to show how the traditional élites and their advisers, acting essentially on prudential motives of statecraft and self-interest, were led to advocate commercialism as the possible antidote to internecine war:

> 'the expansion of commerce and industry in the 17th and 18th centuries has been viewed here as being welcomed and promoted not by some marginal social groups, nor by an insurgent ideology, but by a current of opinion that arose right in the center of the "power structure" and the "establishment" of the time, out of the problems with which the prince and particularly his advisors and other concerned notables were grappling. Ever since the end of the Middle Ages, and particularly as a result of the increasing frequency of war and civil war in the 17th and 18th centuries, the search was on for a behavioral equivalent for religious precept, for new rules of conduct and devices that would impose much needed discipline and constraints on both rulers and ruled, and the expansion of commerce and industry was thought to hold much promise in this regard.'
>
> (Hirschman 1977: 129)

Hirschman therefore, even more than Weber, emphasizes the intimate connection between the new order of capitalism and the prevailing structure of power in early modern Europe. In this he shows the greater sociological realism. Capitalism could not have arisen in total opposition to medieval feudal society, nor could it have been the accomplishment of marginal social groups acting on their own. There is no example of social change of this kind and magnitude that exhibits such a pattern.[1] Revolutionary change – whether or not overtly political – always involves a Frondist element, the collusion or connivance of at least some representatives of the old ruling class. The dominant groups of feudal society were necessarily implicated in the emergence of the system that ultimately undermined their own order. It should be stressed that this relates to a quite different matter from the case of those members of the upper classes, as in England, who went in for capitalist ventures themselves, in trade and agriculture. The upper classes who promoted capitalism in the early modern period did so primarily for reasons of state, and not in order to join in a capitalist free-for-all.

This suggests a further dimension to the question of the origins and development of capitalism. If pre-capitalist groups and preoccupations were so important in the crucial nascent stages, might it not be possible that they remained so in the later stages as well? Might it not be that, in general, 'non-capitalist' elements formed a significant component in the social order of capitalism, not simply as residues or hang-overs but as essential props to its regular functioning? The conventional answer, even among those who give considerable weight to pre-capitalist factors in the origins of capitalism, is to deny them much of a role in its later development. Capitalism, once set going, seems to acquire a logic of its own which governs its further course. For both Weber and Hirschman, the principle of 'unintended consequences' removes to a large extent the significance of the original factors in subsequent evolution. For Weber, Protestants see religion gradually undermined by the secularizing force of the economic system they have helped to create. The pious Richard Baxter is succeeded by the free-thinking Benjamin Franklin. For Hirschman, the principle operates somewhat differently – people intend things that *don't* happen – but the effect is the same. The hopes that capitalism would spell peace were blasted first by the French Revolution and the Napoleonic Wars, and later by the world wars and revolutions of the twentieth century. The social interests associated with those hopes shared the same fate.

It is here that we encounter directly the contributions of Hirsch and Schumpeter. As against these orthodox views, they insist on a degree of relationship between capitalism and its pre-capitalist past that, going well beyond mere overlap and co-existence, amounts to something like an integral symbiosis.

Two

'Market capitalism has never been the exclusive basis of the political economy in any country at any time' (Hirsch 1977: 118). Hirsch's contention is that liberal market capitalism, taken at its own estimation and in its own terms, is unviable. The attempt to make it work according to its principle of 'possessive individualism' – an attempt it is ultimately forced into by the very logic of its own development – drives it into crisis. Hirsch here accepts the view put forward earlier by Karl Polanyi, who postulated that 'the idea of a self-adjusting market implied a stark utopia. Such an institution could not exist for any length of time without annihilating the human and natural substance of society; it would have physically destroyed man and transformed his surroundings into a wilderness' (Polanyi 1957: 3).

Market society therefore never actually functioned according to its own expressed principle of self-regulation through the 'invisible hand'. It could not have done so without destroying itself. How then was the impression created that it had, that the natural order of liberal society was market society? Hirsch argues that there were special historical conditions which made the equation of 'self-love and social' plausible. Part of the predicament of present-day liberal democracies has been to mistake these special conditions for the natural framework of liberal capitalist society. Market capitalism came into being under 'transient inaugural conditions'.

> 'Adam Smith's invisible hand has linked individual self-interest with social need. But the conditions in which this link has been achieved over a wide area can now be seen not as stable conditions that can be relied on to persist or to be readily maintainable by deliberate action. Rather, they can be seen in important respects to have been special conditions associated with a transition phase from an earlier socio-economic system. The generally benign invisible hand was a favourable inaugural condition of liberal capitalism.'   (Hirsch 1977: 11)

What were these favourable but transient 'inaugural conditions'? The first was that 'full participation was confined to a minority – the minority that had reached material affluence before liberal capitalism had set the masses on the path of material growth'. This condition was undermined by the very success of liberal capitalism. Its economic performance made possible the idea of plenty; its liberal principle made it impossible to deny anyone a share – increasingly, an equal share – in that plenty. The frustrations consequent upon the removal of this original condition – the 'crowding' effect – are analysed by Hirsch under the themes (discussed by others in this book) of 'the paradox of affluence' and 'the distributional compulsion'.

The second inaugural condition was that 'the system operated on social foundations laid under a different order of society'. It is these foundations that 'underlie a benign and efficient implementation of the self-interest principle operating through market transactions'. Those who, such as Keynes, have sought to correct the admitted imperfections of the free market by selective acts of public intervention and public provision – e.g. through tax laws and subsidies – have been guilty of a superficial analysis. They have ignored the critical role played by 'the supporting ethos of social obligation both in the formulation of the relevant public policies and in their efficient transmission to market opportunities. Why expect the controllers, alone, to abstain from maximizing their individual advantage?' The fact is that 'the principle of self-interest is incomplete as a social organising device. It operates effectively only in tandem with some supporting social principle.' Both Adam Smith and John Stuart Mill, in their different ways, could more or less take this supporting ethos for granted in the earlier period of capitalism, and so do not comment much on it. Their successors have neglected it at the very time that it is being eroded by the triumph of the individualistic ethic of the market. Hence it is ignored at the time of its greatest need. Keynesian-style interventions to modify the principle of *laissez-faire* have only intensified the problem. 'Correctives to *laissez-faire* increase rather than decrease reliance on some degree of social orientation and social responsibility in individual behaviour. The attempt has been made to erect an increasingly explicit social organization without a supporting social morality' (Hirsch 1977: 11–12, 120).

Hirsch in this account, under the general theme of 'the depleting moral legacy' (Hirsch 1977: 117 ff., 161 ff.), thus directly links the successful operation of capitalism to its pre-capitalist past. The buoyancy of the market system in its initial phase is seen as resting squarely 'on the shoulders of a premarket social ethos' (p. 12). 'The social morality that has served as an understructure for economic individualism has been a legacy of the precapitalist and preindustrial past. This legacy has diminished with time and with the corrosive contact of the active capitalist values' (p. 117). The content of this morality, as well as its direct relevance to market society, is best suggested by Durkheim's crisp rejoinder to the pure market philosophies of nineteenth-century liberals such as Herbert Spencer: 'All in the contract is not contractual.' That is, market relationships depend on non-market norms. 'Wherever a contract exists, it is dependent on regulation which is the work of society and not that of individuals' (Durkheim 1964: 211). Like Durkheim, Hirsch attaches great importance to the restraints on individual appetites and behaviour imposed by traditional morality. For him, these restraints derive largely from the virtues inherent in traditional religious belief which, predating capitalism, were carried over into the capitalist era to act as the necessary checks on unfettered individualism. 'Truth, trust, acceptance, restraint, obligation – these are among the social virtues grounded in religious belief which are . . . now seen to play a central role in the functioning of an individualistic, contractual economy' (Hirsch 1977: 141). The depletion of the moral legacy of capitalism is coupled therefore to the decline of traditional religion. For 'religiously based norms' were a 'fortunate legacy from a set of principles that was being replaced'. The very force and success of market values gradually undermined religious belief and practice. Once more, the result is seen as having a special historical pathos: 'The market system was, at bottom, more dependent on religious binding than the feudal system, having abandoned direct social ties maintained by the obligations of custom and status. Yet the individualistic, rationalistic base of the market undermined the unseen religious support' (p. 143).

It is striking how many current commentators on 'the crisis of liberal society' also discern the core of the problem in the deteriorating moral foundations of the capitalist economy: a problem made well-nigh insoluble by the fact that these foundations are themselves the ruins of older pre-capitalist structures (Brittan 1975: 148; Bell 1976; Habermas 1976: 48–9; Goldthorpe 1978; Gilbert 1981).[2] The keynote was struck as early as 1921 by Tawney when he wrote of 'the nemesis of industrialism'. Industrialism – 'the perversion of individualism' – was destroying itself not through any 'flaw or vice in human nature', but by the very 'force of the idea, which . . . reveals its defects in its power'. Stripped of any concept of a common social or moral purpose, as supplied for instance by medieval Christianity, industrialism (*sc.* capitalism) committed men and nations 'to a career of indefinite expansion, in which they devour continents and oceans, law, morality and religion, and last of all their own souls, in an attempt to attain infinity by the addition to themselves of all that is finite' (Tawney 1961: 47).

The general form of the argument is clear enough. Capitalism, by itself, is essentially amoral and anomic. Individual outcomes are the result simply of the 'free play' of the market. But no social system can work without a morality. Capitalism lives on borrowed time off a borrowed morality. For a long time capitalism has lived off 'the accumulated capital of traditional religion and traditional moral philosophy' (Kristol 1979: 61), elements which are extraneous to the market. Even the secular philosophies of liberalism and utilitarianism were able to offer a sustaining set of values to capitalism only because, as Dunn shows, they were buttressed by 'the shadowy frame of a Christian ideological inheritance' (Dunn 1979: 43). Their own logic and that of the capitalist system they served gradually undermined that inheritance, finally yielding a reductive and mechanical egoism which was as potentially threatening to liberal values of tolerance and democracy as it had once seemed benevolent to them. In a sense therefore we might say that the Protestant ethic was not simply the origin but the persisting condition of capitalism. It restrained the wants and appetites which, in the pure utilitarian felicific calculus, are unlimited and insatiable. 'When the Protestant ethic, which had served to limit sumptuary (though not capital) accumulation, was sundered from modern bourgeois society, only the hedonism remained' (Bell 1976: 224). Generally, then, as Michael Waltzer puts it:

'what made liberalism endurable for all these years was the fact that the individualism it generated was always imperfect, tempered by older restraints and loyalties, by stable patterns of local, ethnic, religious, or class relationships. An untempered liberalism would be unendurable. That is the crisis ... the triumph of liberalism over its historical restraints.'   (Waltzer 1979: 6)

These observations, together with those of Hirsch, all seem to me undeniably true. They are of crucial importance in understanding the development of capitalism: both its expansive growth, and the counter-movement of the 'self-protection of society' which, stemming from other value systems, was necessary to preserve the social conditions for that growth (Polanyi 1957: 130 ff.). But there is a worrying aspect to them. They are couched in vague, general terms. We are offered abstractions such as 'a premarket social ethos', 'a traditional moral philosophy', 'older restraints and loyalties'. The role they are expected to play is central to the drama of capitalism as expounded by these authors. Yet they exist as rather mysterious, free-floating entities, lacking any real material embodiment. What was the social substance of these influences? In what groups were they embodied? Whose interest and outlook did they express? Merely to point to the existence of these non-capitalist factors is a necessary first step towards understanding; but the account remains historically and sociologically in a highly unsatisfactory state if it rests there.

Schumpeter to a good extent supplies the want. In the space of remarkably few writings, Schumpeter sketched a sociology of modern capitalism that in its breadth and brilliance is scarcely inferior to that of Marx and Weber. Re-working 'the ancient truth, that the dead always rule the living' (Schumpeter 1955: 98), he gave an account of capitalism whose distinctive aspect was the stress on capitalism as a *compound* social formation. It was a compound in two linked senses. Historically, it exhibited the features of two epochs, the 'feudal' and the 'capitalist'; sociologically, it carried the impress of two leading classes, the aristocracy and the bourgeoisie, which were the products of those two very different historical epochs. Capitalism in this respect was simply an instance of a more general feature of social systems:

'Every social situation is the heritage of preceding situations and takes over from them not only their cultures, their dispositions, and their "spirit", but also elements of their social structure and concentrations of power. . . . The social pyramid is never made of a single substance, is never seamless. There is no single *Zeitgeist*, except in the sense of a construct. This means that in explaining any historical course or situation, account must be taken of the fact that much in it can be explained only by the survival of elements that are actually alien to its own trends. . . . The co-existence of essentially different mentalities and objective sets of facts must form part of any general theory.'

(Schumpeter 1955: 111)

Applied to the case of capitalism, such a view explains the persistence of a 'premarket social ethos' not as some generalized carry-over from the feudal era but as the class expression of a still powerful aristocracy. As Schumpeter describes the process, the absolutist monarchies of the sixteenth to eighteenth centuries in Europe increasingly shaped their policies according to the needs of capitalist development, the more so as they depended to an increasing extent on revenues created by the capitalist process. But the monarchy, and the aristocracy which – however capriciously – was allied to it, never allowed themselves to become the captives of bourgeois interests, still less politically subordinate to the bourgeoisie. The 'feudal presence' in the structure of the absolutist state was no mere ghost.

'The steel frame of that structure still consisted of the human material of feudal society and this material still behaved according to precapitalist patterns. It filled the offices of state, officered the army, devised policies – it functioned as a *classe dirigente* and, though taking account of bourgeois interests, it took care to distance itself from the bourgeoisie. . . . All this was more than atavism. It was an active symbiosis of two social strata, one of which no doubt supported the other economically but was in turn supported by the other politically.'

(Schumpeter 1976: 136)

This was, says Schumpeter, 'the essence of that society'; and the structure thus established extended well beyond the early phase of capitalist development. 'The aristocratic element continued to rule the roost right to the end of the period of intact and vital capitalism.' Controversial as such a statement is, and subject to many qualifications, it seems to be broadly true. As a perspective on the long-term development of European societies it helps to explain many things which do not fit at all satisfactorily into alternative sociological theories (such as the Marxist). It can explain phenomena as diverse as the French Revolution (Kumar 1971: 52 ff.), the British pattern of industrial development (Wiener 1981), the success or otherwise of English working-class movements in the first half of the nineteenth century (Moore 1976; Kumar 1983), and the nature of German politics and society up to the rise of Hitler (Dahrendorf 1968). In all these cases what is at issue is a cluster of class actions and alliances that do not make sense within the concept of a single unified bourgeois society. Inconvenient 'deviations' and 'archaisms' have to be explained away, as for instance the active role of the French nobility in bringing about the French Revolution of 1789. Schumpeter enables us to see that these are not 'atavisms' or 'cultural lags', but the expressions of the normal pattern of bourgeois politics and bourgeois social development. 'A purely capitalist society – consisting of nothing but entrepreneurs, capitalists and proletarian workmen – would work in ways completely different from those we observe historically if indeed it could exist at all' (Schumpeter 1951: 172).

It is the *normal* order of bourgeois society to be variegated. Its social structure is marked by a fundamental heterogeneity. It is formed not simply by synchronous elements in relationships of conflict and cohesion – bourgeoisie and proletariat – but also by relationships between strata – aristocracy and bourgeoisie – which look towards different historical periods for their characteristic outlook and principles of action. Bourgeois society is Janus-faced, one face turned towards the past, the other towards the future. 'The social pyramid of the present age has been formed, not by the substance and laws of capitalism alone, but by two different social substances, and by the laws of two different epochs' (Schumpeter 1955: 92).

The fact of this structural dichotomy can complicate how classes perceive their 'normal' or 'natural' class interest. Schumpeter gives the example of imperialism. How is it that the bourgeoisie came to be linked, as it was in the late nineteenth century, with an imperialist policy and outlook? The natural tendency of bourgeois society is pacific. The bourgeoisie is 'inclined to insist on the application of the moral precepts of private life to international relations' (Schumpeter 1976: 128). In an ideal bourgeois world, war is irrational and anti-utilitarian, a distraction and a diversion of energy from the central activity of trade and industry (Schumpeter 1955: 69). The bourgeois interest should be the peace interest, and so it often is: as for instance with the Cobdenite English middle class for most of the nineteenth century.

Imperialism in capitalist states is therefore partly explained as the expression of the tendency and outlook of a politically dominant aristocratic class, who owe their very title to rule to their fitness for war, and for whom war once constituted the main business of life. To this extent it represents a persistence of forms of behaviour characteristic of the era of absolutism. But it was not simply the aristocracy that was formed by the absolutist state. The bourgeoisie too carried its stamp. Especially on the Continent, the bourgeoisie was as much brought into being by the absolutist monarchy in the latter's struggles with the aristocracy, as it created itself by its own independent efforts. Systems of tariffs and trading rights were created and regulated by mercantilist states in pursuit of their own autocratic and dynastic interests. The bourgeoisie in its early stages was critically dependent on the patronage and protection of the monarchy against the feudal aristocracy. It became habituated to protectionist and paternalist strategies, and adept at exploiting these to further its own interests against those of other classes and other national bourgeoisies.

> 'Thus the bourgeoisie willingly allowed itself to be moulded into one of the power instruments of the monarchy. . . . Trade and industry of the early capitalist period remained strongly pervaded with precapitalist methods, bore the stamp of autocracy, and served its interests, either willingly or by force. With its traditional habits of feeling, thinking, and acting moulded along such lines, the bourgeoisie entered the Industrial Revolution. It was shaped, in other words, by the needs and interests of an environment that was essentially non-capitalist, or at least precapitalist – needs stemming not from the nature of the capitalist economy as such but from the fact of the co-existence of early capitalism with another and at first over-whelmingly powerful mode of life and business. Established habits of thought and action tend to persist, and hence the spirit of guild and monopoly maintained itself. . . . Actually capitalism did not fully prevail *anywhere* on the Continent. Existing economic interests, "artifically" shaped by the autocratic state, remained dependent on the "protection" of the state. The industrial organism, such as it was, would not have been able to withstand free competition.'
>
> (Schumpeter 1955: 90–1)

Since the bourgeoisie never fully wrested political power from the aristocratic state, 'the state remained a special social power, confronting the bourgeoisie'. But schooled by its past experience the bourgeoisie came to look to the state for 'refuge and protection against external and even domestic enemies. The bourgeoisie seeks to win over the state for itself, and in return serves the state and state interests that are different from its own' (p. 93). Its existence as a child of autocracy makes it highly vulnerable to ideologies which are essentially antithetical to capitalism. It espouses, often with no need of prompting from outside, militarism, nationalism, and imperialism, and so proves itself to be a truly national bourgeoisie. Such readiness 'bears witness to the extent to which essentially imperialist absolutism has patterned not only the economy of the bourgeoisie but also its mind – in the interests of autocracy and against those of the bourgeoisie itself' (p. 94). In the final analysis, then, imperialism is:

'not only historically, but also sociologically, a heritage of the auto-cratic strate, of its structural elements, organizational forms, in-terest alignments, and human attitudes, the outcome of precapitalist forces which the autocratic state has reorganised, in part by the methods of early capitalism. It would never have been evolved by the "inner logic" of capitalism itself.'   (Schumpeter 1955: 97)

It is immaterial, for present purposes, how plausible one may find this account of imperialism; although the imperialist wars of the twentieth-century Leviathan may well seem confirmation rather than refutation of Schumpeter's analysis, and, with the recrudescence of the 'warfare' state, make him appear unduly optimistic as to the waning influence of 'pre-capitalist elements'. What matters more, however, is the method of the analysis. Social theorists have become only too expert at conjuring abstract 'social systems' out of thin air, or out of some undifferentiated substance – 'values', 'power', 'productive mode' – in their conceptual bubble-blowers. Schumpeter is no less theoretical in intent than any of these. But the materials of his 'social system' are the materials of actual history: history as both event and process. He avoids the temptation, succumbed to by most social theorists of the last two hundred years, to impose an evolutionary scheme on social development which conjures up successive stages or states of society, each with their leads and lags, vestiges and residues. By giving due weight and respect to the social elements as actually found and constituted in society at any time, undismayed by 'atavisms' and 'archaisms' which on the contrary he acknowledges as the normal phenomena of any social order, he is able to give an account of modern capitalist society which at the very least passes the test of credibility: a rare achievement in recent social theory. More than that for the moment it is unnecessary to claim.[3] The important thing is that by emphasizing the normality of the non-capitalist elements in the development of capitalism, Schumpeter is able to deal with not simply the familiar features of capitalism but also the irregular and 'aberrant'. Thus he can – in a way that Hirsch for instance cannot – explain how capitalism can be both unboundedly expansive and market orientated, and at the same time sufficiently restrained (at least until recently) to prevent this pure capitalist ethos from tearing the system apart.

For Schumpeter's non-capitalist aristocracy is of course not simply warlike and imperialist. It embodies other traditional values as well. It has an almost religious attachment to the land, it is suspicious or contemptuous of commerce, and it is the upholder of a social philosophy of paternalism which, if its obligations were often carelessly discharged, remained an ideology potentially exploitable by all parties. It preserves, in other words, a rich store of pre-capitalist values and images which can be drawn upon as occasion demands in the social conflicts engendered by capitalism. In alliance with other non-capitalist interests – at various times the church, the army, the bureaucracy, the peasants, and the workers – it intervened, often decisively, in the capitalist process to slow down or otherwise regulate the pure operations of the market system. As the landed interest and the guardian of territorial integrity it resisted, in common with the peasants, the full effects of the commercialization of the soil and international free trade which threatened a complete mobilization of land and the destruction of all small proprietors (Polanyi 1957: 178 ff.). It succeeded in retaining protection until the middle of the nineteenth century in England, and throughout the century on most of the Continent. Together with the workers it fought the factory owners on factory legislation and the utilitarians on poor law reform. The Tory-Radical alliance in England in the first half of the nineteenth century was indeed the source of one of the most successful and sustained counter-movements to capitalism to be found anywhere in Europe (so successful as to deceive Marx and Engels into thinking that they had uncovered the revolutionary proletariat). Elsewhere, as in Germany, a strongly paternalist state run by the traditional landowning class brought in impressive measures of social welfare. In all this, it hardly needs to be said, considerations of class interest were no doubt uppermost in the minds of the protagonists, and social duty often only the public facade. But the effect nevertheless was to save capitalism from itself, at least for the time being. The checks to the market system served to blunt and divert the social forces unleashed by capitalism, which might otherwise have led to social war.

Three

America did not occasion class war; but in other respects it offers a fascinating glimpse of what happens in a largely Europeanized society lacking a feudal tradition. America was a European invention but without a European past. It was forged in the crucible of European thought but not of European social experience. Its development was conditioned by the fact that, as Tocqueville said, Americans were 'born equal, instead of becoming so'. Unlike Europe, it did not gain its democracy through a revolutionary struggle with feudal aristocratic forces. There were few feudal relics in colonial America. Its society of small farmers and small traders, having shrugged off the English crown, was able to develop in relative freedom from a constraining feudal presence. It is one of the few cases we have of a pure bourgeois society, bourgeois in origins and bourgeois in development.[4]

This was in many ways, as Tocqueville declared, a 'great advantage', a beneficent inheritance. It gave to all aspects of American life a uniquely liberal and democratic character. But it had a damaging consequence too. As Louis Hartz brilliantly showed, it led to the enthronement in America of an 'absolutist liberalism', a 'dogmatic Lockeanism', which dominated American politics and which effectively precluded the emergence of a tradition of political thought at all (Hartz 1955). Political thought feeds on political conflict and political diversity. These were the very things denied, in principle and to a good extent in practice, by the force of the prevailing liberal ideology. The result was a dead-weight liberal consensus which killed off for more than a century all significant political speculation and political growth.

In Europe, feudal, bourgeois, and proletarian forces met in 1789. All three continued to interact throughout the nineteenth century and beyond. Their mutual interaction gave rise not just to a rejuvenated conservatism and a militant liberalism, but also to socialism. All three were absent in America. America's 1776 was a purely bourgeois affair. Thereafter the liberal ethos enclosed the American community like a vice. All subsequent developments were the play of variations – Horatio Algerism, Progressivism, New Dealism – on the liberal theme. There were no conflicts between bourgeoisie and aristocracy to generate the conservatism of a Bonald or Burke: 'Southern Toryism' collapsed under the weight of its own contradictions. In this most bourgeois of societies, lacking the social conflicts of Europe, there was not even the growth of a self-conscious and complex liberalism, playing off the people against the aristocracy and the aristocracy against the people, being pushed in one direction – as by James Mill and Macaulay – by fear of the mob, and in a more radical direction – as by John Stuart Mill and Lloyd George – by a sharp reminder of its birth in a popular struggle against the feudal state. The fate of Hamilton's 'high' Whiggery, and the Republican Party's subsequent embrace of the democratic capitalist ideology of Algerism, showed how difficult it was for liberalism of a European kind to gain a foothold in America.

Socialism, as is well known, failed even more dismally to establish itself in American life and thought. This was not simply due to the absence of a truly proletarian class, a dubious enough assertion in any case, still less to the moving frontier. It was at least as much the result of the lack of a feudal tradition and a feudal class, whose presence in Europe provided the explosive matrix for the development of socialism. The socialist movement in Europe was nourished as much by the

aristocracy as by the bourgeoisie in their mutual struggles. The landowning aristocracy could pose – and even act – as the historic protector of the
people against a selfish and rapacious bourgeoisie. Out of the 'feudal
socialism' of a Carlyle and a Disraeli ('half echo of the past, half menace
of the future', as Marx put it), there could develop that Tory Radicalism
that played so important a part in nineteenth-century Europe. As an
ideological component of socialism, indeed, the feudal element remained highly significant. The reception of Proudhon, Ruskin, and
Morris showed that a good part of the appeal of socialism was its promise
to restore something like the communal and craft-based order of the
Middle Ages. Moreover, the aristocracy continued to be serviceable to
socialism when its role shifted from ally to antagonist. Socialism critically
depended for its growth on the presence not simply of the bourgeois
enemy but of the feudal remnant as well. As Marx saw, and as the
Dreyfus affair so well demonstrated, in the conditions of continental
Europe especially, socialism would draw its strength as much from the
struggle against the forces of the feudal order as from the struggle against
capitalism. This was the 'dual revolution' against both feudalism and
capitalism which Marx foresaw would have to be the task of European
socialism, and which Lenin and Trotsky later generalized into a 'law' for
all 'backward' countries (which in practice seems to have been every
country except England and, ironically, America).

The fateful fact of being 'born equal' therefore deprived America of
the fertilizing currents of all the main varieties of European social
thought: conservatism, liberalism, and socialism. This cultural
impoverishment would have mattered less if the rough equality that
prevailed among the early colonial farmers and traders had persisted. It
was a crippling deficiency when, quite apart from the problem of the
'peculiar institution' of slavery, social inequality grew to European
proportions in the second half of the nineteenth century. It meant that
America lacked both the social resources and the ideas with which to
confront the problems of the world's fastest growing capitalist economy.
It is startling to think that America got through the age of the robber-
barons with nothing more impressive to hand than refurbished Herbert
Spencer. But there was a costly price to pay. For all the harshness of the
European patterns of industrilization, there is really little to compare
with the brutality and bitterness of the labour conflicts in America from
the 1870s to the 1930s. Tocqueville had already observed of America in
the 1830s that 'the manufacturing aristocracy which is growing under
our eyes is one of the harshest which ever existed in the world'
(Tocqueville 1961, II: 194). In the mass strike of 1877 over one hundred
strikers were killed by a combination of employers' private armies,

special police, and federal troops. The federal government continued to bless this combination of private and public violence throughout the period. A similar strike-breaking force of 14,000 men was involved in the bloody Pullman strike of 1894 in which thirty-four strikers were killed and hundreds badly wounded. No policy of legal and non-violent strike action was proof against the ability and ready willingness of employers, judiciary, and government to resort to armed force against the strikers. As a result right up to the Second World War nearly every major strike turned into a bloody confrontation, with many dead and wounded (Brecher 1972). Every big strike was treated as incipient rebellion or civil war, every attack on the employers' prerogatives was seen as a challenge to the state.

Marx wrote in the preface to *Capital* that England was the country that showed other industrializing countries the 'image of their future'. It was a poor prediction in more than one respect. Tocqueville judged better in casting America in that role. America is the Hirschian nightmare realized. It is capitalism unleashed, capitalism without the historical restraints that contained its destructive tendencies for so long in Euro-pean societies. Some have argued that, despite the absence of a pre-capitalist class, religion in the form of Protestantism provided a real degree of restraint on the American capitalist system (Bell 1976: 55 ff.; Kristol 1979: 245). The evidence is hard to find; and, in any case, the claim seems to be based on a misunderstanding and misapplication of the Weberian argument. Weber showed that the Protestant ethic restrained the *individual* in his own consumption and style of life, the more freely and efficiently to exploit to the full the resources of nature and society. On the social plane, in other words, the ethic encouraged the most limitless expansion and growth. It provided no compensating social principle to restrict that growth. Hence while Protestantism might have had some regulatory influence on individual psychology, it was quite incapable of containing the capitalist beast at large in society – quite the contrary. It was only, as Schumpeter showed, the existence of social forces with interests and outlooks outside or beyond the market that endowed societies with the capacity to exercise any real degree of restraint on the pace and logic of capitalist development. It was these social forces that America conspicuously lacked. There were no social groups of whom it could truly be said – as it could be said for instance of the landed aristocracy in Europe – that they were in the capitalist system but not of it. All groups were drawn more or less willingly into the struggles of the market-place, and imbibed its ethic to the full. State and society, the public and the private realms, were collapsed into each other. Hence neither within the state nor within the social ethos of a class could there be found a non-market tradition of social responsibility or enlightened paternalism.

What was left to Americans was the freedom of the void: the 'malady of infinite aspirations', as Durkheim defined anomie. 'The limits are unknown between the possible and the impossible, what is just and what is unjust, legitimate claims and hopes and those which are immoderate' (Durkheim 1952: 253). The possibilities were or seemed dizzying; the only unpardonable sin was not to seize them, the only acceptable form of worship was that of the 'bitch-goddess' success. America became classically the land where all that mattered was success or failure. Never mind that 'within the American world there was no escape from the race even for those who won it' (Hartz 1955: 221); or that, as taught by countless examinations of 'the American Dream' from the novels of Scott Fitzgerald to the *film noir* of the 1940s, success remained forever elusive and fleeting. Failure was after all much worse, especially as American society supplied no other values to support an alternative way of life outside the competitive commercial system. And since success was the supreme criterion, how it was achieved could only be a relatively minor concern. Thus not only were the ends of American society 'de-regulated' by the capitalist ethic, so also were the means, making it a perhaps unique case of a social system whose defining principle was anomie (Merton 1957). What distinguished a Carnegie from a Capone was not the ends pursued, or even the means adopted, which were in both cases remarkably similar; it was the success which blessed the enterprise of the former as compared with the *fortuna* that damned that of the latter. It is in this reduction of society to a game in which luck plays a cosmic role that we most clearly see the 'pure logic' of an untrammelled capitalism.

Four

The general message of both Hirsch's and Schumpeter's accounts is that capitalism is killed not by its failure, as Marx expected, but by its success. Its own logic undermines it, by sweeping away all the pre-capitalist and non-capitalist baggage that has accompanied it on its journey. Capitalism itself is unconscious of the necessary labour of sustenance performed by this pre-capitalist inheritance. It sees it at best as an unnecessary burden, at worst as an obstacle to its progress. It regards it therefore variously with indifference or calculated hostility. It saps the force of religion, dissolves all corporate organization such as workers' guilds and village communities, and gradually either eliminates the power and influence of non-capitalist groups or draws them fully into its system. It thereby exposes itself fatally to tendencies within its own system which are preparing its downfall.

> 'In breaking down the pre-capitalist framework of society, capitalism broke not only barriers that impeded its progress but also flying buttresses that prevented its collapse. That process, impressive in its relentless necessity, was not merely a matter of removing institutional deadwood, but of removing partners of the capitalist stratum, symbiosis with whom was an essential element of the capitalist schema.'
>
> (Schumpeter 1976: 139)

The argument, therefore, by a different route, arrives at a general conclusion not so far from Marx's. As Schumpeter urbanely says, 'in the end there is not so much difference as one might think between saying that the decay of capitalism is due to its success and saying that it is due to its failure' (Schumpeter 1976: 162). Hirsch and Schumpeter disagree of course not only with Marx but with each other on what it is about capitalism itself that drives it into crisis. Hirsch picks out particularly the consequences of successful growth in the material economy, forcing upon society a self-defeating struggle for equal shares within the 'positional economy'. For Schumpeter, capitalism's economic success brings about the atrophy of the entrepreneurial function, the bureaucratization of the enterprise, and the disintegration of the bourgeois family. Assailed by a class of alienated intellectuals which is its own creation, it loses both its basic legitimacy and its motivating force.

This is not the place to adjudicate between Hirsch and Schumpeter (for Schumpeter, see Heertje 1981), nor to assess the host of other theories variously contending over the causes of capitalism's current ills. What is interesting is that despite the differences in their analyses, both Hirsch and Schumpeter see emerging out of the strains of developed capitalism what Hirsch calls a 'reluctant collectivism'. For Schumpeter this is 'socialism', but since he defines socialism narrowly as 'control over the means of production by a central authority' (Schumpeter 1976: 167), this is not so far removed from Hirsch's perception of collectivism as a 'trend towards collective provision and state regulation in economic areas' (Hirsch 1977: 1).

Hirsch is concerned to make that collectivism less reluctant, more full-blooded, and so more effective in achieving its ends. The precise measures he suggests are discussed elsewhere in this volume. Here I simply want to observe, by way of concluding, that Hirsch's prescriptions are generally flawed by the same feature that marks his analysis of the pre-capitalist moral framework of capitalism. That is, they hang in the air. They are irredeemably idealist. On the last page of his book Hirsch states the general goal:

> 'the prime economic problem now facing the economically advanced societies is a structural need to pull back the bounds of economic self-advancement. That in turn requires a deliberate validation of the basis of income and wealth distribution that these economies have managed to do without in a transition period that is ending. . . . We may be near the limit of explicit social organization possible without a supporting social morality. Additional correctives in its absence simply do not take . . . the first necessity is not technical devices but the public acceptance necessary to make them work.'   (Hirsch 1977: 190)

It is not too much to say that this either presumes or calls for revolution, or something very similar. This inference is qualified only slightly by the consideration of one of the key mechanisms suggested by Hirsch for achieving this goal: the adoption of an 'as if altruism', whereby self-interested motives are put at the service of collectively orientated behaviour to overcome the felt deficiencies of privately directed behaviour.

> 'the best result may be attained by steering or guiding certain motives of individual behaviour into social rather than individual orientation, though still on the basis of privately directed preferences. This requires not a change in human nature, "merely" a change in human convention or instinct or attitude of the same order as the shifts in social conventions or moral standards that have gone along with major changes in economic conditions in the past.'   (Hirsch 1977: 146)

The fact that Hirsch puts the 'merely' in quotation marks confesses an understandable uneasiness, but it cannot disguise the immensity of the change contemplated, as his parallel with past changes only too clearly underlines.

What social agency is to accomplish so momentous a change? Whose interests are furthered by promoting such a social morality? Everyone's in the end, of course, but that is simply to state the problem in a different form. Is the change to come about by a blinding flash of collective self-enlightenment? For Hirsch himself is only too well aware of the difficulty of getting people to act in a collectively enlightened way while private ends and motivations still predominate (see especially Hirsch 1977: 137 ff.). 'Individuals can perceive a need for themselves and their fellows and yet have no rational basis to act on it in isolation. The socially concerned individual then faces a dilemma between social and individual needs' (p. 179). This brings us back to the need for 'collective means', which remains a highly abstract entity, especially as Hirsch rules out on the grounds of 'primary liberal values' the 'subjugation of individual judgement on moral issues and behavioural choices to the thought of some Chairman Mao' (p. 180). Now that would be a solution, of a kind, but in renouncing it Hirsch is left in the familiar position of having to hoist himself up by his own boot-straps. It is a particularly despairing admission of failure to fall back on the belief that 'the functional need for a change in the social ethic can be expected, over time, to promote it' (p. 179). His own analysis suggests quite otherwise.

Truly, one cannot blame Hirsch for not providing a convincing account of how the change is to come about. Many others have seen the need for comparable changes without being any more successful (see e.g. Hirsch and Goldthorpe 1978: 214–16). For his part, Schumpeter's account of 'the march into socialism' has its own problems, and it is certainly not my intention here to offer it as an alternative to Hirsch. Moreover Schumpeter's task is easier, in as much as he is describing as well as prescribing. But, although his attitude to socialism retains a characteristically detached irony, he clearly sees it not only as more or less inevitable but also as capable of delivering at least as efficiently all that capitalism delivered.

> 'The whole of our argument might be put in a nutshell by saying that socialization means a stride beyond big business on the way that has been chalked out by it or, what amounts to the same thing, that socialist management may conceivably prove as superior to big business capitalism as big business capitalism has proved to be to the kind of competitive capitalism of which the English industry of a hundred years ago was the prototype. . . . As a matter of blueprint logic it is undeniable that the socialist blueprint is drawn at a higher level of rationality.'   (Schumpeter 1976: 195–96)

What is in any case more important, here as in the earlier discussion, is not so much the correctness or otherwise of Schumpeter's view of socialism as the form of analysis he adopts. Schumpeter points to concrete tendencies within late capitalist society which, he argues, whether or not we choose to call the outcome 'socialism', are transforming capitalism to such an extent that it becomes simply erroneous to use the same term for the emerging social order. These include the growth of an interventionist state, a technical and managerial bureaucracy in both public and private enterprises, and a salaried professional middle class with interests and attitudes very different from those of the classic private capitalist and entrepreneur. The exigencies of war and depression further encourage these developments. Socialism is merely the recognition and rationalization of these tendencies. The main work has already been done. 'The capitalist process shapes things and souls for socialism' (Schumpeter 1976: 220).

Simply to mention Burnham's *The Managerial Revolution* and Galbraith's *The New Industrial State* is to indicate the kinship of this argument with that vast concurrence of contemporary social thought to which Schumpeter himself is of course a major contributor. But the very familiarity of Schumpeter's analysis is its strength in the present context. It suggests at the very least that the transforming forces he points to are real observable entities in the recent history of Western societies. Whether or not they can fulfil quite the task that he sets them is disputable, but he certainly presents us with some very plausible means to his designated ends. This is precisely what Hirsch does not do, and on the available evidence the future seems to lie much more with Schumpeter's commissars than Hirsch's 'jaded social democrats'.

Comparisons can be artificial as well as invidious. Actually Hirsch and Schumpeter go together very well. Both break through the conventional categories of discipline and ideology to cast a refreshing and revealing perspective on the development of Western capitalist societies. Both emphasize important features of that development too often ignored or treated as peripheral. In contemplating the future, Schumpeter is the greater realist, as is consistent with the greater sociological realism of his treatment throughout; but he is a realist at the cost of the sacrifice of values he obviously cherishes. Hirsch, however, is certainly no wild-eyed visionary. The impressiveness of his achievement lies in the sense of a man grappling with some of the most intractable problems of modern society without abandoning his commitment to liberal and humane values. Who has yet done more?

Notes

1. The view that there was no radical break of any kind – in England at least – in the sixteenth and seventeenth centuries has been provocatively put by Macfarlane (1978). Space, as well as general competence, forbids any discussion of that theme here. But one might at least say that Macfarlane takes a very restrictive and narrow view of what is implied by 'the rise of capitalism', and the question cannot be resolved by a concentration on legal or customary definitions of land ownership and tenurial rights. A good deal more is involved by way of changes in social values, attitudes to work and religion, and the sense of communal ties. Macfarlane does not discuss any of these.
2. John Goldthorpe has seen in this a key difference in the treatment of capitalism by economists and sociologists:

'There are, and have been historically, clear differences between economists and sociologists in their evaluations of the capitalist market economy. Economists tend to see this as having an inherent propensity towards stability or, at least, as capable of being stabilized through skilled management on the basis of the expertise that they can themselves provide. Sociologists, on the other hand, tend to view the market economy as being inherently unstable or, rather, to be more precise, as exerting a constant destabilizing effect on the society within which it operates, so that it can itself continue to function satisfactorily only to the extent that this effect is offset by exogenous factors: most importantly, by the integrative influence of some basic value consensus in the society, deriving from sources unrelated to the economy; or by some measure of "imperative coordination" imposed by government (or other agencies) with the ultimate backing of force.'

(Goldthorpe 1978: 194)

3. Perhaps one might add, as a particularly telling example of the undogmatic quality of Schumpeter's thinking, that even in his most 'purely' economic analysis, *The Theory of Economic Development*, he concedes so important a role to 'accidents' – i.e. history – in the aetiology of the crises of the business cycle as calmly to suggest the possibility that no general theory might be needed at all (Schumpeter 1961: 222).
4. America is only the best studied example of a fascinating exercise in comparative analysis that can be undertaken by looking at societies such as those of Latin America and Australia, which have been formed out of 'fragments of Europe'. See, e.g., the studies in Hartz (1964).

References

BELL, D. (1976) *The Cultural Contradictions of Capitalism.* London: Heinemann.

BRECHER, J. (1972) *Strike!* Boston: South End Press.

BRITTAN, S. (1975) The Economic Contradictions of Democracy. *British Journal of Political Science* 5: 129–59.

DAHRENDORF, R. (1968) *Society and Democracy in Germany.* London: Weidenfeld and Nicolson.

DUNN, J. (1979) *Western Political Theory in the Face of the Future.* Cambridge: Cambridge University Press.

DURKHEIM, E. (1952) *Suicide: A Study in Sociology.* Trans. J. A. Spaulding and G. Simpson. London: Routledge and Kegan Paul.

—— (1964) *The Division of Labor in Society.* Trans. G. Simpson. New York: Free Press.

FORBES, D. (1954) 'Scientific' Whiggism: Adam Smith and John Millar. *Cambridge Journal* 7: 643–70.

—— (1966) Introduction to his edition of Adam Ferguson, *An Essay on the History of Civil Society.* Edinburgh: Edinburgh University Press.

GELLNER, E. (1979) The Withering Away of the Dentistry State. In his *Spectacles and Predicaments: Essays in Social Theory.* Cambridge: Cambridge University Press.

GILBERT, M. (1981) A Sociological Model of Inflation. *Sociology* 15 (2): 185–209.

GOLDTHORPE, J. H. (1978) The Current Inflation: Towards a Sociological Account. In Hirsch and Goldthorpe (eds) *The Political Economy of Inflation*. London: Martin Robertson.

HABERMAS, J. (1976) *Legitimation Crisis*. Trans. T. McCarthy. London: Heinemann.

HARTZ, L. (1955) *The Liberal Tradition in America*. New York: Harcourt, Brace and World.

—— (1964) *The Founding of New Societies*. New York: Harcourt, Brace and World.

HEERTJE, A. (ed.) (1981) *Schumpeter's Vision: Capitalism, Socialism, and Democracy after Forty Years*. New York: Praeger.

HEILBRONER, R. (1973) The Paradox of Progress: Decline and Decay in *The Wealth of Nations*. *Journal of the History of Ideas* 34: 243–62.

HIRSCH, F. (1977) *Social Limits to Growth*. London: Routledge and Kegan Paul.

HIRSCH, F. and GOLDTHORPE, J. H. (eds) (1978) *The Political Economy of Inflation*. London: Martin Robertson.

HIRSCHMAN, A. O. (1977) *The Passions and the Interests*. Princeton: Princeton University Press.

HUME, D. (1903) Of Money. In his *Essays: Moral, Political and Literary*. London: Grant Richards.

KRISTOL, K. (1979) *Two Cheers for Capitalism*. New York: Mentor Books.

KUMAR, K. (ed.) (1971) *Revolution: The Theory and Practice of a European Idea*. London: Weidenfeld and Nicolson.

—— (1983) Class and Political Action in 19th Century England. *European Journal of Sociology* 24 (1).

LOW, J. M. (1952) An Eighteenth Century Controversy in the Theory of Economic Progress. *The Manchester School* 20: 311–30.

MACFARLANE, A. (1978) *The Origins of English Individualism*. Oxford: Basil Blackwell.

MERTON, R. K. (1957) Social Structure and Anomie. In his *Social Theory and Social Structure*. Revised edn. Glencoe: Free Press.

MOORE, D. C. (1976) *The Politics of Deference*. London: Harvester Press.

POLANYI, K. (1957) *The Great Transformation*. Boston: Beacon Press.

ROSENBERG, N. (1968) Adam Smith, Consumer Tastes and Economic Growth. *Journal of Political Economy* 76: 361–74.

SCHUMPETER, J. A. (1951) Capitalism in the Post War World. In R. V. Clemence (ed.) *Essays of J. A. Schumpeter*. Cambridge, Mass: Addison Wesley.

—— (1955) *Imperialism and Social Classes: Two Essays*. New York: Meridian Books.

—— (1961) *The Theory of Economic Development*. New York: Oxford University Press.

—— (1976) *Capitalism, Socialism, and Democracy*. 5th edn. London: Allen and Unwin.

SMITH, A. (1910) *The Wealth of Nations* 2 vols. London: Dent and Sons.

—— (1969) *The Theory of Moral Sentiments.* Indianapolis: Liberty Classics.

TAWNEY, R. H. (1961) *The Acquisitive Society.* London: Fontana.

TOCQUEVILLE, A. de (1961) *Democracy in America* 2 vols. New York: Schocken Books.

WALTZER, M. (1979) Nervous Liberals. *New York Review of Books* 11 October.

WEBER, M. (1930) *The Protestant Ethic and the Spirit of Capitalism.* Trans. T. Parsons. London: Allen and Unwin.

WIENER, M. J. (1981) *English Culture and the Decline of the Industrial Spirit 1850–1980.* Cambridge: Cambridge University Press.

9 Classical liberalism, positional goods, and the politicization of poverty

JOHN GRAY

In its uses in political argument, the idea of a positional good and the theory of the emergent positional economy has been deployed as part of a radical critique of liberal democratic welfare capitalism. This is un-equivocally clear, not only in the reception which Fred Hirsch's *Social Limits to Growth* (1977) received in academic circles and in the media, but also in the book's argument itself. Hirsch's chief object throughout is to contest the belief, widely invoked in defence of the managed capitalist economy which came to prevail in all Western nations after the Second World War, that economic growth – the continuous expansion of the aggregate of goods and services – can indefinitely secure a widening circle of opportunities for all, including the worst-off. Hirsch's principal arguments against this belief are not, as were those of the Club of Rome, Malthusian arguments aiming to identify ultimate physical limitations of food, space, and natural resources on further growth. Rather, Hirsch sought to identify a neglected dimension of social scarcity, not to be analysed primarily in terms of absolute overcrowding, which was bound to render vain and delusive the promise of further economic growth to bring about an endless enhancement of opportunities. Further, Hirsch was at pains to spell out how this curtailment of the promise of growth threatened to shatter the fragile legitimacy of post-war capitalism.

Widespread disappointment of the hopes reposed in further economic growth, Hirsch concluded, could only stimulate the distributional struggle in the advanced societies and, in the end, compel a transformation of their capitalist economic foundations.

Hirsch's argument in support of these conclusions is complex, subtle, and sometimes confused, but its main outlines are easily discerned and it can be summarized in three main claims. First, there is the claim that growing affluence carries with it the paradoxical expansion of a certain sort of social scarcity – that generated by competition for positional goods. Now the idea of a positional good is never very explicitly or systematically elucidated in Hirsch's book, but it seems to denote, centrally and fundamentally, any good whose value to its consumers is inversely related to its general availability. This relationship between a good's accessibility and its value to those who possess it, in terms of which any good's positionality is to be understood, is far from being a determinate one. Hirsch recognizes that positionality may have various sources and may assume a diversity of forms. As with membership of a prestigious club, a good's positionality may result almost wholly from its socially exclusive character, or else it may have a decisive physical aspect (as with congestion in popular tourist resorts, perhaps). A good's positionality may result mainly from conventional and institutional factors or it may express some sort of physical constraint, but however this may be, the positional goods have become the chief objects of social competition in the advanced capitalist nations.

The very nature of the positional goods entails that most of those who compete for them are bound to be disappointed, and it is the inherently frustrating character of competition within the positional economy that bring Hirsch to his second thesis. This is the claim that advanced capitalist orders are increasingly governed by a distributional imperative which motivates the reluctant resort to collectivist procedures for resource allocation. It is the intense competition for positional goods, in conjunction with the sharp distributional conflicts thereby engendered, which gives Hirsch his third thesis – that the moral legitimacy of advanced capitalism is diminishing to a critical level, and that the legitimation crisis which this erosion of capitalism's moral capital embodies can be resolved only by the construction of a co-operative and socialist economic order governed by a new moral consensus.

The nub of Hirsch's argument, then, is in the claim that the emergence of the positional economy has generated a severe crisis of legitimacy for our societies – a crisis for which socialism is, apparently, the only or at least the obvious solution. It will be seen at once, of course, that it is the structure of Hirsch's argument as a whole, rather than any of its constitutive elements, that is original. It is in his use of the idea of a positional good that Hirsch can make his least implausible claim to originality, but the idea of a good which is scarce by its very nature – the goods of power and prestige being those most often instanced – is a long-standing theme of social theory, recurring in various forms in the writings of Hobbes and Rousseau, for example. Again, the claim that modern mass societies are fated to suffer severe distributional conflicts is a prominent feature of nineteenth-century liberal and conservative thought, with writers as different as J. S. Mill and A. V. Dicey seeing the sources of such struggles in the necessities of political competition in mass democracy rather than in any paradox of economic growth. Last, the suggestion that capitalist enterprise depends upon a legacy of moral practices which its very operation tends to corrode and in the end to destroy is made, not only by such recent writers as Joseph Schumpeter and the neo-conservatives, Daniel Bell and Irving Kristol, but also by the founding fathers of classical liberalism, Adam Ferguson and Adam Smith. It is well to remember the deep current of pessimism about the long-run prospects of liberal society expressed in the writings of its most distinguished early defenders in England and Scotland.

Hirsch's argument is not a new one in any of its several components, then, but these are fused into a synthesis which commands our attention and merits our critical scrutiny. Hirsch's argument demands serious analysis and assessment for a variety of reasons, but not least because it embodies important fallacies and errors and suggests policy implications which are bound to be disastrously self-defeating. The idea that the dwindling moral capital of liberal-democratic welfare capitalism opens up the real possibility of a morally consensual socialist order contains a manifest contradiction and depends on a highly disputable interpretation of the history of industrial capitalism. The idea of positionality which Hirsch deploys is very poorly specified and it gives a thoroughly misleading reading of the sources of current social scarcity. There is much to support the conjecture that the positionality of many of the goods that Hirsch mentions derives from the politicized and collectivist mode of their provision, so that their positionality would be increased, not diminished, by any further move to collectivism of the sort that Hirsch commends. Twentieth-century experience, inexplicably ignored by Hirsch and his disciples, shows that it is in socialist orders that goods such as education, housing, and access to favoured occupations acquire a degree of positionality beyond any possessed in societies containing a powerful market sector. Hirsch errs disastrously in his argument, not only in the account he gives of the sources of modern scarcity in the rise of the positional economy, but in his account of the forces which sustain the positional economy itself and, above all, in his prescriptions for resolving the distributional conflicts which the rise of the positional economy has engendered.

Let us look in greater detail at the weaknesses of Hirsch's argument, starting with the interpretation of history it rests upon. Much in Hirsch's book turns on the view, derived from the writings of Marx, and especially Engels, but popularized in such influential books as Karl Polanyi's *The Great Transformation* (1957), that the moral culture of possessive individualism, which is supposedly distinctive of our own societies, was engendered by the break-up of a feudal order and its replacement by capitalist industrialism sometime within the sixteenth, seventeenth, and eighteenth centuries. Before then, it is supposed by Hirsch and almost everyone else, men lived in extended families and small, exclusive communities, hierarchically organized and geographically almost immobile. With the expansion of trade in the sixteenth century in various parts of Europe and the emergence of a powerful bourgeoisie in Europe (to continue the conventional story), the old traditional order yielded to the new forces and its communal form of life was dissolved into an atomistic and proprietary individualism. Nor was the dislocation of the old order without hardship, for, on this conventional account, the rise of industrial capitalism precipitated a fall in the standard of life of the labouring classes. Any improvement in the living standards of the poor that undeniably occurred in the nineteenth century is explained, if not by reference to philanthropic endeavour, then by reference to the political pressures exerted by organized labour, which at length gave birth to the welfare state. The late twentieth-century crisis of capitalist legitimacy is then explained in terms of the exhaustion, after two centuries of strain, of its pre-capitalist moral foundations.

I think I do not exaggerate when I say that this immensely influential story, now revealed as utterly banal and commonplace, is an amalgam of half-truths, falsehoods, distortions, and groundless assertions. It is not at all clear, in the first place, that the social and geographical mobility and moral culture characteristic of possessive individualism came into being only with the rise of industrial capitalism. In England, at any rate, as Alan Macfarlane has shown in his brilliant *Origins of English Individualism* (1978), an individualist culture antedates the industrial revolution and goes back at least as far as the yeoman economy of the thirteenth century. There is little reason to suppose that a feudal order of the sort theorized by Polanyi in crudely Marxian terms everywhere preceded industrial capitalism, and much to suggest that, when industrial capitalism first appeared in England, it did so after centuries of agricultural, commercial, and social development on an individualist model. The great explosion of wealth and trade and the efflorescence of industrial innovation in the eighteenth and nineteenth centuries occurred in England, and arguably could only have occurred, against a background of long-standing political stability and civil liberty. Political institutions and the legal framework figure in this history, not as the passive reflections of autonomous economic developments pictured in the fables of historical materialism, but as the indispensable pre-conditions of the initiation and continuation of economic growth. Again, the forces of economic growth released in England in these times, far from wreaking havoc on a stagnant and immobile feudal order, accelerated greatly the slow improvement in general living standards, including those of the poorest classes, which had been going on for some time. As R. M. Hartwell (1977: 73–93) has convincingly argued, the massive growth in population and the increased consumption of former luxuries by ever larger sections of the population in England during the period of the early Industrial Revolution should make us suspicious of the entrenched assumption, fostered by Engels and by writers in the Romantic Tory tradition of anti-capitalist sentiment, that the poor were the losers by the early stages of capitalist industrial growth in England. Finally, and perhaps most crucially, the immemorial stability of individualist moral culture in England – at least six centuries long, if Macfarlane is to be believed – should make us reluctant to assent to the view that late twentieth-century economic and political difficulties are to be explained by reference to the alleged erosion of capitalism's basis in individualist morality and culture. If (as Hirsch and the rest suppose), liberal capitalism is a transitional political and economic order, the period of transition has in England been inordinately prolonged, stretching over just about the entirety of our recorded history.

If the pattern of historical interpretation, taken for granted in Hirsch's account, is deeply contestable, his use of the notion of a positional good to illuminate contemporary distributional conflicts is forced and unpersuasive. Consider, first, certain truisms about positional goods. It is clear that any imaginable human society will contain some positional goods. Wherever a conception of physical beauty is found, the genetic lottery will advantage some people over others in respect of the necessarily scarce attributes graded by the notion of beauty. (I leave aside here the possibilities of redistributive or compensatory cosmetic surgery explored in L. P. Hartley's anti-egalitarian dystopian novel, *Facial Justice*.) Any society stratified by reference to differences in prestige – that is, all known human societies – will contain competition for the roles or statuses conferring prestige. It cannot be Hirsch's argument that positional goods were unheard of before the advent of industrial capitalism.

Rather, we must interpret him as arguing that goods which did not have the property of positionality have acquired it in contemporary times. Or, more modestly and more plausibly, Hirsch may be arguing that the positionality of a good may be a matter of degree, as is the publicness of a good in public choice theory, when he asserts that the positionality of education, say, has been heightened in post-war capitalist orders. If this is Hirsch's claim, however, we are still left in the dark as to the *mechanism* whereby the positional character of education has of late been heightened. Certainly, there is nothing in Hirsch's book to render plausible the claim that economic growth alone exacerbates the positionality of key goods.

Consider in these respects the heyday of *laissez-faire* capitalism in Britain and the USA in the mid-nineteenth century. These were periods in which tremendous social mobility was combined with phenomenal economic growth. The goods of education, housing, and so on did not become noticeably more positional – rather the contrary. During this brief episode of unhampered market processes, British and American societies resembled closely Hayek's conception of the market order as a *catallaxy* in which a game of exchange combining skill and chance constantly redistributes income and wealth (1976: ch. 10). Such a catallactic order cannot help minimizing the positional character of the goods it contains, since there is no single path to their acquisition and no single power structure which distributes them. Education will still have a positional aspect and it will assist in the on-going competitive struggle, but it will not be the case that a person's whole future in life will be decided by the accident of his early education. The element of lottery distribution in the dispersion of positional goods in an unhampered market order itself does something to diminish their positional character, or at the very least, it tends to break or weaken the link between possession of one positional good (a superior education, say) and acquisition of another (a prestigious or lucrative occupation). The economic theorists of the free market have shown that it is to this period of unregulated market competition that the advanced nations owe much of their current wealth. My point is slightly different: I contend that it was during the brief episode of *laissez-faire* capitalism that the inevitable positionality of many important social goods was most diminished and rendered most palatable to genuine sentiments of justice.

What, then, if not any paradox of affluence or self-defeating effect of economic growth, does account for the sharp distributional struggles which have recently come to disfigure social life in the advanced capitalist societies? Before we can answer this question properly, we must pause and clear our mind of the cant surrounding the welfare state in Britain. Conventional historians of the welfare state have reinforced the moral complacency of their readers by representing the growth of state welfare institutions and policies as a result of disinterested altruism and moral will from which the poorest have been the greatest net gainers. Recent studies, undertaken at once by radical Marxists and by Friedmanites, have demonstrated that there is almost no shred of truth in this conventional view (Nozick 1974: 274–75). The greatest net beneficiaries from the welfare state in Britain have been the professional middle classes, whose political pull and social skills have enabled them to create and then to exploit a vast range of services largely sustained by tax subsidies derived from the poorer majority. The largest net losers from British welfarism, on the other hand, have been the working poor and the victims of the artificial poverty trap created by the extremely high marginal tax rates to which they are subject. Far from being a monument to altruism and moral disinterestedness, the welfare state in Britain has been a product of group self-interest in combination with the imperatives of party competition.

Perhaps a couple of examples taken from recent policy will help to demystify the processes which generated and now sustain the welfare state. In the field of housing policy, tax relief on mortgage interest payments, favourable treatment of capital gain on house sales, rent control, and the virtual disappearance of the private market in rental accommodation have together conferred on the home-owning majority in Britain a substantial windfall gain. (A similar situation exists in the USA, where zoning law has created opportunities for sizeable local profits on the part of business interests with political clout.) In education policy, the phasing out of selective grammar schools and their replacement by neighbourhood comprehensive schools has had the predicted result of closing the window of educational opportunity on the ablest offspring of the poor, and reinforcing the competitive advantage of less able children whose parents can afford housing in catchment areas containing schools with strong academic traditions. The effect of these recent policies in housing and education has been to enhance the positionality of these goods, and to link possession of the one with acquisition of the other. The end-result of policies of this sort can only be a new variant in the caste system, with little or no downward or upward social mobility. In the societies of the Soviet bloc, indeed, such a caste system has already been approximated, with only the black economy and the institution of the political purge providing some limited leeway for the redistribution of positional goods and the circulation of élites.

Far from satisfying any Rawlsian test of bettering the lot of the worst-off, the reluctant collectivism of modern capitalist states has merely institutionalized poverty by politicizing resource allocation. The politicization of poverty is, after all, an inevitable outcome of mass democracy unconstrained by constitutional limitations, in which the logic of party competition is bound to benefit majority interest groups. The single most important result of modern welfarism may thus be that, in reinforcing and rendering cumulative and rigid the inequalities of the market, it has transformed the advantages of market success into goods whose positional character is guaranteed by their political protection. The bitterness of current distributional conflicts is to be accounted for, not by any paradox of affluence, but by reference to the realities of party competition during a period of economic stagnation, and of almost zero growth. Regressive redistribution by the welfare state is tolerable politically when a booming market leaves almost everyone better-off, but its political price rapidly escalates when every transfer payment leaves someone absolutely worse-off. Contemporary distributional struggles only serve to confirm the insights of the nineteenth-century liberal critics of mass democracy, who anticipated the mutual predation it would allow but failed to foresee the long period of middle-class hegemony and self-enrichment through the political process which continuing economic advance permitted.

If Hirsch's diagnosis of current difficulties is so wide of the mark, it is only to be expected that his prescriptions for reform are misguided. It may be worth commenting at this point on the manifestly paradoxical character of Hirsch's call for a new economic order embodying a new moral consensus. If it were true, as Hirsch supposed, that post-war capitalism witnessed a dwindling moral consensus, what reason is there to think that a new consensus will replace the one that has disappeared? Remember that this new consensus will have an even more decisive legitimating role in any new socialist order, since in any such order all important resource allocation will be public and political. Agreed moral norms must be at hand to resolve allocational dilemmas which need never be faced in market societies. Ideas of social justice and of basic needs, which form the threadbare clothing of contemporary social democratic movements, are of minimal help here. Criteria of desert and merit, such as enter into popular conceptions of social justice, are not objective or publicly corrigible, but rather express private judgements grounded in varying moral traditions. Conceptions of merit are not shared as a common moral inheritance, neutrally available to the inner city Moslem population of Birmingham and the secularized professional classes of Hampstead, but instead reflect radically different cultural traditions and styles of life. It defies experience to suppose that any consensus on relative merits can be reached in a society so culturally diverse (and, for that reason, so free) as ours. Even if agreement could somehow be reached on the various ingredients of deserving or meritorious behaviour, people in different moral traditions would weigh these elements differently in the many instances where they came into practical competition with each other.

The objectivity of basic needs is equally delusive. Needs can be given no plausible cross-cultural content, but instead are seen to vary across different moral traditions. Even where moral traditions overlap so as to allow agreement to be reached on a list of basic needs, there are no means of arriving at an agreed schedule of urgency among conflicting basic needs. Again, not all basic needs are even in principle satiable. Think only of medical needs connected with senescence. These are surely basic needs in that their non-satisfaction will result in death or a worthless life, but (contrary to the quietly apocalyptic hopes which inspired the writers of the Beveridge Report) there is no natural limit on the resources which could be devoted to satisfying them. There is an astonishing presumptuousness in those who write as if hard dilemmas of this sort can be subject to morally consensual resolution. Their blindness to these difficulties can only be accounted for by their failing to take seriously the realities of cultural pluralism in our society, or (what comes to the same thing) to their taking as authoritative their own traditional values. One of the chief functions of the contemporary ideology of social justice may be, as Hayek intimates, to generate an illusion of moral agreement, where in fact there are profound divergencies of values. It remains unclear how such divergencies are to be overcome, save by the political conquest of state power and the subjugation of rival value systems.

The traditional defence of market freedom – that it permits different cultures and value systems to live in peaceful co-existence – has never been more relevant or more neglected than it is now. The appeal of social democracy, and of Hirsch's fantasy of a new economic order expressing a new moral consensus, depends upon a blindness to the incommensurable value systems expressed in the many moral traditions which our society contains. It presupposes a degree of moral solidarity unknown in contemporary Europe except in war-time. If the idea that the market could be supplanted by democratic procedures of resource allocation is nothing but a chimera, we should not (on the other hand) neglect the political difficulties of any attempt to free the market from political regulations. The project of reviving the unhampered market as envisaged in classical liberalism and refined by Hayek and Friedman does not confront all of the dilemmas faced by Hirsch in as much as the agreement the free market needs if it is to work is only on procedural rules and not on substantive outcomes. No one should underestimate, however, the obstacles to be encountered in gaining general assent to procedural principles of market justice. Apart from the purely intellectual problems in the theory of initial property rights and of rectificatory justice (Nozick 1974: ch. 7), there is a massive political obstacle in the entrenched privileges of groups that benefit from the prevailing order. The anti-capitalist mentality of the dominant intelligentsia itself creates a climate in which it is unrealistic to expect political efforts at the restoration of free markets to be judged fairly. And the sheer contingencies of political and economic life mean that attempts to end inflation or to curb union power as prolegomena to the restoration of a viable market order are bound to inflict undeserved losses on some sectors of the population.

The political prospects of a revival of classical liberalism are bleak, even if the intellectual foundations of such a project are sounder than any social democratic project oriented around conceptions of basic needs or positional goods. The deep-rooted collectivist prejudices of the modern intelligentsia, in conjunction with the economic interests which benefit from interventionism, together form a formidable obstacle to any pro-gramme of limiting the state and depoliticizing resource allocation by returning it to the unhampered market. Public choice theory itself, which explains the losses inflicted by group interest politics, also shows how difficult it is to reverse the process of increasing state intervention in economic life once it has started. (A good treatment of this question is found in Tullock 1974.) It may well be that the development of democratic institutions has over the long run a self-defeating effect seeing that it generates demands for the political control of economic life which are inconsistent with the continued functions of democracy. This view has been argued for by a distinguished lineage of liberal thinkers, including our contemporary, Samuel Brittan (1977). The upshot of my argument, however, is that if, as contemporary libertarians and the Marxian theorists of legitimation crisis both believe, the political institu-tions of welfare capitalism cannot for long stand the strain currently being placed upon them, the way out is not towards the chimera of new co-operative order imagined by Hirsch. Whatever the difficulties, we must search for constitutional limitations on political intervention in economic life, if we are not to be saddled with the permanent legitimation crisis of real-world socialism, and all the Hobbesian competition for the supreme positional good of power that that brings with it.

References

BRITTAN, S. (1977) *The Economic Consequences of Democracy*. London: Temple Smith.

HARTWELL, R. M. (1977) Capitalism and the Historians. In *Essays on Hayek*. London: Routledge and Kegan Paul.

HAYEK, F. A. (1976) *Law Legislation and Liberty: The Mirage of Social Justice* vol 2. London: Routledge and Kegan Paul.

HIRSCH, F. (1977) *Social Limits to Growth*. London: Routledge and Kegan Paul.

MACFARLANE, A. (1978) *The Origins of English Individualism*. Oxford: Blackwell.

NOZICK, R. (1974) *Anarchy, State and Utopia*. Oxford: Basil Blackwell.

POLANYI, K. (1957) *The Great Transformation*. Boston: Beacon.

TULLOCK, G. (1974) *The Social Dilemma*. Blacksburg: University Publications.

10 Market failure: Fred Hirsch and the case for social democracy

COLIN CROUCH

An author who addresses politically sensitive themes on his own terms, avoiding the clichés of the day, must expect to be variously interpreted. For some conservatives, *Social Limits to Growth* spoke to the mood of pessimism they were adopting in the late 1970s: since the workers have forgotten how to keep their places, and growth cannot satisfy their strivings for certain kinds of goods, why put so much effort into the inflationary pursuit of growth? And so there can be what one might call 'right-wing Hirschians'.[1] Others on the right have been more aware that Fred Hirsch had opened a seam of vulnerability in the intellectual defence of the free-market economy, and disliked it. John Gray in this volume is among those more discerning observers.

This does not mean that Hirsch has been generally welcomed as a friend on the left, as Peter Taylor-Gooby's reading of his work in this volume shows. He sees Hirsch as expressing conventional views about the damaging consequences of a pursuit of equality that is erroneously seen (by Hirsch) as having been successful, and the ill consequences of a collapse of Victorian morality which, Taylor-Gooby believes, is also prematurely announced. This, too, I shall try to show, is a mis-reading of Hirsch. In my view his achievement was to demonstrate many of the social costs of the extension of market rationality, not by pitting an emotional and moral appeal against that rationality, as do so many social critics, but by using the methods of modern economic analysis itself. The individual arguments are not necessarily original – he acknowledges a wide range of sources – but they are marshalled powerfully and cumulatively.

The political implications of Hirsch's arguments are not simple; it is incorrect for Gray to describe him as a utopian socialist. One is at liberty to accept many of his arguments about the costs of the market and still decide the price is worth paying. In other cases the forces that gain and lose from an extension of commercial calculation are ranged on unexpected sides of the political divide. In other cases again he is simply pointing out some of the follies of human behaviour that are likely to be beyond the reach of political or economic remedy. (This is neither a useless nor a nihilistic lesson; knowledge of one's limitations is highly practical if frequently unheeded knowledge.) In the main, however, the political contribution of *Social Limits to Growth* lies in its analysis of the costs of reliance on the free market as the main means of pursuing human ends, that is the cost of the policies of the so-called new right, that political force currently dominant in Washington, Bonn, London, and several major international economic agencies.

Hirsch grouped his arguments under three main headings: the question of social scarcity, or the pursuit of positional goods; the commercialization bias of the market economy; and the depleting moral legacy of capitalism. I agree with some of the reservations of his critics concerning both the historicism and the explanatory power of the first and third of these, though the critics exaggerate the strength of their attack. In contrast, Hirsch underplayed his second theme, treating it rather as a secondary consequence of the positional problem. Rather, I see in this theme of commercialization a powerful general analysis of the ways in which the free market often opposes or inhibits free choice, a phenomenon of which his other two themes can in fact be seen as particular cases. In the following I shall try to re-assess the arguments on positional economy and moral legacy and then to demonstrate what I see as his larger argument.

The positional economy

By positional goods Hirsch means those goods (or, more commonly, those aspects of goods) the enjoyment of which is dependent on their non-possession by others. This may happen either (a) because satisfaction is derived *directly* from the fact that others do not have the good (e.g. the satisfaction that derives from being a trend-setter in fashion), or (b) because although the good is sought for its own sake, possession of it by others *incidentally* interferes with its enjoyment (i.e. through the phenomenon of crowding or congestion).

Thus, the demand for a good has potentially two components: an intrinsic one for the good as such, and a positional one, which is the demand to be able to enjoy it without congestion. In the case of large numbers of goods (such as potatoes, newspapers, underwear) we can ignore positional quality. Now, as affluence grows, demand for goods rises, and this demand includes both that for the intrinsic qualities of goods and that for any positional qualities they have. However, increased supply can meet only the intrinsic demand; by definition it cannot increase the positional component – indeed, it gradually *destroys* it. This might not happen in the very early stages; as Ellis and Heath point out (in this volume), a small increase in the number of people adopting a fashion will not spoil its fashionability. Similarly, the initial increases in traffic on empty roads cause no congestion. In these early stages positional supply does in fact rise; this is the moment of optimal satisfaction from growth. But this cannot continue for long; *gradually* crowding becomes evident.

Supply of positional qualities can only be increased alongside continuing affluence if the number of people contending for position is reduced by the opening of *new, substitute, but non-competitive arenas of consumption.* Ellis and Heath, in effect, describe such processes. However, they are wrong to see this as a long-term solution. First, the demand elasticity of the development of new arenas will typically be much lower than that of the supply of the initial goods through longer production runs. But even when the new arenas are developed, they may be disappointing. If they are substitutes, they are probably able to be compared, and hence the condition of non-competitiveness will not be fulfilled; there will be positional competition for access to the best arenas. Further, as new arenas multiply, there may arise a congestion of arenas, alongside the original problem of congestion *within* individual arenas.

These abstract points can be illustrated. An increase in demand for travel facilities/urban residence/holidays/dresses will comprise an *intrinsic* component (the desire to move around/to be near urban amenities/to relax in a pleasant natural environment/to be presentably clothed) and a *positional* component (to do so without being slowed by traffic jams/without overcrowding/without being surrounded by thousands of other people/with what will be generally recognized as distinctive taste). Supply responds by increasing production of cars/flats and houses/hotels at holiday resorts/and mass-produced dresses. This meets the intrinsic demand but *at the same time* generates crowded roads/over-populated cities/crowded beaches/undistinctive, run-of-the-mill physical appearances. Positional quality can only be regained by construction of new roads (which takes longer than production of new cars)/design of new cities (which takes longer than adding flats and houses to existing ones)/development of new holiday resorts (which takes longer than adding hotels to existing ones)/designing new dress styles (which takes longer than producing more copies of old ones). However, eventually, the new roads/cities/resorts/styles appear. But some roads are found to be faster and generally better/some cities have better amenities/some resorts are more beautiful or sunny/some dress styles are considered to be superior. Competition for the inherently limited favoured cases becomes intense. Furthermore, people begin to complain that the countryside is over-run by roads/there are just too many conurbations/there are no longer any unspoiled beaches/there are so many dress styles that it is impossible to distinguish good taste. Affluence has everywhere increased; nearly everyone has more of all sorts of goods, but there is a general feeling that many of them are shoddy and 'not what they were'.

When the demand for the intrinsic qualities of a good slumps as it becomes widespread, the trend-setters will move on to something new until they are followed there by everybody else, and so on, leaving behind a debris of unwanted, temporarily enjoyed products. This is the case of those markets heavily dominated by fashion, such as popular music, clothes, and certain kinds of art.[2]

Leadership positions may be similarly analysed. If there is a growth in the number of leadership positions, we must ask: do these occupy space which used to be monopolized by existing sources of power, or do they open completely new areas of organizational activity with which existing sources had been entirely unconcerned? If it is the former, then congestion of leadership space will occur; only the latter constitute the opening of new arenas. For example, the organization of workers in firms previously without unions; the emergence of a new pressure group lobbying an existing government department; the establishment of a new charity within a field already occupied by existing charities[3] – will all create conditions analogous to crowding. Existing leadership groups will experience less room for manoeuvre and autonomy; the newcomers will find less scope for wielding power than they had expected on the basis of their prior observation of the behaviour of existing power-holders. It is interesting that, following the rise of a large number of pressure- and interest-groups during the 1960s, we heard precisely complaints of this kind on behalf of established political élites; the whole literature on 'ungovernability' and 'pluralistic stagnation' can be seen as the political equivalent of complaints about traffic jams by those accustomed to have the roads to themselves (see, for example, Crozier, Huntingdon, and Watanaki 1975; Dahl 1982; Rose and Peters 1978).

But the opening of new arenas for leadership activity does occur. The biggest single example was probably the settlement and government of colonies during the eighteenth and nineteenth centuries. Less dramatically, new issue areas can be opened where few existing groups are trying to exercise leadership: a recent example would be gay rights. However, similar problems occur as with the more physical examples of attempts to relieve congestion. First, fields of leadership will be ranked. Second, and probably more important here, even groups in different arenas of life are competing for some important resources: membership and members' time, money, political attention, publicity within established media. Just as an increasing number of roads leads to complaints about the country becoming covered with tarmac, so there are complaints that governments have to respond to masses of different issues, that too many areas of life are being politicized, that too many charities compete for public attention and money. Power need not be strictly zero-sum for political space to become congested.

Economic growth and rising affluence enable increasing numbers of us to enjoy more goods; but wherever part of the enjoyment of the good is impaired by the presence of many others doing the same, there will be a concomitant decline in the quality of the goods, leading to disappointment and disenchantment. Since there will always be some people who reach the head of the queue, this disappointment will lead to efforts to be among these few. This leads to what Hirsch calls the 'distributional struggle' for higher income and to the acquisition of wasteful 'secondary goods'.[4] As Hirsch shows, to the extent that our striving for goods is positional, it is rational to seek to earn *more than other people* rather than simply to earn *more*, as positional struggle is by definition relative. Taylor-Gooby, in his contribution to this volume, takes 'distributional struggle' to mean 'tendency towards equality', and therefore tries to refute Hirsch by showing how weak any such tendency has been. But clearly there need be no assumption of egalitarianism in distributional struggle; it might concern one vice-president of the Ford Motor Company striving to earn more than the other vice-presidents.

The implications of the positional goods argument are varied, and no one can make unequivocal political capital from them. To a large extent Hirsch is pointing to the ineluctable hopelessness of much human striving, to the folly of pretending that material effort can produce human happiness. This gives point to some of his later arguments, when he considers the opportunity costs of the pursuit of growth through extensions of economic efficiency and market rationality; some of the gains from that growth which we are invited to weigh in the scales are offset by the fact that expanding material wealth will not bring the satisfaction it seems to promise.

But he strikes in particular at some key tenets of free-market doctrine. First, he shows that competition will not always have the productive consequences claimed for it: the expenditure on secondary goods which positional competition generates is wasteful.

Second, the injunction of defenders of market forces and their consequent inequalities that people should look to the overall size of the cake, and not worry about the size of individual slices, is shown to be futile. If I seek, say, not just a comfortable and roomy house, but one that will be generally recognized as the 'best in the neighbourhood', then no amount of *general* improvement will satisfy me. I need to know that my income is going to be able to buy me a *better* house than those with whom I compare myself.

Third, the claim that the free market, by improving efficiency and therefore growth, will realize many of man's wants, is shown to be limited in scope; the intensity of market competition for possession only sharpens the appetite for positional goals which must always prove elusive for the many.

Hirsch's proposals for alleviating part of our predicament constitute a novel reformulation of certain socialist ideas. First, he argues for less inequality, though on more substantial grounds than the usual socialist claim that somehow equality seems right. He proposes alleviating the excessive competition for positional goods by disengaging the positional component from more intrinsic goals (1977: 182–87). In this way those who are mainly interested in the positional component should expect to be able to enjoy little more than that. The main example he gives, and it is the most important, concerns the pursuit of 'top' jobs.[5] Given that people desire these jobs for their positional qualities, it is unnecessary to attract candidates to them by the offer of large salaries; a reduction in their salaries would therefore reduce wasteful competition.

Similar arguments can be applied to concentrations of *power* in leading positions. To the extent that it is the label of occupying the leading post that matters, there can be considerable delegation of the substantive power wielded by its holder, so that those who mainly seek power can be diverted from the contest. This is after all how Europe's surviving monarchies made themselves safe.

Second, Hirsch argues for the public provision of certain goods and services on a basis that escapes much of the charge of paternalism usually thrown at such advocacy by defenders of the free market. If a good is owned publicly and made readily available, its positional quality disappears altogether; no one may 'possess' it. Furthermore, there is no need for people to strive for increased income which they spend on wasteful secondary consumption in order to get it. This argument does not just make the case for public art galleries and public parks, but also for some aspects of the welfare state. The positional nature of education as a means of gaining qualifications for jobs is stressed by Hirsch. But the demand for education, health, and other goods characterized by their being (a) considered 'important' and (b) difficult to assess, may also have a further positional component. People wishing to do 'the best possible' (that is, making an intrinsic demand) for themselves or their families with respect to one of these goods, may have difficulty knowing what constitutes the best possible. They solve this information problem by doing 'at least as much' as they can see being done by those they take as their reference group; as others spend more, so do they, without necessarily considering what is being gained. The good has acquired an incidental positional component, and increments in spending on it may considerably outweigh any gains in the intrinsic good being obtained.

As Hirsch himself points out (1977: 106–07), certain kinds of public spending are themselves an aspect of positional competition: for example, the pursuit of education as a means of improving job prospects or the construction of roads to relieve traffic congestion. But high-quality public provision can reduce the pressure on people to indulge in wasteful private expenditure in order to obtain the good in question. Of course, so long as people are able to enter private markets for, say, education, existing alongside public provision, they will do so as part of positional competition; even if few real benefits are to be gained that way, people will be convinced that if they spend extra money they must be getting some benefit for it. Hirsch's expectation that an extension of public provision would reduce positional competition is therefore likely to be valid only if alternative private provision is prevented, made difficult, or forced by a demonstrably excellent public service to compete in what become obviously increasingly trivial ways. What Hirsch gives us here is a guideline for public intervention: where the pursuit of a good through private means is clearly leading to demonstrably wasteful secondary competition, there is an *a priori* case for public provision. Of course, it remains to be decided in each case whether the competition is occurring in an area of life sufficiently important to justify public-policy concern; some may argue that that is still paternalism, though others may contend that it is simply political decision making.

The moral legacy

The nub of the 'moral legacy' thesis, which claims an ancestry going back to Adam Smith himself, is that, while capitalism is considerably assisted if certain assumptions can be made about behaviour (trust, restraint, honesty), it cannot itself generate such norms, but has historically depended on their inculcation by pre-capitalist moralities (such as religion).[6] Worse, capitalist conduct actively erodes and destroys these underpinning values, not because of the moral depravity of capitalists, but because these values are public goods. Hirsch's argument here is strikingly similar to that of Daniel Bell (1976) in *The Cultural Contradictions of Capitalism*, though strengthened in its explanation of capitalism's corrosive effect on morality by the use of public goods theory.

As stated by Hirsch, the historicism of the argument is vulnerable to attack, and on this point Gray's critique strikes home. Commercialization is now very old, at least in Britain. Exactly when was the moral legacy acquired: before the Tudor period? Yet Adam Smith thought it was just coming under threat in his day; while contemporary bewailers of a decline in moral restraint usually look back to a Victorian moral high-water mark – a century after Adam Smith! Arguments about once-and-for-all historical shifts tread slippery ground. In the late nineteenth century sociologists spoke of the once-and-for-all loss of community as people moved from rural villages to the anonymity of industrial working-class urban settlements (see the account of these themes in Nisbet (1966)); in the 1950s Young and Wilmott (1957) wrote of the loss of community as people moved from nineteenth-century industrial working-class urban settlements to suburban council estates. It is easy, when observing a powerful process of social change, to overlook man's capacity to reconstruct and re-invent. Hirsch overlooked the fact that the rationality of calculative commercialization is opposed by a rationality of trust and community.

The rationality of calculation leads us to assess scrupulously our gains and losses, but the suspension of this process is not necessarily non-rational. Calculation takes time and effort: it is a transaction cost that is by no means negligible. As Shonfield (1982: 63–4) has pointed out, even ordinary buyers and sellers in the market often rely on mutual trust rather than 'shop around' for each new transaction in true market fashion. Further, when we are objects of calculation by others we are mistrusted and subject to suspicion, and we may offer trust in the hope of reciprocal action which will reduce this burden. It is probably possible to write the history of most human institutions in terms of alternations between trust and calculation, with bursts of the latter (based on the need to adjust to change and innovation or on evidence of past bad faith) being followed by attempts by the parties to relax again and allow trust to grow. Major periods of social change, such as the industrial revolution itself, or a smaller process of economic and social adjustment such as the west has been experiencing for several years, will involve particularly strong extensions of calculation or commercialization, but they do not necessarily invade all corners of life without resistance, neither are they irreversible.

The important antagonism at the heart of Hirsch's discussion is that between (a) pure rational calculation of the costs and benefits that actors derive from a relationship, and (b) a willingness to maintain and strengthen a relationship *per se*, at the expense of calculation of the costs and benefits incurred. It is only under the latter conditions that the parties to a relationship can develop such qualities as trust for their own sake, that is as public goods and not as part of the coinage of exchange. It is the same opposition that Alan Fox (1974) made central to his very similar theory of industrial relations. We can set out this antagonism in abstract terms, without initially specifying the context in which the relationship exists. Actor A, from whose point of view we shall consider the situation, comes into a relationship with actor B. As exchanges occur in this relationship, A is suspicious that he/she/it/they[7] may get the worse of them; he therefore calculates carefully what he is getting from B and what he is giving in exchange, and will try to ensure that he does not give more than is necessary to maintain the exchange. If he feels he is losing from these exchanges, he may try to reduce his contributions or contemplate leaving the relationship altogether. However, whether he can do this will depend upon the obstacles in his way of so doing and upon the availability of alternative means of securing those gains which he has been getting from B. (This point is crucial; without recognition of it one tends to assume that, if exchange relations are continuing, they must in some ways be 'equal'. *A contrario*, if it is easier for one partner to leave the relationship, or if the relationship is less central to his fulfilment of needs, or if he has more alternatives available, or if he can coerce the other partner to remain, then the relationship will continue on one-sided terms, the weaker partner making the best of a bad job. For a full discussion of unequal exchange relations, see Blau (1964).

Two developments may happen to relax the degree of calculation which the actors bring to their relationship.[8] First, the interactions between A and B may become so great in number and heterogeneous (and therefore difficult to measure) that the effort of calculating gains and losses may not be worth making. A's experience to date tells him that he is making many gains as well as incurring losses; that what he loses today he will make up some time in the future; and that he and B are so intertwined with each other than it is unlikely that B will trick him. He therefore continues to make his exchanges on the basis of *trust* that overall he is not losing. A relationship of this kind can be called a community.

Alternatively – or additionally – the relationship may be so durable, and/or so intense (that is, important to A), and/or extensive (that is, touching so many aspects of his life), that his own *experience of himself* includes the relationship with B; the relationship has become 'part of himself', and he feels part of it. In such a situation, the very notion of an exchange with B alters; one can have an exchange only with an external 'other'. To the extent that A *identifies* with the relationship with B, then exchanges become internal transfers and the idea of calculation becomes irrelevant. Such a situation goes beyond trust, incorporating it, and can be called love.[9] (Blau (1964: 76–85) provides a different account of love analysed in terms of exchange.)

Provided some of the criteria of frequency of interaction, some gains to offset losses, duration, intensity, and extensiveness are met, the most unequal, even compulsory exchanges may generate trust and even love. Trust and love may also be quite one-sided; history has provided many examples of these paradoxes: serfs and lords, workers and employers, unrequited lovers. It is notable that Fox's (1974) examples of high-trust industrial relations include paternalistic employers as well as participative co-operatives.

Relations of trust, community, and love are those in which calculations of partisan advantage have been suspended by at least one of the parties to it. In each case there are potential gains to be had by an attempt to quantify and assess contributions against rewards and to measure different balances that might be obtainable within alternative relationships; and in each case the introduction of such calculation will diminish trust, love, and community. This is a fundamental choice which confronts us all the time in all our relationships. We evaluate trusting as opposed to calculative behaviour differently in different contexts, and we disagree with each other about some of these evaluations. The reader may test this by re-reading the account given above of A and B while evaluating the propriety of the advice to A never to relax his calculative approach to B, having replaced the abstract relationship A:B by, successively, the following: wife: husband; conscripted soldier:military authorities; parent:child; shareholder:company in which he has shares; worker:employer; businessman:loss-making factory owned by him.

Such an exercise raises awkward problems for everybody's politics: there is little scope in the real world for a 'calculative' party advocating easy divorce, the right of soldiers to disobey orders, the trading of children, normal stock-exchange activity, militant trade unionism, and the closure of all loss-making factories; nor for a 'community' party advocating the opposite. This is however a difficulty which the political right can solve far more easily than the left. I have stressed the possibility of at least one-sided trust developing in situations where the weaker party to a relationship has little chance to leave it however disadvantageous the exchanges – this would include those situations that Ellis and Heath call coerced exchanges. If it is possible to structure a society so that all the 'As' in relationships who one wishes to see develop attitudes of trust towards their various 'Bs' have poor opportunities for leaving those relationships, one may blithely commend highly calculative approaches everywhere else in society without fear of 'calculative contamination'. Provided divorce is made difficult, soldiers subjected to ruthless discipline, unemployment kept high, and trade unions subordinated to repressive legislation, a reactionary will have little to fear from an extension of commercialization. It is difficult to put together an equivalent package of constraints from the left, as the positions which the left defends are by definition those of subordinates.

Hirsch considered such a reversion to this 'conservative strand of liberalism' as 'now morally and politically unthinkable' (1977: 188–89), but he wrote that a few years before the rise of Ronald Reagan, Margaret Thatcher, and Franz-Josef Strauss. However, we have yet to see for how long the rethinkable can become the practicable.

What emerges most forcefully from this consideration of the reactionary alternative is that, in order to pursue it, the free-market doctrine is required to relinquish its claim to be the high road to freedom of choice. The market is able to permit freedom only within a carefully limited area ringed by coercion over those who might wish to make disapproved choices as a result of their rational calculation. This leads to the general theme of the market's opposition to free choice which I regard as having been Hirsch's major under-recognized contribution in *Social Limits to Growth*.

The market as the enemy of free choice

To extend market rationality to an area of life means to provide only those goods within it, the gains from which can be privately appropriated. Goods are therefore stripped to their bare, tradable essentials. In many cases this makes them inferior, even 'spoiled' goods compared with what they might have been under systems of provision that could avoid this problem. The example of this cheapening effect of commercialization which Hirsch deploys to greatest effect is that of sex (1977: appendix to ch. 6). He also uses it to give a needed theoretical base to Titmuss's arguments (1970) that commercial supplies of blood for medical transfusions are likely to be inferior to the publicly organized voluntary system typical of the British National Health Service (1977: 94, 141).

To the extent that we are dependent on market provision, we are unable to demand non-tradable goods or the non-tradable aspects of goods; that is one limitation on freedom that the market requires. But the limitation goes further. Within the realm of market transactions it is impossible for consumers to register their dissatisfaction with this process, because of what Hirsch calls the 'tyranny of small decisions' (1977: 79). The market makes available certain options, and in choosing among them we make incremental, short-term decisions. He provides some good examples of how this prevents us making larger decisions or from perceiving the long-term consequences of our small choices:

> 'purchase of books at discount stores eventually removes the local bookshop. Yet bookbuyers can never exercise a choice as between cheaper books with no bookshops and dearer books with one. The choice they are offered is between books at cut price and books at full price; naturally they take the former. The effective choice of continuance of a bookshop at the expense of dearer books is never posed.'
> (1977: 40)

He goes on to give a similar account of the effect on cities and suburbs of an apparent choice between living in the one or the other.

It must be acknowledged that this inability to make strategic choices is in part a valid defence of the market system's democracy: in such a situation none of us can impose his will on everybody else, as happens in command economies. Nevertheless, it remains relevant to consider the lesser tyranny of small decisions. (Indeed market democracy is somewhat spoiled by the fact that very large consumers – not just governments, but also large corporations – are able to get beyond the problem of small decisions by ordering highly specific goods designed to meet their precise needs. In order to do this they develop close *organizational* relationships with suppliers, replacing market mechanisms with what Williamson (1975) calls 'hierarchy'.)

Hirsch's argument here is similar to that developed by his near namesake, A. O. Hirschman in *Exit, Voice and Loyalty* (1970). 'Exit' and 'voice' are contrasting ways in which people may express dissatisfaction with what they are offered.[10] Exit is the mode characteristic of market behaviour: we can buy a good or leave it on the shelf. The attractions of this are that the consumer's action is immediate and individual; it requires no organization or co-operation. Its disadvantages are its passivity; if no suitable good is available, one has no opportunity of suggesting one and there is no chance to propose improvements to the poor goods. This is virtually identical to Hirsch's tyranny of small decisions. Voice is the mode characteristic of participative politics:[11] we have a chance actively to speak our minds about what is wrong with the goods on offer, to suggest improvements to them, and voice ideas about goods not being offered. Voice acts collectively; this is a strength in so far as it frees us from the limitations of the lone individuals, but it is also its weakness. The exercise of voice is vulnerable to all the well-known problems of exercising collective action (see Olson 1965), as well as those of securing consensus or at least appropriate majorities.

To limit freedom of choice to those alternatives which the market and exit are able to provide is to restrict them severely. The only solution to this problem within the logic of commercialization is to find ways of privatizing as many of the gains from initially public goods as possible; but this too brings constraints on freedom. For example, if a neglected piece of common land is taken into private ownership,[12] it will be improved by the new owner, who may then let people have access to it in return for payment of an entry charge; but this requires controls and restrictions to prevent non-paying use. As Hirsch points out:

'a common facility can give satisfaction in itself. Its loss through commercialization involving exclusion both removes one item in the circle of economic choice and curtails personal liberty in various dimensions, for example of movement. This restriction needs to be put in the scale against the increase in narrow efficiency. . . . Privatization will also affect the distribution of income. Unless the system of tax or other form of finance supporting the public good is extremely regressive, privatization will be detrimental to the poor, by removing what to them (though not of course to society) was a free good.'

(1977: 92)

A recent example of this process occurred early in 1983, when the owner of Land's End decided to commodify this unique English landmark by charging for entry to it. So, in the name of extending freedom of choice through the market, turnstiles and barriers are erected and a little bureaucracy of ticket inspectors established. Of course, we still have the freedom of exit – to choose not to visit Land's End; but the market does not allow the public to decide whether this kind of exclusion should be permitted at all – that requires voice and 'interfering' politics.

Sometimes we may opt for expensive, regulated entry to a privatized facility in preference to either not having it at all or having it provided in polluted or neglected form. But the uncontrolled extension of markets does not give us the option: if private owners buy up all the best beaches, then so be it. To acquire more freedom of choice than this requires (a) government regulation of the conduct of private ownership, for example to prevent the pollution of public goods; and/or (b) government guarantee of the provision of public goods.[13] As with positional goods, we are led to a reformulation of socialist policies, this time presenting public intervention as a means of extending choices that the market does not permit.

However, it remains true that political action, spurred by the voice mechanism, is an unwieldy device, and capacity to have recourse to it is unequally and arbitrarily distributed (as indeed is ability to compete in the free market). Olson, who earlier (1965) formulated the difficulties that stood in the way of constituting the interest organizations which are needed to give effect to voice in pluralist societies, has recently (1982) argued *against* the role of such organizations as are able to form. His argument becomes a defence of the free market. Such bodies as trade unions or business cartels are, according to Olson, highly likely to inhibit economic growth, because for them it is a public good. Their purpose is to defend existing interests; existing interests will be threatened by change; growth means change. These organizations, which appropriate the gains which flow from keeping their membership intact and looking after its immediate interests, but which can appropriate no gain from contributions they might make to promoting growth, will oppose growth-related changes that contribute to the general good.

Much of this deserves to be taken seriously. However, following Hirsch's analysis, we should carefully inspect what it is that special interests are defending against market forces; are there some further public goods lurking there that will be swept away if the cold winds of the free market blow unchecked? It should be noted that the freedom of Olson's market economy enables man to choose just one goal: economic growth. To return to Hirsch's bookshop example, Olson (1982) would take a low view of an organization of bookshop owners seeking retail price maintenance to protect them from discount stores, even though their success would preserve greater choice of book outlets for consumers. It may be a poor world in which we are left dependent on the serendipitous public goods buried within the special pleading of organized lobbies; but often the free market would deny us even that. The answer lies in improving the quality of our pluralism so that a greater number of interests receive expression and influence, not in cutting out the process altogether.

A similar argument applies to inflation when this is seen as a consequence of the politicization of economics. On this account, inflation occurs because governments have responded to pressures to provide a range of spending programmes which they are unwilling or unable to finance without deficit. The solution widely canvassed among free-market economists is that, to prevent this recurring, there should be permanent limits on governments' ability to spend money, expressed either through constitutional provisions or the power of some such non-elected body as the central bank. Such limits constitute a constraint on freedom of choice: they prevent governments responding to pressures to provide high levels of spending, spending which will usually be used to pursue goals not possible through the market; and they prevent the temporary use of inflation as one of the options for alleviating social tensions. True, a government that allows inflation to take place will eventually be forced to take deflationary action, and some damage may be done to the economy in the process. But the freedom to make mistakes may be considered a freedom with which it is 'paternalist' to interfere. And again, to use inflation as the pretext for imposing permanent constraints on governments is to prevent people having the chance to choose those goods which free markets cannot provide.

Attempts at working out an appropriate division of labour between market and political processes are bedevilled by the polemic of free-market advocates that feeds on the uneven nature of the institutions' tasks. This is unfortunately a point that is omitted by Robert Lane (in this volume) in his appraisal of the two. The market demonstrates its great precision because it eschews the production of public goods and all choices that cannot be embraced within the tyranny of small decisions. When the omissions and flaws of the issues which then get neglected become blatant, special lobbies develop to try to engender action to deal with them; the polity receives as its agenda those tasks which the market has failed to accomplish; and is then compared adversely with the market for its inability to tackle its agenda with the efficiency that the market brought to bear on those issues it did accept! If heavy goods vehicles break up the roads, people do not blame the haulage companies or the firms whose goods are being transported; after all, they have to earn their living. They blame the county council for not repairing the roads quickly enough, though they will also complain if it charges higher rates in order to maintain larger road-repair staffs.

The whole matter is further confounded by the fact that the political process does not just represent the interests of the people who want something done about market failures, but also those who have an interest in ensuring a low level of government intervention – who go on to use the polity's inability to perform its functions as evidence of the superiority of market forces. Perhaps the most blatant single example of this would be Conservatives comparing private health care favourably with the National Health Service after they have reduced the latter's budget.

Conclusions

None of these arguments make possible a blanket rejection of market processes. In each case we can weigh the costs and benefits of commercialization. While in many areas of our lives we may be willing to sacrifice a good deal of calculative efficiency for some human trust and community, there are other transactions we would prefer to be as minimal and specific as possible so that we may conserve our resources for those relationships to which we choose to commit them. The erection of barriers and policing is an infringement of liberty, but without them many goods would not be produced. We have to tread with care and try to define the contexts where the market's gains in efficiency outweigh its losses in alternative goods, and *vice versa*. Doing this is the stuff of politics.

That last simple assertion says a good deal. It is only if politics are allowed to enter that the possibility of making many choices arises; and by politics one means, not just the actions of governments and parties, but the whole array of interest organizations that make voice possible. But at the present time the difficulties of this process, and the problems it presents for interests dominant in the free market, have led to a powerful pressure to put society on automatic pilot by clearing away whole areas of political intervention and allowing market forces to run free. This is always done in the name of freedom of choice. But the more the logic of the market, of commercialization, and of pure accountancy judgements is allowed to be the unimpeded criterion for decision-making, the less able we are to make those choices which the market inhibits and which politics alone make possible; and the less able we are to pursue those values which the market destroys. This is the fallacy at the heart of the claim of men like Hayek and Friedman[14] that the market facilitates choice while state intervention regulates choice away. Certainly a full-blown command economy excludes choice, but a heavily market-dominated one limits and trivializes it. So far the most sensitive, though still inadequate, mechanism which human society has developed for improving the scope of human choice is that combination of amended markets, state intervention, and active group politics that has generally become known as social democracy. It is that approach which has been so heavily reviled by the recent revival of the advocates of the *laissez faire* economy. Fred Hirsch's book has many messages, but the one which is most urgent and timely now is that which demonstrates the false basis of so much of that attack and makes possible a revised defence of social democracy.

Notes

1. Examples might include those who analysed the conflicts of the late 1960s and 1970s in terms of the inability of the market economy to cope with a combination of raised expectations among the masses of their entitlements, together with the collapse of traditional deference. See, for example, Wiles (1973: 378, 392); Mishan (1974); Brittan (1975).
2. Those who make it their priority to pursue the positional element of artistic taste, i.e. fashion, may sometimes sacrifice intrinsic goals for its sake – e.g. the people who profess to find Beethoven's fifth symphony 'hackneyed'. It is important for the suppliers of goods to fashion-dominated markets that their goods should not be of high quality, otherwise people may retain them for their intrinsic qualities and not move on to new position-conferring goods when fashions become stale.
3. The desire for leadership positions may take the form of the establishment of new businesses; the market deals with overcrowding here by bankruptcy and takeover. The casualty rate among new small businesses is notoriously high, and some of the waste incurred by this can be debited to the account of positional competition.
4. It must be borne in mind that before an apparent secondary good is written off as waste it must be demonstrated that there is *neither* intrinsic satisfaction from its pursuit *nor* is the overall level of performance in the position improved as a result of its use. If I require all candidates for a job to have passed A-level Latin merely in order to reduce the number of applications I have to read, I encourage wasteful secondary consumption of Latin courses (unless the students enjoy them); if the successful candidate can make good use of the Latin in the job, I have acted reasonably.
5. Outside the field of employment it must be pointed out that the market itself can perform some of this 'repackaging' of goods in order to separate intrinsic and positional demand. Hirsch does not acknowledge this. For example, the availability of excellent reproductions of Old Masters lessens the positional advantage of owning an original; public access to stately homes and gardens enables non-possessors to enjoy their intrinsic qualities.

   It is important to ask why the market cannot do this with jobs; given the positional desirability of top jobs, why is their remuneration so high? This can be explained by asking who decides the level of pay of top jobs. The answer of course is: other holders of top jobs. Since the proportion of total expenses of an organization represented by its top salaries will almost always be negligible, there is little constraint from product markets over what they can be paid. Of course, once such a system has begun, new organizations have to pay high salaries to their top job-holders to remain competitive within the job market, like the crowd standing on tip-toe.

6. One of the best examples of this is the history of financial institutions in the City of London. Especially in the days before modern communications, these institutions depended on a high degree of personal trust. It is significant that families and strongly integrated religious groups played a major part in their development, complementing the calculative relationships of what is often regarded as one of the purest areas of market activity with a different kind of bond.

7. For convenience I shall henceforth restrict myself to the masculine singular pronoun; but the parties to a relationship may be not only feminine but also neuter collectivities or pluralities.

8. In very durable relationships where new generations replace their predecessors in highly similar roles, relations of trust and community may be 'inherited', and there may not be much calculation even in the early stages.

9. This is presumably the meaning of the phrase 'flesh of my flesh and bone of my bone' in the marriage service. At the climax of their love duet in Act II of Wagner's *Tristan und Isolde* he calls her Tristan and she calls him Isolde.

10. Hirschman's third term, loyalty, is the device used by those seeking to prevent exit (e.g. producers of goods trying to keep customers) or quieten dissenting voices (e.g. organizational leaders trying to get their own way). In terms of my preceding analysis loyalty is the exercise of trust by clients, customers, members, etc.

11. But not necessarily of mass parliamentary elections. The invitation to vote for one of two or more offered party packages has more of the characteristics of exit than of voice.

12. Private ownership is the purest case, but it is with market processes that we are here concerned rather than ownership as such. A public body providing the good and charging an economic price for it would be in the same position as a private owner.

13. Because of its authority, revenue-raising powers, and, in democracies, its responsiveness to public opinion, the state is the most important source of such interventions; but a similar role may sometimes be played by charitable organizations, such as that of the National Trust in acquiring large tracts of outstanding countryside, conserving them, and leaving them open to public access.

14. Friedman's most recent contribution to this ideological literature is Friedman and Friedman (1980); for Hayek it is the collection of his earlier works in Hayek (1982).

References

BELL, D. (1976) *The Cultural Contradictions of Capitalism*. London: Heinemann.

BLAU, P. (1964) *Exchange and Power in Social Life*. New York: Wiley.

BRITTAN, S. (1975) The Economic Contradictions of Democracy. *British Journal of Political Science* 5: 129–59.

CROZIER, M., HUNTINGDON, S. P., and WATANAKI, J. (1975) *The Crisis of Democracy*. New York: Trilateral Commission.

DAHL, R. A. (1982) *Dilemmas of Pluralist Democracy*. New Haven: Yale University Press.

FOX, A. (1974) *Beyond Contract: Work, Power and Trust Relations*. London: Faber and Faber.

FRIEDMAN, M. and FRIEDMAN, R. (1980) *Free to Choose*. London: Secker and Warburg.

HAYEK, F. A. (1982) *Law, Legislation and Liberty*. London: Routledge and Kegan Paul.

HIRSCH, F. (1977) *Social Limits to Growth*. London: Routledge and Kegan Paul.

HIRSCHMAN, A. O. (1970) *Exit, Voice and Loyalty*. Cambridge, Mass.: Harvard University Press.

MISHAN, E. J. (1974) The New Inflation. *Encounter* 42 (May): 12–24.

NISBET, F. (1966) *The Sociological Tradition*. London: Heinemann.

OLSON, M. (1965) *The Logic of Collective Action*. Cambridge, Mass.: Harvard University Press.

—— (1982) *The Rise and Decline of Nations*. New Haven: Yale University Press.

ROSE, R. and PETERS, G. (1978) *Can Government Go Bankrupt?* New York: Basic Books.

SHONFIELD, A. (1982) *The Use of Public Power*. Oxford: Oxford University Press.

TITMUSS, R. (1970) *The Gift Relationship*. London: Allen and Unwin.

WILES, P. (1973) Cost inflation and the State of Economic Theory. *Economic Journal* 83 (June): 377–96.

WILLIAMSON, O. (1975) *Markets and Hierarchies*. New York: Free Press.

YOUNG, M. and WILMOTT, P. (1957) *Family and Kinship in East London*. London: Routledge and Kegan Paul.

Name index

Subject index